The Systemic Nature of the Economic Crisis

T0304124

The most prominent aspect of the current financial crisis is its systemic character which manifests itself in high levels of inequality, rampant unemployment, economic and social insecurity and environmental decay. This book explores the potential of a pluralistic and interdisciplinary approach for a deeper understanding of the manifold aspects of the economic crisis.

This book examines the potential of a number of contributions from heterodox economics and psychoanalysis in providing a deeper understanding of these problems. The book analyses some of the most debated aspects of the concepts of market, democracy and socialism and explores the role of structural ties between economic, social and psychological aspects of collective life. It also addresses the main economic aspects of the crisis and pays particular attention to a number of structural imbalances, and to the psychological interpretation of these phenomena.

By drawing together approaches from heterodox economics and psychoanalysis, this book adopts a pluralist and interdisciplinary approach to the study of these phenomena and manages to overcome the fragmentation so often present in social sciences.

Arturo Hermann is a Senior Research Fellow at the Italian National Institute of Statistics (ISTAT), Rome, Italy.

Routledge frontiers of political economy
For a complete list of titles in this series, please visit www.routledge.com

The Systemic Nature of the Economic Crisis

The perspectives of heterodox economics and psychoanalysis

Arturo Hermann

Routledge
Taylor & Francis Group

LONDON AND NEW YORK

First published 2015
by Routledge
2 Park Square, Milton Park, Abingdon, Oxfordshire OX14 4RN

and by Routledge
711 Third Avenue, New York, NY 10017

First issued in paperback 2016

Routledge is an imprint of the Taylor & Francis Group, an informa business

British Library Cataloguing in Publication Data
A catalogue record for this book is available from the British Library

Library of Congress Cataloging in Publication Data
Hermann, Arturo.
The systemic nature of the economic crisis: the perspectives of heterodox
economics and psychoanalysis / Arturo Hermann. — First Edition.
pages cm
Includes bibliographical references and index.
1. Financial crises. 2. Economic history—21st century. 3. Social change.
I. Title.
HB3722.H47 2015
330.9'051—dc23
2014041466

ISBN 13: 978-1-138-22053-9 (pbk)
ISBN 13: 978-1-138-80022-9 (hbk)

Typeset in Times New Roman
by Swales & Willis Ltd, Exeter, Devon, UK

A Gabriella, i miei genitori, Palma, Giovanni, Giuliana, Mariarosaria

Contents

Illustrations

Acknowledgements

Various chapters of the book develop issues also treated in previous contributions and, for this reason, present a number of similarities with the works listed below.

Chapters 1, 3, 5, 9, 12 and 13 are related to the chapters of the book *Towards a Sustainable and Equitable Society: Insights from Heterodox Economics and Psychoanalysis*, Rome, Aracne Editrice, November 2012.

Chapters 1 and 3 have a number of similarities with the article 'Institutionalism and Psychoanalysis: a Basis for Interdisciplinary Cooperation', *International Journal of Pluralism and Economics Education*, vol. 1, no. 4, 2010.

Chapter 9 and 10 display various links with the articles 'The Institutional Analysis of the Market', *International Journal of Green Economics*, vol. 2, no. 4, 2008; and 'Market, Socialism and Democracy in an Interdisciplinary Perspective', *International Journal of Pluralism and Economics Education*, vol. 4, no. 4, 2014.

Chapters 12 and 13 partly draw on 'Policy Responses to Economic and Financial Crises: Insights from Heterodox Economics and Psychoanalysis', *International Journal of Pluralism and Economics Education*, vol. 3, no. 1, 2012.

The issues treated in Chapters 6, 7, 11, and 15 are partly related to articles written in Italian in the journals *Studi Economici e Sociali*, *Il Pensiero Economico Moderno* and *Nuova Economia e Storia*.

I thank the publishers and the editors for the granted permission to use this material.

To avoid overburdening the text with hundreds of references, only essential references have been included. Many interesting contributions can be found in the Conferences organized by the following Associations: AFIT, AHE, AFEE, AISPE, ASE, ASSA, EAEPE, IAFFE, IIPPE, SASE, SCEME, STOREP, URPE, WEA, WSSA and the Green Economics Institute. I wish to thank Chris Brown, Katia Caldari, Stefano Carrara, Marcella Corsi, Guglielmo Forges Davanzati, Wolfram Elsner, Fred Jennings, Miriam Kennett, Fred Lee, Maria Alejandra Madi, Romano Molesti, Simon Mouatt, Cristina Nardi Spiller, Cosimo Perrotta, Bruce Philip, Nick Potts, Jack Reardon, Andrew Trigg, Shann Turnbull, Gianfranco Tusset, John Watkins and Stefano Zamberlan for the interesting discussions on some of the issues addressed in the book.

I wish to thank Andy Humphries and Lisa Thomson at Routledge, and two referees for their useful advice and support in the preparation of the book.

The views expressed in the book are solely the author's. Arturo Hermann can be reached at ahermann@istat.it and a.hermann@libero.it.

Introduction

The systemic character of economic crisis and the need for an interdisciplinary approach

As is known, the world is experiencing an unprecedented economic crisis, for which no easy solutions seem close at hand. The most prominent aspect of the crisis is its systemic character, as it involves several dimensions that reach out to the whole social fabric. There are, then, various crises that involve (i) growing disparities of income between people and economic areas, which are often accompanied by severe forms of poverty and destitution; (ii) environmental problems, which include global warming, destruction of natural habitat, various forms of pollution, urban congestion and decay; (iii) economic life, through the negative effects on the security of jobs, the opportunity of employment, the stability of economic and social relations; (iv) last but not least, the crisis exerts very negative effects on the stability of international relations, with a resurgence of nationalisms and armed conflicts.

This situation poses a major challenge to economic theory and policy action. In fact, the inadequacy of the mainstream[1] (or neoclassical) policies to effectively address these imbalances is by now evident. By remarking this, we do not deny the progress realized in some provinces of the neoclassical domain and even the circumstance that assuming simplified hypotheses can be useful in some cases. But we wish to underscore that progress so realized is one-sided and incomplete and generally takes the form of 'exceptions' to the basic neoclassical model of perfect competition. A good instance can be the application of the theories of imperfect information to the analysis of economic phenomena.

In fact, in our view the weak aspect of neoclassical economics is not so much that it relies on too simple hypotheses but in the circumstance that these hypotheses, as formulated in the form of 'prime postulates', do not allow for much pluralism, as they do not leave room for any real verification.

For this reason, any divergence of real phenomena from these hypotheses does not invite a closer analysis of their reliability but is considered as an unwelcome exception having its cause in 'exogenous factors'. A typical instance in this respect is public intervention which, except for a handful of strictly necessary functions, tends to be appraised as a negative factor for economic development.

In that vision, the only thing we need to do in order to restore the perfect world of neoclassical vision is to reduce or eliminate such 'disturbing factors'. In this respect, we believe that in the analysis of economic crisis there is a strong need for an alternative interpretative framework, based on interdisciplinarity and pluralism.

This also suggests a broader concept of empirical analysis, which should include not only statistics and econometrics but also historical analysis, case-studies and social surveys. In order to provide a contribution towards the realization of this objective, we have addressed the contributions of heterodox economics[2] and psychoanalysis.

The book is organized as follows: in the first part we provide a general introduction (which cannot replace the reading of the psychoanalytic contributions) to the main concepts and developments of psychoanalysis. We pay particular attention to how these insights can be employed in the analysis of economic and social phenomena. In this light, we also consider some of the most debated aspects of psychoanalysis.

The second part is centred on the main contributions of institutional economics, especially in its 'old' and more heterodox tradition. After providing an outline of the distinguishing features of institutional economics, considered also in their historical dimension, we focus attention on the theoretical perspectives of Thorstein Veblen and John Rogers Commons and on their relevance for understanding the economic imbalances of today. In the subsequent chapter we explore the reasons for the decline of institutional economics in the post Second World War period and the perspectives of today by centring attention on the following, and very debated, issues: (i) the links with other heterodox economics' traditions; (ii) the relations between theoretical and empirical analysis; (iii) the interdisciplinary orientation.

In the third part we continue our heterodox journey by addressing the institutional character of the market and its implications for the analysis of the notions of market imperfections, competition, and public and private action. Then, we explore a number of aspects related to the complex and evolutionary links between economic, cultural and psychological aspects.

In the fourth part we analyse – also building on important aspects of Keynes's macroeconomics – the manifold aspects of the crisis together with some relevant theoretical and empirical explanations. In particular, after underscoring the role of policy co-ordination in structural problems, we try to identify the main reasons for the steady increase over many decades of public spending and credit creation. Such reasons have little to do with a supposed failure of 'Keynesian' policies but have found their pivotal reason in the role of public spending and credit creation in sustaining aggregate demand. In the subsequent chapter we consider the psychological interpretation of these phenomena and the role of *superego* in shaping the perception that public spending is 'too high' and that the only thing we should do is to comply with 'the needs of the market'.

In the fifth part we investigate the structural transformations of economic and social systems and their effects on economic and social life. We draw attention to the contradictions of our societies and to the reasons underlying the growing difficulty of aggregate demand to reach the level of full employment, however defined. We also examine the opportunity for economic systems to move towards a society in which the exclusive search for monetary gain will gradually lose relevance and be replaced by a system of activities which better express the needs and inclinations of individuals.

Then, in the next chapter we pursue this line of enquiry by analysing the contradictions of our societies as appraised in John Kenneth Galbraith's *The Affluent Society*. In this light, our approach is not focused on the identification of the ideal characteristics of a new society: whether, for instance, such society should approach a particular type of socialism or social justice and should be oriented towards a de-growth, a moderate growth, or a steady state. This is because we concentrate more on the ways to overcome the shortcomings of our economic systems and then on how to steer the creation of a really sustainable and equitable society. Such society can be in accordance with various economic organizations based on co-operative and equitable relations, which are likely to vary according to the unique characteristics of any context we may consider.

We conclude that part by pointing out that the main difficulty in accomplishing the transition towards a more equitable society is likely to reside not in an economic but in a psychological difficulty. It may relate to our long-standing habits of thought centred on the notion of 'physical scarcity' which makes us think that the real economic and social problem is one of 'supply-side': namely, how to produce more and more on quantitative terms, as if we were constantly on the brink of famine. And this despite the overwhelming evidence to the contrary highlighted[3] by many authors.

For this reason, any attempt to orient the economic system in a direction more conducive to the real needs of individuals tends be hampered by a feeling of guilt, more or less unconscious, that tends to equate the activities unrelated to the classic 'economic motive' to idleness and indifference.

The final chapter addresses, on the basis of these insights, the manifold ways of interaction between heterodox economic and psychoanalysis, with particular attention to policy implications.

The most important conclusion of this analysis pertains to the necessity of overcoming the fragmentation (or limited collaboration) so often present in social sciences. We try to make evident the potential of these theories, still largely unexplored, for the analysis of many aspects of the economic crisis, and in particular, (i) how economic and psychological factors combine to shape social systems, (ii) the problematic aspects of these processes, (iii) how people can react to these problems and with what effects on point (i). Needless to say, in an interdisciplinary approach it is neither possible nor advisable to consider all the disciplines with the same weight.

In this and other instances, a choice needs to be made. What seems important in this respect is to make explicit the choices adopted by acknowledging, in a pluralistic perspective, the existence and relevance of other approaches and disciplines. As observed by the famous sociologist Karl Mannheim, a landscape can be seen only from a determined perspective and without perspective there is no landscape. In this sense, observing a landscape (or phenomenon) from different angles (or disciplines) can help to acquire a much clearer insight into the features of the various perspectives.

Therefore, an interdisciplinary perspective does not imply that each discipline would lose its distinctive features. Quite the contrary, a more comprehensive approach such as this, by broadening the horizon of the observer, can also contribute to a better appraisal of the specific characteristics of his/her main fields of specialization. In this way, a more comprehensive social value process can ensue which, as we try to show, lies at the heart of the effectiveness of policy action.

Notes

1 By mainstream economics we refer to the theories which build their analyses on the basic neoclassical hypotheses of maximizing economic agents and perfect and self-sustaining markets. Hence, for the purpose of our work, we consider mainstream economics chiefly as synonymous with neoclassical economics. A broader definition would also include classic economics. In fact, too, this theory is based, in particular in its Ricardian version, on rather simple hypotheses related to the working of the capitalistic system. And furthermore, that theory was undoubtedly mainstream in its time. However, nowadays such a theory tends to be considered, if not properly heterodox, at least less mainstream and more compatible with some strands of heterodox economics (in particular Marxism). We agree in large part with this appraisal, but we also think it necessary to critically address the basic premises of this theory.

2 According to a fairly common definition, heterodox economics would include institutional economics (in particular in the 'old' tradition), Marxist oriented contributions and other theories of socialism and social justice, Keynesian theories, Sraffian and other versions of neo-Ricardian theories, critical realism, some strands of Austrian economics, the 'neo-Schumpeterian' theories of path-dependency and technological accumulation, and environmental economics, in particular in the field of 'bio-economy'.

3 This is well expressed in the concluding passage of J.K. Galbraith's *The Affluent Society* 'To furnish a barren room is one thing. To continue to crowd in furniture until the foundation buckles is quite another. To have failed to solve the problem of producing goods would have been to continue man in his oldest and most grievous misfortune. But to fail to see that we have solved it, and to fail to proceed thence to the next tasks, would be fully as tragic.'

Part I

The psychoanalytic approach and its potential for a better understanding of economic and social phenomena

In this part we provide in Chapter 1 an outline of the main psychoanalytic concepts.

Then, in Chapters 2 and 3 we focus attention on their potential for the study of economic and social phenomena and for the analysis of the social change.

Also in connection with these issues, in Chapter 4 we address some controversial aspects of psychoanalysis.

1 The perspective of psychoanalysis

An outline

1.1 Introduction: the origin of psychoanalysis and the controversy between Freud, Adler and Jung

The aim of this and the subsequent chapters is to provide an account of the psychoanalytic approach and its relevance for a better understanding of economic and social phenomena. As we shall see, the psychoanalytic perspective, by helping acquire a deeper understanding of the complex interaction between persons and society, can be particularly useful in the analysis of the systemic character of the crisis and the process of social change.

In this account we refer in particular to the theories which maintain a reference to the Freudian approach. The reason for this is that we believe that these psychoanalytic contributions, although highly amenable to an interdisciplinary collaboration, have been largely overlooked in the analysis of societal phenomena.

Three groups of factors may have contributed to this situation: (i) the difficulty for social scientists and psychoanalysts to go beyond the methodological scope of their complex disciplines; (ii) a tendency among social scientists to interpret Freud's work as being chiefly based on 'biological needs' and thus, on these grounds, to be rather sceptical of its usefulness for analysing social phenomena; (iii) furthermore, the intrinsic multifariousness of psychoanalytic issues and the partly different views of 'psychoanalytic schools' may have contributed to making it difficult for social scientists and psychoanalysts to build a sufficiently integrated 'conceptual core' for the study of economic and social phenomena.

Let us now address briefly the well-known divergences in the early stage of the psychoanalytic movement,[1] which ended up in the creation by some members of the former 'Psychoanalytic Committee' – in particular, Alfred Adler and Carl Gustav Jung – of new psychological schools.

We can stress here, without entering into a detailed analysis of these theories, some interesting aspects: (i) by seeing that controversy in retrospect, the personal element related to the formation of 'transference' feelings seems to have played a relevant role. In this regard, Freud was considered by Adler and Jung as authoritarian and intransigent whereas he regarded them as 'stubborn and rebellious sons'.

Probably, both sides were partly right, but the result was one of intense 'transference' which ended up in a permanent estrangement. (ii) These aspects were reinforced by the circumstance that in these instances, as often happens in the case of a new theory, the issues at the stake tend to be stretched to the extremes. In this case, the most controversial point was the role of psycho-sexuality in the formation of psychological disturbances. As is known, Freud stressed its role whereas Adler and Jung downplayed it. However, both sides employed, especially in the emphasis of the debate, a simplistic notion of sexuality. As we will make clear later on, Freud's account of this issue is not always clear, but it is important to note that his concept of sexuality was much broader than a simple bodily dimension as it involved the role of feelings and emotions.

On the other hand, Adler and Jung, although critical of Freud's notion of psycho-sexuality, never denied its role in the development of personality. (iii) These aspects have been greatly elaborated by the subsequent development of psychoanalysis, in particular within the theories of 'object' and 'interpersonal' relations, which highlight the complexity of relations between the bodily and mental aspects of personality and the paramount need for the person of establishing sound interpersonal relations. (iv) Considered in this new light, the theories of Freud, Adler and Jung do not seem so incompatible as they appeared before. Of course, they remain different, but pivotal concepts developed by Adler and Jung can be jointly employed in the analysis of social issues.

The main concepts elaborated by Adler [2011 (1925)] pinpoint, in particular, (i) the feeling of inferiority and the corresponding will for power, (ii) the creative self and the finalism of existence, (iii) the importance of a 'social sentiment', which implies the need for the person to establish sound interpersonal relations.

The perspective expounded by Jung [1968 (1964)] centres, in particular, on (i) the notion of 'complex', which pertains to a system of conscious and unconscious representations of a person embodying a strong affective orientation; (ii) the concepts of collective unconscious and archetypes, which describe the ideals, symbols and representation typical of many societies; (iii) the notion of individuation and finalism as a way to express the authentic needs and orientations of personality.

As can be easily seen, Adler's and Jung's perspectives can complement in significant ways Freudian (and in particular, post-Freudian) contributions, and also the contributions that pinpoint the role of psychological sciences in the analysis of social phenomena. We can mention, among others, the contributions[2] of social psychology, of cognitive psychology, of 'humanistic psychology', of Pragmatist psychology (cf. also the second part), of psychology and sociology of emotions. Moreover, a useful collaboration can be established also with experimental economics as new insights can be gained by simulating in an 'experiment' what economic behaviour could be in the real world.

On the basis of our approach, we believe that the 'experiments' need to be integrated with the analysis of individual-society dynamics. This implies, on the one side, the analysis of the emotions and motivations of single persons, and on the other, the study of the characteristics of the broader collective context. Of course, we are aware that it is not always easy to carry out these kind of analysis and that some simplifications can be expedient in some instances. However, in our view, this should not become the rule and researchers should always be aware of the complexity of the issues under investigation.

1.2 The basics concepts

In order to illustrate the basic concepts of psychoanalysis, the first question we need to answer is: what is psychoanalysis?

Psychoanalysis can be defined (see, in particular, Freud, 1924, 1933. Also Fenichel, 1945; Fine, 1979; Laplanche and Pontalis, 1967; Nagera, 1969) as a discipline, founded by Sigmund Freud, characterized by a method of enquiry consisting in explaining the unconscious meaning of speech, actions and imaginative productions of a person. This method can be employed: (i) for the treatment of neurotic disturbances and, in this case, rests on the free associations of the person which constitute the basis for an open and tentative interpretation of the possible reasons lying behind such conflicts; (ii) for the analysis of human activities in their social context for which free associations may not be available.

One key question raised by the previous definition is: what is neurosis? A concise and very effective definition of neurosis – formulated by Freud for the first time in 1894 – is that of a defence against incompatible representations. As observed by Fine (1979), psychoanalytic theory can be considered a development of this first insight.

A broad definition of neurosis is that of a psychological disturbance, where symptoms are the symbolic expression of a psychic conflict, which has its roots in the person's infantile life and constitutes a compromise between a desire and a corresponding defence.[3] A central feature of neurotic disturbances is that they bring about a hindrance, more or less severe, to the normal psychological development of a person. The reason for this is that the neurotic person is, to varying degrees, unable to overcome the conflicts associated with his or her development stages.

However, neurotic disturbances should not be regarded as something 'bad or abnormal' but as the typical expression of the structure of human personality, with all the related problems, weaknesses, contradictions and ambivalence. In that connection, one central insight of psychoanalytic theory is that much of our psychic life possesses an unconscious character.

In Freud's theory the definition of the unconscious assumes different meanings,[4] one of them referring to the area of mental activity (feelings, emotions, thoughts) of which the person is unaware as a consequence of a process of 'repression'. But, why does a person need to activate such a 'repression' process? One answer is the infantile development of a person is a highly complex process that is likely to undergo several conflicts.

The conflict considered central by Freud within the scope of his theory of libidinal stages[5] of development is the *Oedipus* complex. In broad terms, the *Oedipus* complex can be defined as the organized whole of a child's loving and hostile feelings toward its parents.

In the paradigmatic example, the affective desire and sexual fantasies[6] of a child towards the parent of the opposite sex may trigger intense feelings of jealousy, rivalry and anger toward the 'rival' parent. As a consequence of these feelings, the child is likely to fear punishment, also because it tends to feel guilty for experiencing such feelings. All the emotions associated with this situation can become highly distressing for the child, and, therefore, it tries to repress all the related feelings. As a result of the attempt to repress (mostly at an unconscious level) the emotional conflicts associated with the *Oedipus* complex, much of its contents become unconscious.

Of course, the attempts to repress all the feelings associated with the *Oedipus* complex cannot be very effective, and so cannot help to relieve the emotional distress. As a result of this situation – in which there is a desire, considered 'bad', and a corresponding defence trying to repress it – a neurotic disturbance arises, which may express itself in many different forms of behaviour and fantasies.

The purpose of such a disturbance is, according to the previous definition, to realize, in a symbolic, distorted and unconscious way, both the instances of the desire and the defence. In this sense, it represents a defence from incompatible representations.

Needless to say, the dynamics of the *Oedipus* complex are far more tangled than could appear from this brief description. Owing to this complexity, throughout his research activity, Freud identified many aspects and forms of the *Oedipus* complex and many neurotic disturbances which may be caused by it.[7] In this regard, it is important to note that Freud himself and later psychoanalytic contributions stressed the importance of every stage of life[8] for the formation and evolution of personality and of the related psychological disturbances (cf. also the next chapters).

Freud's conclusion that the *Oedipus* complex tends to represent a universal experience for human beings has received much criticism.[9] We will discuss this issue in more detail in the next chapters. Now, we can observe that Freud was well aware that the *Oedipus* complex involves many aspects and may assume various forms and intensity according to the culture, society and family situations in which a child's life develops. An interesting analysis of these aspects is contained in *Totem and Taboo* (1912–1913), *Civilization and Its Discontents* (1939) and others.

As shown in these studies, the *Oedipus* complex will acquire different forms and intensities according to, among other factors, the personalities and conflicts of the child's caretakers. Since these individual aspects also interchange with cultural factors, the role of the latter (and, more generally, of the collective dimension of life) is likely to play a central role in shaping the characteristics of the *Oedipus* complex. As observed before, Freud considers individual and collective psychology as two complementary aspects of the same phenomenon – owing to the circumstance, stressed in particular in his *Group Psychology and the Analysis of the Ego* (1921), that in ancient times group life was preponderant and that only subsequently the person has gradually come to assume a more distinct role within the various groups of society.

In this respect, the concept of the *superego* represents the psychological instance through which cultural values are internalized by the child. For this reason, it constitutes a fundamental link between individual and collective psychology.

The *superego* can be considered as the heir of the *Oedipus* complex, since it arises from the internalization of the prohibitions and of the moral and cultural values – as perceived by the child – of the child's parents and also of later institutional figures such as teachers and other opinion leaders. In the early stage of psychoanalysis, many important contributions to these issues were also provided by Karl Abraham, Sándor Ferenczi, Ernest Jones, Otto Rank.

1.3 Further developments

Freud's theory has been greatly extended to significant aspects of human development. A common pattern of these studies, though widely different in several respects, can be identified in the importance they attribute to the role of affective relations in the dynamics of human action and motivation.

Within this perspective, numerous studies have analysed key elements of infantile development and in particular the child–mother relationship in the early stages of infancy. Pivotal contributions were provided by, among others, Erik Erikson (1968), Anna Freud (1936), Heinz Hartmann (1964), and Melanie Klein (1964, 1975). These authors have cast light on aspects that are crucial for a fuller understanding of human psychology. A. Freud, Hartmann and many others spelled out the structure of the *ego* as a mediating factor between instincts and society, while Erikson took up these insights for analysing the role of identity in the formation of personality. In his work, *Identity, Youth and Crisis*, he considers the concept of identity and the factors which may concur to determine it. Identity is regarded both as an individual and a social concept. Hence, the analysis of individual behaviour would demand a study of the characteristics of social setting in which individual action takes place; and, in that connection, social enquiry should consider important features of psychoanalysis.

M. Klein[10] analysed, from a new perspective, the mechanisms underlying the child–mother relationship in the early stages of infancy. Particularly important are the mechanisms of internalization, scission and projection, through which the child tries to cope with its ambivalence and aggressiveness towards the mother. These feelings are likely to be particularly intense in the first months of life. As a matter of fact, in this period the child, after experiencing the trauma of birth (first expounded by Otto Rank in 1924) is in a situation of extreme dependency on its mother (or prime caretaker). In this stage, every real or imaginary shortcoming in the fulfilment of its need – for instance when it is hungry and the mother is absent – is likely to be experienced by the child as a hostile act of abandonment. In this stage, the child does not clearly distinguish itself from others. Therefore, it tends to regard the mother, and in particular her feeding breast, as a part of itself.

In its attempt to cope with the anxiety and aggressiveness related to this early relation, the mother is divided into 'a good and a bad object', which are unconsciously 'internalized', through an identification process, by the child. This stage is denoted as 'the schizo-paranoid position', because in this way the child tends to split its personality into two mutually incompatible elements. The child tries to retain all its 'good qualities' through the following defence mechanisms: internalizing the 'good and protecting mother' and, at the same time, projecting its aggressiveness into the 'bad and aggressive mother' who is therefore – as result of this process, named 'projective identification' – felt as a hostile and persecutory figure.

Subsequently, as the child grows up, this stage may be overcome to varying degrees as the child recognizes that the mother is just one person and, as a consequence, it tries to compensate for the imaginary attacks made against her. This stage is indicated as 'the depressive position', which corresponds to the process of (psychic) differentiation from the mother and the parallel discovery of the father, other persons and, more generally, the external world.

It is from this first neurotic structure that the *Oedipus* complex – about which M. Klein posited its beginning earlier on than Freud – and the following stages of life develop. Depending on many circumstances – and, in particular, on the characteristics of family setting – these later stages may help reinforce or partially overcome these earlier, more or less traumatic, experiences.

M. Klein's theory sheds new light on many social phenomena by providing a deeper understanding of the conflicts that, while arising in the infantile development, may heavily impinge upon the type of relations adults establish within groups and institutions.

In particular, one of the great insights of her theory is the further elaboration of the role of unconscious representations in the psychic life of the person. As appears from the previous outline, the core of neurotic disturbances lies in the relation of the child with an 'internal object', which constitutes the internalization of its early relations and experiences. These relations take largely the character of fantastic objects. The problem is that these objects, however fantastic,[11] are very real in the 'psychic reality' of the person and so are likely to heavily impinge on every aspect of the later life.

1.4 The 'object and interpersonal relations' theories

Other noteworthy contributions – indicated as object relations theories,[12] even though it is difficult to identify for them a completely unitary framework – have been provided by the so-called 'Independent Approach' (the former 'Middle Group') in British psychoanalysis, some of whose most important exponents are Michael Balint, John Bowlby, Marjorie Brierly, Ronald Fairbairn, J.C. Flugel, John Rickman, Ella Sharpe and Donald Winnicott. This approach has many parallels with the American contributions to this field – some of the most relevant authors being Edith Jacobson, Heinz Kohut, Otto Kernberg, Hans Loewald, Margaret Mahler and Arnold Modell – and also with most of the 'cultural psychoanalysts' quoted in the next chapter.

Such contributions have been, in various ways, critical of both Anna Freud's, Sigmund Freud's and Melanie Klein's theories on the grounds that, notwithstanding their differences, they all tend to focus attention mainly on the 'biological' side of instincts. And, for this reason, they do not fully consider the role of affection and object relations in individual development.

Although these contributions have occasioned a lively debate, they hold important aspects of Freud's theories of instinct and libidinal stages of development and also adopt, in many cases, a Kleinian framework in the explanation of the first stages of development. In this sense, they try to integrate and deepen these theories[13] rather than dismissing them.

We would like to note (see also later) that Freud built his instincts theory in order to have a basic interpretative framework of human behaviour but he was well aware of the complexity of the issue. Indeed, throughout his research activity he continuously enlarged and restructured his theories.[14] Within this ambit, Freud's theory of instincts has always assumed a dualistic character, and underwent a complex evolution, which we do need to follow here in its detail, in which two stages can be identified: (i) the first, in which the two main instincts are sexuality and self-preservation (the latter also labelled as the 'instincts of the *ego*' (see, in particular, Freud, 1905, 1915).

This theory was superseded by another theory of instincts, in which the main instincts are life and death (see, in particular, Freud, 1920; Laplanche and Pontalis, 1967; Nagera, 1969). As we shall see presently, the latter theory has triggered many controversies and is now dismissed or put in the background by many psychoanalysts.

One important reason why Freud remained attached to a 'biological' concept of instinct[15] resides in his purpose of underlining the role of psycho-sexuality in human psychology. He feared that, were psycho-sexuality not sufficiently stressed, this concept would be overlooked, or unconsciously 'repressed', in the analysis of human development.

However, Freud has always underscored the role of feelings, object relations and cultural factors in driving individual behaviour, providing important contributions in which he stresses that – mostly in an unconscious and sublimated way[16] – libidinal relations are the necessary instance for the existence of society. In this regard, as already observed, he tends to employ the term *eros* or *libido* as synonymous with love.[17] Besides, he stressed that the unconscious is mainly constituted by representations which have been repressed as a result of a neurotic conflict. Therefore, the objective of the psychoanalytic method is to help turn the 'unconscious' into 'conscious' – *es into ego* – through the person's understanding of his or her conflicts.[18]

Of course, this is not to say that Freud's theories were perfect and that he considered all the importance of object relations and cultural factors in driving individual behaviour. In this regard, these new theories have provided important contributions to the role of affective life for a sound development of the person.

Considering the complexity of these aspects, many 'object relations' oriented researchers believe that the supposed contrast between instincts and object relations theories is for many aspects groundless as these theories are, rather than in opposition, complementary to each other. These authors have adopted a more integrated view of the human personality, which more explicitly embraces its complex needs and orientations. Hence, the distinction between 'biological', affective and intellectual needs tends to be considered as an expression of the various aspects making up the human personality, which, therefore, need to be studied in their complex interaction.

On the basis of this approach, it seems reasonable to posit that human needs are complex and interrelated and, as a consequence, a child needs: (1) to be fed and protected; (2) to establish sound object and interpersonal relations; (3) more generally, to develop in an integrated way all the aspects of its personality.

In this sense, psychoanalysis, especially in these new developments,[19] is acquiring a more distinct evolutionary character (cf., in particular, Rayner, 1991; Sandler and Dreher, 1996). This suggests that, as these relations cannot unfold in a *vacuum*, the analysis of characteristics of the related Institutional and Socio-Economic Framework[20] (ISEF) becomes more and more pertinent. For this reason, there is arising a growing area of collaboration between psychoanalysis and social sciences.

1.5 Psychoanalysis, cultures and societies

Related to these strands of research which, as we have tried to show, bring to the fore the importance of the symbolic and actual relations of the person within his or her ISEF, there arises the issue of analysing cultures and societies by utilizing psychoanalytic concepts.

Within anthropology, a strand of research fairly close to psychoanalysis has tried to verify the extent to which psychoanalytic concepts can be applied to the study of primitive populations. Pioneering studies were carried out by Abram Kardiner and Geza Roheim. One of their findings has been that psychoanalysis can help to explain a number of common patterns in the psychology of these populations, even though their cultures may greatly vary from one another. For instance, regarding the *Oedipus* complex, these authors find its dynamics in every culture considered, although its expression may differ according to the characteristics of cultures and family organizations.

However, as we shall see presently, other contributions to these issues have taken a critical stance towards psychoanalysis on the grounds of its supposed 'determinism and biologism'.

The 'Cultural Psychoanalysts'

In relation to these issues, a strand of research has stressed the role of cultural forms in the study of the psychological orientation of society. Leading members of this group are Erich Fromm, Karen Horney, Harry Stack Sullivan and Clara Thompson. These authors investigated the structure and conflicts of contemporary societies and the role of interpersonal relations, with their related cultural values, in the formation of psychological disturbances.

A lively debate,[21] still in progress, arose between this group and the more 'orthodox' psychoanalysts, and in 1956 some 'Culturalists' (also referred to as the neo-Freudians) created a new institution, the American Academy of Psychoanalysis. These authors have the great merit of bringing to the fore the relation between culture and psychological disturbances. If society requires the individual to pursue contradictory objectives – for instance, individual success based on an egoistic quest for money and power, together with the virtues of friendship and altruism – this may cause a corresponding tension on the part of the person which may reinforce his or her inner conflicts.

With regard to psychoanalytic theory, their common heading is that Freud's view, owing to his stress on the role of instincts, would rest on a universal and deterministic theory of human development in which, therefore, there is little room for an adequate account of the variety of cultural factors. In our view, the unconvincing aspect of this approach is that it tends to posit a dichotomy between 'instincts' (or, more generally, 'nature'), and 'culture'.

This happens because, in such view, instincts tend to be considered as elemental bodily-based phenomena whereas cultural formations are supposed to house, in various degrees, the more elaborated expressions of the person. But in Freud's theory the bodily aspects gain significance for psychological life on account of their symbolic connection with the emotional sphere. For instance, the act of feeding acquires importance for the child not only because it fulfils a biological need but also because it tends to be interpreted by the child as an expression of affection. And the child, through the elaboration of this and other symbolic connections, also expresses and develops its affective and intellectual potential. In that connection, by considering the different social contexts in which these experiences are rooted, the surprising element is that, whereas cultures vary widely in the characteristics of their eating habits, virtually all seem to attribute to them special importance in many family and social situations.

In this regard, as we will also try to evidence in the following chapters, we can note that: (i) in Freud's theory, instincts constitute complex entities which embody the need for affection and the whole dynamics of emotional life; (ii) for this reason, his (continually evolving and tentative) theory of instincts, as being rooted in the dynamics of interpersonal relations, cannot show, for its very nature, any deterministic pattern but, on the contrary, can contribute to explain the variety of cultural expressions.

As already noted, this more comprehensive concept of instinct has significant parallels with Veblen's notion that 'all instinctive action is teleological. It involves holding to a purpose', and also with important aspects of the philosophy and psychology of Pragmatism.

Certainly, there are some unclarities and contradictions in Freud's theory, but the solution would lie not in dismissing every tangled aspect of the theory but in casting more light on these issues, as many later psychoanalysts have done.

All that said, we think it pertinent to stress the richness of the Cultural Psychoanalysts' contributions, their awareness of social contradictions and the importance they attach, also through the help of psychoanalysis, to the process of social change. Let us quote the following passages, which synthesize brightly the Cultural Psychoanalysts' orientations on the matter of social change:

In a world in which time is of the essence, in which we can scarcely defer great constructive changes unless we shall have raised a new generation to political power, the most searching scrutiny of the dynamics of favorable change in personality becomes utterly imperative. . . . The less of parents' work that has to be corrected, the quicker man moves ahead. The surer our aid to parents in preparing their young for life, the more geometrically expanding will be the resulting good to the great number. . . . Freedom of information is meaningless unless it is used for a purpose, namely, to promote the peace and well-being of humanity. . . . The thinking-out of constructive, functionally coherent, revisions of any one of the major cultures of the world . . . shall be less restrictive on understanding and more permissive of social progress; that, truly, is a task to which unnumbered groups of the skillful may well apply themselves.

There will remain the intimidating task of implementing the better, once it shall have been designed; but for the first time in the history of man, there is a world-wide, if often most unhappy, realization of the necessity, and at the same time a set of administrative agencies clearly charged with the responsibility. I say to you with the utmost seriousness of which I am capable that this is no time to excuse yourself from paying the debt you and yours owe the social order with some such facile verbalism as 'Nothing will come of it; it can't be done.' Begin; and let it be said of you, if there is any more history, that you labored nobly in the measure of man in the twentieth century of the scientific, Western World.

(Sullivan et al., 1953: 382, 383, 384)

1.6 'Cultural anthropology' and the 'irrelevance'of the *Oedipus* complex

Another related strand of research, often referred to as 'cultural anthropology', stresses the importance of recognizing the variety of cultural forms. A rather common feature of these studies is that the variety of cultural forms would demonstrate the 'irrelevance' of the *Oedipus* complex. A famous instance is Malinowski's *Sex and Repression in Savage Society* (1927), in which he claims that the *Oedipus* complex is not a universal tendency but a cultural product of Western society. This conclusion – which has triggered a lively debate – is based on his field-study in the Trobriand islands, where he noted that the typical aspects of the *Oedipus* complex, limited to the boy's perspective, are shifted to the uncle and the sister: the boy admires, but, at the same time, fears and hates the uncle, who stands as an authoritarian father figure in a matrilinear type of family. At the same time, he desires his own sister and has a friendly relation with his natural father who, however, plays a limited role in his upbringing and, more in general, in family life.

However, this interpretation is based (as shown by, among others, Fine, 1979) on a misunderstanding of the nature of the *Oedipus* complex. In fact, this complex – defined above as the organized whole of a child's loving and hostile feelings toward its parents – assume many forms and may also involve other caretakers of the child.

The 'universality' of the *Oedipus* complex is not a consequence of the working of some abstract 'natural laws' but stems from the circumstance that the child – owing to a prolonged dependency upon its caretakers – establishes with them its first significant affective relations, which, in their complex vicissitudes and transformations, will constitute an important model of reference for the child's future development.

In this sense, the universality of the *Oedipus* complex implies nothing less than that a child, in its process of growth and differentiation, is likely to experience complex feelings which may also involve trouble, contradiction and difficulty.

To begin with, birth itself, as stressed in particular by Otto Rank, constitutes a trauma for the child. Then, the child feels 'fused and identified' with the mother, and, hence, the subsequent process of differentiation and discovery of another person, the father, is likely to engender complex relations of identification, but also of fear, rivalry and conflict. The child understands that it is no longer 'at one' with the mother, and, therefore, that the parents may even 'leave it aside' in their common life. Of course, the child loves its parents and needs their affection and protection but, at the same time, can desire to be 'at one' with the mother or the father and so, on these grounds, may develop a feeling of rivalry towards the parent of the opposite sex and also – in connection with its feeling of being 'left aside' – of hostility and mistrust for both.

The consideration of these factors is not tantamount to downplaying the variety of cultural expressions. On the contrary, a better understanding of the needs and difficulties of human development can contribute to bring attention to the numberless ways through which cultural evolution takes place.

As a matter of fact, the specificity of every cultural context plays a central role in shaping the forms of the early relations of the child. In this regard, the aspect we deem important to point out is that these cultural forms do not exist apart from the individuals involved but are partly shaped by their thoughts and actions. This means that the entire set of experiences, orientations, values, needs and conflicts making up the human personality concur to shape the related cultural forms as well.

In this respect, it seems appropriate to observe that the *Oedipus* complex, as occurring in most cases within a cultural context, and as involving people of different generations, constitutes an utterly cultural phenomenon, which, of course, has an important link with the orientations of each person involved. Therefore, culture is not something standing apart from these orientations, since it constitutes the 'institutional way' for their collective expression.

In order to explain the remarkable differences in the characteristics of neurotic disturbances, Freud introduced (in particular, 1905, 1924 and 1933) the concept of 'complemental series'. This theory considers the joint action of the following factors in the formation of neurotic disturbances[22]: (i) a person's 'innate' constitution, including the entire set of his or her 'innate' biological and intellectual traits; (ii) the influence of 'accidental events', by which he chiefly means the role assumed by the family and socio-cultural contexts.

As already noted, the role of the family and social context is likely to play, through their influence on the formation of a person's *superego*, a relevant role in these dynamics.

Notes

1 For more details on all these aspects refer in particular to Jones (1953) and Fine (1979).

2 Cf. for a more detailed account of these theories Goleman (1995); James (1890); Kahneman and Tversky (2000); Maslow (1971); Nisbett and Ross (1980); Pervin and John (1997); Ross and Nisbett (1991); Turner and Stets (2005).

3 It is important to note that in Freudian theory neurosis does not comprise all the psychological disturbances, which include also perversions and psychoses. However, as psychoanalysis stresses that the above definition of neurosis constitutes the common ground for all psychological disturbances and that, furthermore, even 'normal' minds undergo the same processes in their development – in this sense, the difference between the normal and neurotic personality tends to be more a question of different forms and degrees of psychological disturbances than one of sharp distinctions between "pure neurosis" and "pure normality" – we employ the term neurosis, only for the purpose of our work, as a synonymous with psychological disturbances.

4 Cf. in particular Freud (1915, 1923, 1924 and 1933).

5 Although the theories on the issue differ to some extent, the *Oedipus* complex is generally assumed to have its main development, approximately, between the ages of 2 and 5 years. Freud (1926a and 1926b).

6 In this regard, Freud hypothesized a sexual instinct (for the multifarious meaning of instinct refer to the following notes) in the person acting from the beginning of life. He stressed the importance of such instinct for the development of the person and the etiology of neurosis. These assumptions have perhaps constituted the most controversial and 'scandalous' aspects of his theory. In this respect, anticipating our subsequent discussion, we can observe that: (i) sexuality assumes in Freud a complex meaning – extending well beyond the merely biological dimension – which embraces all aspects of the affective life of a person. In this sense, as remarked by Freud (in particular in his work on the unconscious of 1915), sexuality, in its mature and non-neurotic expression, is synonymous with *eros* or love. (ii) In this meaning, infantile sexuality cannot be correctly regarded through our adult-based vision, as it presents a complex evolutionary pattern which psychoanalysis tries to understand as regards its effects on child development. For a more detailed analysis of these aspects refer in particular to Freud (1900, 1905, 1915, 1923, 1924, 1933, 1937), Fenichel (1945), Fine (1979), Laplanche and Pontalis (1967), and Nagera (1969).

7 For an analysis of the characteristics of these disturbances refer, among others, to Freud's renowned case studies, Fenichel (1945), and the quotations in the next chapter.

8 However, it remains true that the stage of infancy plays a relevant role in the formation of neurosis. The reason for this is twofold: (i) the child, owing to its dependence on its caretakers and the long period needed for reaching adulthood, is particularly exposed to external influences; (ii) also for these reasons, the child tends to interpret the external experiences in a simplistic and dichotomic way. For instance, if a child asks for food and the mother does not turn up in short time, this behaviour can rapidly be interpreted as a sign of persecutory abandonment, even if this in the vast majority of cases does not correspond to the reality.

9 For a discussion of these issues refer, among others, to Bastide (1950), Elliott (1994) and Fine (1979).

10 In this regard, we can recall the conflict that occurred between Anna Freud and Melanie Klein on the role of *pre-Oedipal* stages of developments (the so-called *controversial discussions*). However, apart from these aspects, M. Klein accepted the basic concepts

of Freud's analysis, including his theory of the death instinct that, as we shall see later, has been widely criticized among later psychoanalysts. However, it is important to note that both A. Freud (1936) and M. Klein (1964, 1975) provided important contributions to the analysis of aggressiveness. See also Klein, Heimann and Money-Kyrle (1955); Nagera (1969); Rayner (1991). Cf. also the next section.

11 As already noted, the real aspects of the experiences play a central role, but the relevant point is that they tend to be biased by the fantasies of the child. So, if the mother is absent when the child is hungry this is a real experience but if, out of that, the child builds in its mind a figure of the persecutory breast and mother, this implies that such experience has been internalized as a fantastic 'bad object'. In the same way, positive experiences can constitute the basis for building an internal 'good object'.

Needless to say, there is always a relation with reality, hence, these feelings are likely to be reinforced in the presence of a real inadequacy on the part of the care-takers. However, what makes these early experiences so important for the life of the child is that – owing to the child's limited knowledge of the world around it and the primitiveness of its defence mechanisms – they are internalized, through a process of identification, in its psychic life. As we have seen, it is from this process that originates the 'scission' between 'good' and 'bad' in the personality which is then projected on persons, groups and institutions which, as a result, are perceived, to a greater or lesser extent, according to our unconscious fantasies.

12 For a deep analysis of these theories refer to, among others, Fine (1979); Greenberg and Mitchell (1983); Rayner (1991); Sandler and Dreher (1996); Tyson and Tyson (1990).

13 Anna Freud's contributions also played a significant part in the formation of these new theories, even if her major influence was on the formation of the '*ego* psychology' school, mainly developed in the American context.

14 In particular, the very definition of 'instinct' has always been extremely problematic to formulate not only in Freud's analysis but also in every other theory dealing with this issue. As is known, Freud's instinct theory is highly complex, as he distinguishes between *instinkt* and *trieb*. *Instinkt* tends to refer to the prevailing concept of instinct existing at his time, whereas the notion of *trieb* – which was formulated with the main aim of identifying a theoretical framework for his theory of sexual development and of psychoneuroses – can be defined (see in particular Freud 1905, 1915, 1923, 1924, 1933) as a dynamic process consisting of a pressure – having its source in a state of bodily excitation – which pushes the organism to discharge it (the aim of the *trieb*). However, Freud was well aware that the distinction between *instinkt* and *trieb* presents many problems also because the definition of these two concepts is very difficult to draw. Consequently, he continuously enlarged and restructured these definitions throughout his research activity, even if, as observed by subsequent studies, his theory of sexual development can be accommodated also within the classical theory of instinct. Within this scope, Freud's central contribution lies in having discovered the role of psycho-sexuality in human psychology. For a deep analysis of these issues refer, among others, to Fenichel, 1945; Fine, 1979; Greenberg and Mitchell, 1983; Laplanche and Pontalis, 1967; Klein, Heimann and Money-Kyrle (1955); Nagera, 1969; Tyson and Tyson, 1990). It is also interesting to observe that *trieb* has been translated in the English version of Freud's complete work as 'instinct', although the term 'drive' can also be employed. In our work we prefer to employ the term 'instinct' to indicate both *instinkt* and *trieb*.

15 As we shall also see in Chapter 4, an important qualification is in order: namely, that his theories of instincts have never acquired a deterministic character, in the form of

unmodifiable 'postulates' or 'prime principles'. Freud (in particular, 1915) explicitly made clear this central methodological aspect by saying that psychoanalysis (as well other sciences) start their analysis by employing a set of tentative hypotheses that are continually revised and modified over time as the observation of real life experiences goes on.

16 The theory of sublimation plays an important role in Freud's theory but, as also observed by Freud himself and by subsequent authors, presents complex aspects that require further investigation. For our purpose, we can observe that Freud defines sublimation as a psychological orientation toward human activities apparently not in relation with sexuality – for instance, intellectual and artistic creations – which nonetheless draw most of their inner force from the psycho-sexual instinct. As far as we understand Freud's analysis, sublimation plays such a complex role because it may constitute, in manifold combinations, (a) a means for the expression of neurotic conflicts, and (b) a means for the expression of normal motivations of human personality. These different concepts of sublimation are outlined but not always clearly distinguished in Freud's analysis, and this may be one of the reasons, as we shall see later, for some entangled aspects of his analysis of society.

17 For more details on the complex evolution of Freud's terminology on these issues refer to Fenichel (1945), Fine (1979), Laplanche and Pontalis (1967), Nagera (1969).

18 For an interesting account of how, in relation to the emergence of new theoretical insights, the objectives of psychoanalysis have been clarified and refined, refer in particular to Sandler and Dreher (1996).

19 Recent contributions, in particular in the field of 'objectual and interpersonal relations', have elucidated relevant aspects of the child's early relations. Particular attention is devoted to the analysis of primary fantasies and to the defence mechanisms activated for coping with traumatic experiences, also in their implications for later interpersonal relations. Cf. among others Britton et al. (1989), Gazzillo (2012), Grotstein (2009), Kernberg (1976, 1992, 1998, 2004), López-Corvo (2006), Rosenfeld (1988), Tyson and Tyson (1990).

20 We can define the ISEF, in a broad sense, as the entire set of institutions and of socio-economic structures of a given reality, with its related cultural orientations, values, habits, knowledge, customs and working rules.

21 See, among others, Elliott (1994); Fine (1979); Greenberg and Mitchell (1983); Kernberg (2004); Rayner (1991); and Tyson and Tyson (1990).

22 As already observed, the concept of innate biological constitution seems to refer in Freud's analysis to the inborn traits (biological and intellectual) of the person and, in particular, to the qualitative and quantitative characteristics of his or her instinctual endowment. These concepts are complex to formulate and, in this regard, Freud always stressed that it is very difficult to be precise in an acceptable way about the real characteristics of any biological constitution under consideration.

Bibliography

Adler, A. (2011) *The Practice and Theory of Individual Psychology*. Eastford, CT: Martino Fine Books. First edition 1925.

Bastide, R. (1950) *Sociologie et Psychoanalyse*. Paris: P.U.F.

Britton, R., Feldman, M. and O'Shaughnessy, E. (1989) *The Oedipus Complex Today: Clinical Implications*. London: Karnac Books.

Elliott, A. (1994) *Psychoanalytic Theory*. Oxford: Blackwell.

Erikson, E.H. (1968) *Identity, Youth and Crisis*. New York: Norton.
Fenichel, O. (1945) *The Psychoanalytic Theory of Neuroses*. New York: Norton.
Fine, R. (1979) *A History of Psychoanalysis*. New York: Columbia University Press.
Freud, A. (1961) *The Ego and the Mechanisms of Defence*. London: The Hogarth Press and the Institute of Psycho-Analysis. Original German edition 1936.
Freud, S. (May and June 1894) Die Abwehr-Neuropsychosen. *Neurologisches Zentralblatt*. 13, nn. 10 and 11, pp. 362–364 and 402–409. English version, *The Neuro-Psychoses of Defence*. Cologne, Germany: The White Press, 2014.
Freud, S. (1900) *Die Traumdeutung*. Leipzig and Vienna: Deuticke. English version, *On Dreams*. Standard Edition. New York: Norton, 1990.
Freud, S. (1905) *Drei Abhandlungen zur Sexualtheorie*. Leipzig and Vienna: Deuticke. English version, *Three Essays on the Theory of Sexuality*. New York: Basic Books, 2000.
Freud, S. (1912–1913) *Totem und Tabu*. Leipzig, Vienna and Zurich: Internationaler Psychoanalytischer Verlag. English version, *Totem and Taboo*. Standard Edition. New York: Norton, 1990.
Freud, S. (1915) *Das Unbewusste*. *Internationale Zeitschrift für ärztliche Psychoanalyse*. English version, *The Unconscious*. London: Penguin, 2005.
Freud, S. (1920) *Jenseits des Lustprinzips*. Leipzig, Vienna and Zurich: Internationaler Psychoanalytischer Verlag. English version, *Beyond the Pleasure Principle*. Standard Edition. New York: Norton, 1990.
Freud, S. (1921) *Massenpsychologie und Ich-Analyse*. Leipzig, Vienna and Zurich: Internationaler Psychoanalytischer Verlag. English version, *Group Psychology and the Analysis of the Ego*. Standard Edition. New York: Norton, 1959.
Freud, S. (1923) *Das Ich und das Es*. Leipzig, Vienna and Zurich: Internationaler Psychoanalytischer Verlag. English version, *The Ego and the Id*. Standard Edition, New York: Norton, 1990.
Freud, S. (1924) Vorlesungen zur Einführung in die Psychoanalyse. *Gesammelte Schriften*, vol. 7. English version, *Introductory Lectures on Psycho-Analysis*. Standard Edition. New York: Norton, 1990.
Freud, S. (1926a) *Die Frage der Laienanalyse. Unterredungen mit einem Unparteiischen*. Leipzig, Vienna and Zurich, Internationaler Psychoanalytischer Verlag. English version, *The Question of Lay Analysis*. Standard Edition. New York: Norton, 1990.
Freud, S. (1926b) *Hemmung, Symptom und Angst*. Leipzig, Vienna and Zurich: Internationaler Psychoanalytischer Verlag. English version, *Inhibitions, Symptoms and Anxiety*. Standard Edition. New York: Norton, 1990.
Freud, S. (1930) *Das Unbehagen in der Kultur*. Leipzig, Vienna and Zurich: Internationaler Psychoanalytischer Verlag. English Version, *Civilization and Its Discontents*. Standard Edition. New York: Norton, 1990.
Freud, S. (1933) *Neue Folge der Vorlesungen zur Einführung in die Psychoanalyse*. Leipzig, Vienna and Zurich: Internationaler Psychoanalytischer Verlag. English version, *New Introductory Lectures on Psycho-Analysis*. Standard Edition. New York: Norton, 1990.
Freud, S. (1937) Die endliche und die unendliche Analyse. *Internationale Zeitschrift für Psychoanalyse* vol. 23. English version, *Analysis Terminable and Interminable*. International Psychoanalytical Association. First edition 1987.
Gazzillo, F. (2012) *I sabotatori interni*. Rome: Cortina Editore.
Goleman, D. (1995) *Emotional Intelligence*. New York: Bantam Books.
Greenberg, J.R and Mitchell, S.A. (1983) *Object Relations in Psychoanalytic Theory*, Cambridge, MA: Harvard University Press.

Grotstein, J.S. (2009) *But at the Same Time and on Another Level*. London: Karnac Books.
Hartmann, H. (1964) *Essays on Ego Psychology*. New York: International Universities Press.
James, W. (1950) *The Principles of Psychology*. New York: Dover Publications. First published in New York by Holt and Company, 1890.
Jones, E. (1953) *The Life and Work of Sigmund Freud*. London: Collins.
Jung, C.G. (1968) *Man and His Symbols*. New York: Dell Publishing. Originally published by Aldus Books in 1964.
Kahneman, D. and Tversky, A. (eds.) (2000) *Choices, Values and Frames*. Cambridge: Cambridge University Press.
Kernberg, O. (1976) *Object Relations Theory and Clinical Psychoanalysis*. New York: Aronson.
Kernberg, O. (1992) *Aggression in Personality Disorders and Perversions*. New Haven, CT: Yale University Press.
Kernberg, O. (1998) *Ideology, Conflict and Leadership in Groups and Organizations*. New Haven, CT: Yale University Press.
Kernberg, O. (2004) *Contemporary Controversies in Psychoanalytic Theory, Technique, and Their Applications*. New Haven, CT: Yale University Press.
Klein, M. (1964) *Contributions to Psychoanalysis 1921–1945*. New York: McGraw-Hill.
Klein, M. (1975) *Envy and Gratitude and Other Works 1946–1963*. New York: Delacorte Press.
Klein, M., Heimann, P. and Money-Kyrle, R. (eds.) (1955) *New Directions in Psycho-Analysis*. London: Tavistock Publications.
Laplanche, J. and Pontalis, J.B. (1967) *Vocabulaire de la Psychoanalyse*. Paris: P.U.F.
López-Corvo, R.E. (2006) *Wild Thoughts Searching for a Thinker: A Clinical Application of W.R. Bion's Theories*. London: Karnac Books.
Malinowski, B. (1927) *Sex and Repression in Savage Society*. London: Kegan Paul.
Maslow, A. (1971) *The Farther Reaches of Human Nature*. New York: Viking Press.
Meltzer, D.W. (1994) *Sincerity and Other Works. Collected Papers of Donald Meltzer*. London: Karnac Books.
Nagera, H. (1969) *Basic Psychoanalytic Concepts on the Libido Theory*. London: Allen & Unwin.
Nisbett, R.E. and Ross, L. (1980) *Human Inference: Strategies and Shortcomings of Social Judgement*. New Jersey: Prentice-Hall.
Pervin, L.A. and John, O.P. (1997) *Personality. Theory and Research*. New York: Wiley.
Rank, O. (1929) *The Trauma of Birth*. London: Kegan Paul. Originally published in German by the Internationaler Psychoanalytischer Verlag in 1924.
Rayner, E. (1991) *The Independent Mind in British Psychoanalysis*. London: Free Association Books.
Rosenfeld, H. (1988) *Psychoanalysis and Groups: History and Dialectics*. London: Karnac Books.
Ross, L. and Nisbett, R.E. (1991) *The Person and the Situation: Perspectives of Social Psychology*. New York: McGraw-Hill.
Sandler, J. and Dreher, A.U. (1996) *What Do Psychoanalysts Want?* Abingdon and New York: Routledge.
Sullivan, H.S., Perry, H.S. (ed.) and Gawel, M.L. (ed.) (1953), *The Interpersonal Theory of Psychiatry*. New York: Norton.
Turner, G.H. and Stets, J.E. (2005) *The Sociology of Emotions*. Cambridge: Cambridge University Press.
Tyson, P. and Tyson, R.L. (1990) *Psychoanalytic Theories of Development*. New Haven, CT and London: Yale University Press.

2 Implications for the study of economic and social phenomena

2.1 The 'public' and 'private' dimensions of human aggressiveness

As is known, human aggressiveness[1] constitutes a relevant source of trouble in human life. It is very difficult to deal with, as it is often ingrained in well-established habits of thought and life. In several cases it is also difficult to locate, as it often expresses itself in a subtle and disguised way.

An important distinction that can be drawn between the types of aggressive behaviour refers to its degree of 'public' or 'private' dimension. In the 'private' dimension, which we can conventionally identify in the sphere of life not directly involving a social purpose (e.g., personal dimension, family and friends), we can observe countless forms of aggressive behaviour.

They can refer, in particular, to a person's difficulty in giving affect and consideration to his/her fellows, which is accompanied by a parallel difficulty in recognizing and appreciating the affect and consideration they receive. This picture is often accompanied by other signs of aggressiveness: we can mention, in addition to overt cruel and sadistic behaviour, egoism, excessive narcissism, egocentrism, loftiness, authoritarianism, a tendency to marginalize and/or exploit and/or control others, also by trying to hamper and/or downplay their accomplishments.

There are also other, more disguised but no less dangerous, forms of aggressiveness, such as indifference, defeatism, excessive tendency to complain, obsessive preoccupation for others' well-being, passivity, lack of self-esteem and assertiveness. And, last but not least, aggressiveness can find expression in the classic neurotic symptoms like anxiety, depression, phobias, compulsive and obsessive behaviour. These symptoms are likely to be linked in various ways to the other aggressive traits outlined above.

Of course, all these personal expressions of aggressiveness are heavily interlaced with their more public or collective expressions. These are ingrained in the related ISEF, which is characterized by complex frameworks of rules, organizations and actions and by multiple systems of feelings and beliefs. These 'emotional' systems tend to be much articulated, as they range from the 'general mood' of a society to the specific institutional and organizational 'cultures'.

From these remarks a fundamental conclusion ensues, which calls for a systematic interdisciplinary approach in social sciences: namely, that, owing to the intrinsic multifariousness and complexity of social life, every attempt to inter-pret economic and social phenomena in a 'one-dimensional' way by means of a single and 'homogenizing' criterion will produce a very unrealistic and distorted picture of reality.

Let us now consider the psychoanalytic theory of aggressiveness and its impli-cations for the analysis of social life.

2.2 The psychoanalytic theory of aggressiveness

The psychoanalytic theory of aggressiveness did not go through an easy path-way. As is known, Freud, especially in his later work, tended to regard instincts as opposing forces which, out of their conflicts, are supposed to drive human behaviour in a rather ineluctable way. This conception, especially as set forth in his theory of the death instinct, led him to a pessimistic[2] view of human develop-ment, in the sense that such a view tends to imply that little can be done to reduce human aggressiveness.[3]

In this regard, his formulation of the theory of the death instinct – which, it is important to remember, Freud set out with the main aim of providing an explana-tion of human aggressiveness[4] but was nonetheless never completely convinced about its real validity[5] – triggered many controversies among psychoanalysts and is now largely dismissed chiefly as a result of an improved psychoanalytic under-standing of the role played by neurotic conflicts in the formation of aggressive behaviour (see, for instance, Fine, 1979).

In this respect, we believe that Freud's theory of the death instinct[6] hindered him from carrying out a deeper analysis of human aggressiveness and, also for this reason, one important strand of psychoanalytic research after Freud has brought the interpretation of aggressiveness to the fore.[7]

Thus, aggressive behaviour (including that aimed at causing the death of the person concerned or of others) is not considered as an inevitable outcome of 'nat-ural' instincts but as a dramatic expression of neurotic conflicts which, as we have seen, have their roots in the infantile life of the person.

Obviously, aggressiveness could not develop without an individual's inborn ability to develop this feeling, which can vary from person to person. However, the point is that, given these innate endowments, neurotic conflicts can play a great role in reinforcing aggressiveness, which, for this reason, cannot be realisti-cally regarded as an ineluctable expression of 'natural' instincts.[8]

Considering neurotic aggressiveness solely as an expression of immutable natural instincts is tantamount to regarding well-recognised neurotic symptoms, depression or phobias for instance, as a 'natural' expression of human nature sim-ply because man has an innate ability to experience sorrow or fear.

In this regard, it is notable that Freud and many other authors have stressed the role of (mostly unconscious) aggressiveness in causing depression, pho-bias and virtually any other neurotic disturbance. Furthermore, as we will see later on, aggressiveness may play a central role in shaping social and cultural contexts.

Within this ambit, several authors have underlined the articulated role of aggressiveness in institutional and cultural contexts: (i) on the one hand, it concurs to shape in many ways the ISEF through the mutual dependent actions of its members; (ii) on the other hand, cultural values are likely to foster the development of aggressiveness especially in the early stages of individual life – for instance, indirectly through their influence on the child's caretakers and directly through their role of 'cultural models' to be imitated and internalized by the child.

2.3 The psychoanalysis of groups and organizations

As already noted, Freud considers individual and collective psychology as two complementary aspects of the same phenomenon – owing to the circumstance, that in ancient times group life was pre-eminent and that only subsequently the person (and the institution of family) has gradually acquired a more defined role within the various groups of society.

As noted by Freud (in particular, 1912–1913, 1921 and 1930) and by subsequent psychoanalysts (see below), group cohesion tends to be based on the following processes: (i) emotional bonds among the members of the group; (ii) projection of individual aggressiveness into people and/or institutions lying outside the group; (iii) identification with the group leader – who symbolizes the parental instance (typically, the father) – in order to repress the conflicts related to the *Oedipus* complex.

These processes – which operate in part at an unconscious level and may be partly driven by neurotic conflicts – can help explain the scission that often occurs within groups between 'the good and right', lying inside the group, and 'the bad and mistaken', lying outside its boundaries. Building on these insights, there has been among psychoanalysts a growing attention to the collective dimension of psychological phenomena.

By using the Kleinian framework, Bion (1970) investigated unconscious group dynamics by means of the 'Therapeutic Group', while Kernberg (1998) made significant contributions to the analysis of group behaviour by employing his approach based on the object relations theory. Another remarkable contribution was provided by Ammon (1971), in which he stresses the importance of the 'therapeutic groups' as a key linking factor between the individual and the institutional dimension of psychological conflicts, with particular attention to aggressive behaviour.

All these contributions stress the role of groups and organizations for expressing the needs and conflicts of the person. For instance, to the person, the group may represent an idealized *ego*. And, in this connection, its 'morals' and 'code of conduct' symbolize[9] parental figures who, through a process of 'internalization', play the role of *superego*.

In this regard, it is important to note that the instance of *superego* discussed before, certainly, stems also from a normal human tendency to establish sound interpersonal relations, and, accordingly, to behave with affection and solicitude towards each other and continually improve the 'bright aspects' of personality.

However, whereas in non-neurotic situations the 'code of conduct' emerging from such tendencies asserts itself as a genuine behaviour, in neurotic situations leading to the formation of *superego* things run in a completely different way: here, the tendency of improving personality tends to be, under an appearance of goodness and morality, subordinated to the expression of neurotic contents at cross-purposes with such tendency.

As a matter of fact, on account of the sense of guilt arising from the child's aggressiveness towards its caretakers, a good portion of such aggressiveness is directed towards the child's *ego* in the role of a controlling and punitive instance for its aggressiveness. From this origin stems the severity, rigidity and inflexibility of the *superego*.[10] These characteristics of *superego*, however, as being based on the expression of neurotic conflicts, are able neither to create a better environment for the person nor to solve his or her problems.

Rather, as stressed by the authors just mentioned and many others,[11] quite often the severity of *superego* leads – through the so-called paranoid and narcissistic transformation of personality, extensively studied in psychoanalysis – single individuals, groups or societies to do nasty and persecutory actions towards other individuals, groups or societies into which their aggressiveness has been projected, and so to sabotage, in the meaning reviewed before, the possibility of establishing sound interpersonal relations.

These psychological processes can help explain – and history is full of such instances – the neurotic roots of racism, xenophobia and other phenomena of exclusion and marginalization. As we will see later, these phenomena tend to be reinforced by economic and social crises.

In this regard, after Freud's contribution on the subject (1914), the various aspects of narcissism have been deeply investigated especially within the object relations theories. These theories interpret the neurotic aspects of narcissism – often referred to as 'malign or pathological narcissism' as opposed to the normal narcissism, which corresponds to a normal process of self-assertion – as a severe incapacity of the person to establish sound interpersonal relations, which finds its origin in the *Oedipal* and pre-*Oedipal* stages of development.

This disturbance, therefore, does not imply that the narcissistic person expresses more self-love. Conversely, in such instance the underlying conflicts have pushed the person, through the scission and projection (largely unconscious) mechanisms described before, to negate and give up his or her real needs and orientations and, in their place, to find a meagre surrogate in compulsory fantasies of self-aggrandizement and omnipotent control of the external world.

The foregoing discussion implies that, for a deeper understanding of these phenomena, in the study of these conflicts both individual and collective dimensions should be considered, whatever be the particular focus of the analysis. For instance, in the study of individual conflicts, the characteristics of economic, social and cultural forms should be taken into account; whereas, in the study of collective forms, the psychological orientation of the individuals composing them should also be brought into focus.

2.4 Observing economic and social phenomena from a psychoanalytic perspective

As can be easily noted, the psychoanalytic perspective can be employed for the study of a countless range of economic and social situations. For instance, first an foremost, how do we perceive our society? Let us recall some pivotal psychoanalytic insights: (i) the significance for the person of the early stages of development and of the characteristics of family setting; (ii) the role of conflicts and fantasies in the formation of the unconscious life with its typical defence mechanisms – identification, internalization, scission and projection; (iii) the need of the person to give and receive affect, which, however, can be distorted and frustrated by neurotic conflicts.

On that basis, a first generic but important insight is that many persons tend – to a greater or lesser degree and mostly at an unconscious level – to perceive society as a kind of 'extended family'. In such 'family', the King or the President of the Republic plays the role of father, and powerful people that of elder brothers. But where is the maternal figure in society? Of course, this can lie in the Queen or in the President of the Republic, if it is a woman. However, in these instances it may happen that these women tend also to be perceived as masculine and father-like figures,[12] especially if they carry with them an idea of intransigent power.

Apart from these situations, there are many instances which can symbolize a maternal figure: in general, they can be identified in the protecting, gratifying and reassuring aspects[13] of society. Thus, the maternal role can be represented by society itself, by welfare provisions, by public goods and other forms of public spending.

In the analysis of these phenomena, we wish to point out the great potential of psychoanalytic theories for a better appraisal of the reasons and conflicts of such behaviour at individual and collective level. Now, we draw attention on a number of issue which can be addressed by this approach:

Considering that the economic action of the person – consumption, work, saving, investment – does not unfold in a *vacuum* on the basis of an abstract principle of maximization but is, rather, heavily embedded in the institutional, social and cultural domain, psychoanalysis can be of particular interest in illuminating the profound reasons underlying economic action.

For instance, considering an act of individual consumption, psychoanalysis can help identify the profound reasons, often unconscious, which can underlie this action. For instance, if persons buy a product chiefly out of imitation, emulation, and conformism to the prevailing social canons – a pattern well depicted by Veblen's theory of 'conspicuous consumption' – it can hardly be the case that they are maximizing their behaviour.

But the advocates of 'rational choice' theory will reply that this is the consumer's choice, and we should suppose that that choice is rational. In fact, they would add, why should we claim that people would not act rationally?

2.5 Rational choice and 'excess of cultural relativism'

This debate is very interesting but, in the absence of a psychological approach, tends to end up in a kind of stalemate. In fact, on the one hand, rational choice's theorists insist on the 'logical' supposition that individuals should act rationally. On the other hand, many contributions at variance with this approach underscore the importance of cultural factors in driving individual behaviour, and the role of habits of thought and life in forming the prevailing socio-cultural trajectories. For such reasons, these critics say, reducing all individual behaviour to the dichotomy rational/irrational constitutes a gross simplification of the variety of social and cultural forms.

However, the danger of this perspective is that it easily leads to what we can define (see also later) as 'the excess of cultural[14] relativism'. In fact, it could seem that, on the grounds of ensuring equal consideration to each context considered, equal legitimacy should be allowed to any kind of individual and social behaviour, no matter how ethical and psychologically sound we consider these patterns of behaviour to be.

For these reasons, both perspectives – rational choice and cultural relativism – however interesting in some respects, provide little aid in providing a deeper understanding of the multiplicity of factors underlying individual-society dynamics. In fact, these theories, each in its own way, do not allow the enquiry to go beyond their basic premises. In this sense, both theories 'do not care much' about why people feel and act in a certain way and, in particular, whether a given social system is conducive to the real developments of its members. As a matter of fact, every behaviour is allowed and considered 'normal' because, in one case, people 'behave rationally' and, in the other, their behaviour is a 'true expression' of a particular culture.

However, since many individual and social situations appear to be very far from an optimal or even satisfying condition, the central question becomes how to identify suitable policies for improving these situations. We will address these aspects later in the work: for now we can note that they are related to the ontological foundations of social value and policy action, with particular attention to the ethical and psychological dimensions. On that matter, the ethical foundations of social value and policies can be found not so much in some kind of abstract universal principles of kindness and solidarity but, rather, in latching these principles on the actual needs of the person.

For instance, if we assume, following Veblen and many contributions from social and psychological sciences (cf. also the second part), that the propensities of workmanship and parental bent – or, in psychoanalytic terminology, the capacity 'to work and love', which relates to the need for the person to establish sound interpersonal relations – lie at the heart of the true expression of the needs of the person, the ethical principle of solidarity would be endowed with a more precise content since it becomes engrained in a continual scientific oriented observation of the characteristics of human needs in their social and cultural unfolding.

Notes

1 Needless to say, we employ the term aggressiveness only in its neurotic connotation, as implying all kinds of hostile feelings and behaviour involving both the individual and the collective dimension.
2 As we shall see later in this part, Freud's pessimism is not so complete as his vision also allows for the possibility of social change.
3 This point was effectively addressed by Karen Horney. She notes that linking aggressiveness to an inner desire for death is against the evidence that in nature aggressiveness, for instance in predatory activities, is 'for the sake of life and not for the sake of destruction', (Horney, 1939: 131). But, if this is the case, a fundamental conclusion follows: namely, that all the unnecessary and neurotic aggressiveness should be regarded as a distorted expression of a basic instinct for life. We attack because we have a feeling, more or less neurotic-based, of being threatened or abused in our needs and rights. The following passages express these concepts clearly, 'The theory of a destruction instinct is not only unsubstantiated, not only contradictory to facts, but is positively harmful in its implications. In regard to psychoanalytical therapy it implies that making a patient free to express his hostility is an aim in itself, because, in Freud's contention, a person does not feel at ease if the destruction instinct is not satisfied. It is true that to the patient who has repressed his accusations, his egocentric demands, his impulses of revenge, it is a relief if he can express these impulses. But if analysts took Freud's theory seriously, a wrong emphasis would have to ensue. The main task is not to free these impulses for expression but to understand their reasons and, by removing the underlying anxiety, remove the necessity of having them. Furthermore, the theory helps to maintain the confusion that exists between what is really destructive and what essentially pertains to something constructive, that is, self-assertion. For example, a patient's critical attitude toward a person or cause may be primarily an expression of hostility arising from unconscious emotional sources; if, however, every critical attitude suggests to the analyst a subversive hostility, interpretations expressing such possibilities may discourage the patient from developing his faculties for critical evaluations. The analyst should try instead to distinguish between hostile motivations and attempts toward self-assertion. Equally harmful are the cultural implications of the theory. It must lead anthropologists to assume that whenever in a culture they find people friendly and peaceful, hostile reactions have been repressed. Such an assumption paralyzes any effort to search in the specific cultural conditions for reasons which make for destructiveness. It must also paralyze efforts to change anything in these conditions. If man is inherently destructive and consequently unhappy, why strive for a better future?', (Horney, 1939: 131, 132).
4 Needless to say, we employ the term aggressiveness only in its negative connotation, as implying all kinds of hostile feelings and behaviour involving both individual and collective dimension.
5 For more details on these issues refer to Freud (1920). In this regard, it can be interesting to note that Freud, in his first theory of instincts, explicitly linked the feeling of hate to self-preservation instincts. This is because hate, and the aggressive feeling associated with it, is considered as a reaction to an external frustration. In this sense, hate 'as an expression of the reaction of unpleasure provoked by objects, it remains forever closed related to self-preservation drives, so that ego drives and sexual drives readily form an opposition replicating that between hate and love' (Freud, 2005: 30; original edition 1915). As can easily be seen, this dualism is more pronounced in neurotic

situations. In this sense, Freud came near to – and indeed was about to realise – a full integration of aggressiveness in his theory of instincts. In fact, in order to complete the framework, perhaps only two, and relatively straightforward steps, were needed: (i) An explicit acknowledgement of neurotic aggressiveness in the formation of sadistic and destructive behaviour (including that directed towards the person in the form of masochism); and (ii) A clear distinction between the normal and neurotic aggressiveness. Both have their roots in the self-preservation instinct, but the latter, as being linked to neurotic disturbances, can find expressions that are, in various degrees, at cross-purpose with the instinct of self-preservation. For this reason, the introduction of a death drive in his second theory of instincts has created a notable gulf in respect to his first theory. There can be various reasons for this shift, but their analysis goes beyond the scope of our work. In this respect, it is likely that both internal and external reasons had played a significant role. As for the former, we may mention his psychological conflicts, also related to the 'technical' and emotional difficulty involved in the discovery of a new discipline; and, as for the latter, we can consider the feelings of disappointment and pessimism that were harboured in Freud's mind in relation to the events of the First World War.

6 However, as death constitutes an important factor in our life, the analysis of our psychological reaction and adaptation to such an event, which presents in any case a traumatic character, becomes relevant. In this regard, the following elements would require further investigation: for instance, the circumstance that a person's desire for death, rather than expressing a kind of inborn instinct, may constitute a defence mechanism against the fear of death. In this sense, if we perceive death as a persecutory and aggressive instance, the defence mechanism of identification with the aggressor – discovered by Anna Freud, who has stressed its importance in neurotic process and in particular in the formation of *superego* (cf. also Chapter 9) – can lead us to (apparently) 'desire' death. Likewise, considering as the basis of death instinct the desire to return to a previous state (in Freud's theory, from organic to inorganic) is not convincing. For example, it is true that the child, after experiencing the trauma of birth, may wish, as a defence mechanism, to go back to its protective experience as a *foetus*, but this does not imply that, for this reason, it desires 'to die' but only that it wants to release the anxiety associated with the growth process. The desire to abate tension and so become more 'relaxed' necessarily presupposes a form of life for experiencing and enjoying relaxation and, therefore, cannot be linked with death experience which means the end of our existence with all the related perceptions, feelings and emotions.

7 Among the numerous contributions which address, from different perspectives, the analysis of aggressiveness, refer to A. Freud (1936), Fine (1979), Kernberg (1976, 1992, 1998, 2004), M. Klein (1964, 1975), Rayner (1991), Winnicott (1958, 1974, 1988). From a partly different perspective see also May (1972).

8 However, it is important to note that Freud was aware of this process even though he had not fully developed this insight. See, for instance, the final part of *Civilization and Its Discontents* (1930), where, although within the death instinct framework, he suggests that the child's aggressiveness could be reinforced by the anger experienced within the *Oedipus* complex.

9 Within a different approach, the role of symbols and fantasies in the dynamics of psychological conflicts has been stressed by Jacques Lacan's theoretical perspective.

10 It is interesting to observe that the presence of *superego*, though being easily identifiable in instances of rigid moral systems, may acquire many forms often aimed at disguising its real repressive and punitive nature. A typical example can be that of an alcoholic

who claims that drinking is a way of 'being free', of not caring about the world. True, this can certainly be one side of the coin, but, conversely, the other side may rest in the circumstance that the *superego* is so severe and unbearable as to compel the person to try to escape – by impairing, as a way of punishment, his or her potentialities – from any action which can symbolize, in one way or another, its presence.

11 Within an interdisciplinary perspective embracing many fields of social and psychological sciences, T.W. Adorno and other researchers carried out a seminal enquiry on the characteristics of 'the Authoritarian Personality'.

12 As investigated by psychoanalytic theory, in the infantile perception power situations tend to be associated with the father (cf. also the next note). This happens especially in the presence of a patriarchal family.

13 Needless to say, such role can be performed also by the father. However, it is likely that the child tends to attribute different roles to its parents and that this attitude can be transposed in adult life, especially in neurotic situations. Of course, these attitudes depend on cultural values, but these, in turn, express profound psychological needs and conflicts. In this sense, a better comprehension of these conflicts can contribute to overcoming the rigid division of the roles typical of the patriarchal family.

14 We can employ the notion of culture in its common definition (cf. for instance, Dewey, 1939, and Ogburn, 1964) as the complex system which includes knowledge, beliefs, values, the economic and social arrangements and any other habits or capability acquired by a person in the social context.

References

Adorno, T.W. et al. (1950) *The Authoritarian Personality*. New York: Harper & Row.

Ammon, G. (1971) *Gruppendynamik der Aggression*. Berlin: Pynel-Publicationen.

Bion, W.R. (1970) *Attention and Interpretation: A Scientific Approach to Insights in Psycho-analysis and Groups*. London: Tavistock Publications.

Dewey, J. (1989) *Freedom and Culture*. New York: Prometheus Books. First edition 1939.

Fine, R. (1979) *A History of Psychoanalysis*. New York: Columbia University Press.

Freud, A. (1961) *The Ego and the Mechanisms of Defence*. London: The Hogarth Press and the Institute of Psycho-Analysis. Original German edition, 1936.

Freud, S. (1912–1913) *Totem und Tabu*. Leipzig, Vienna and Zurich: Internationaler Psychoanalytischer Verlag. English version, *Totem and Taboo*. Standard Edition. New York: Norton, 1990.

Freud, S. (1914) Zur Einführung des Narzissmus. *Jahrbuch der Psychoanalyse*, vol. 6. English version, *On Narcissism: An Introduction*. Cologne, Germany: White Press, 2014.

Freud, S. (1915) Das Unbewusste. *Internationale Zeitschrift für ärztliche Psychoanalyse*. English version, *The Unconscious*. London: Penguin, 2005.

Freud, S. (1920) *Jenseits des Lustprinzips*. Leipzig, Vienna and Zurich: Internationaler Psychoanalytischer Verlag. English version, *Beyond the Pleasure Principle*. Standard Edition. New York: Norton, 1990.

Freud, S. (1921) *Massenpsychologie und Ich-Analyse*, Leipzig, Vienna and Zurich: Internationaler Psychoanalytischer Verlag. English version, *Group Psychology and the Analysis of the Ego*. Standard Edition. New York: Norton, 1959.

Freud, S. (1930) *Das Unbehagen in der Kultur*, Leipzig, Vienna and Zurich: Internationaler Psychoanalytischer Verlag. English version, *Civilization and Its Discontents*. Standard Edition. New York: Norton, 1990.

Horney, K. (1939) *New Ways in Psychoanalysis*. New York: Norton.

Kernberg, O. (1976) *Object Relations Theory and Clinical Psychoanalysis*. New York: Aronson.

Kernberg, O. (1992) *Aggression in Personality Disorders and Perversions*. New Haven, CT: Yale University Press.

Kernberg, O. (1998) *Ideology, Conflict and Leadership in Groups and Organizations*. New Haven, CT: Yale University Press.

Kernberg, O. (2004) *Contemporary Controversies in Psychoanalytic Theory, Technique, and Their Applications*. New Haven, CT: Yale University Press.

Klein, M. (1964) *Contributions to Psychoanalysis 1921–1945*. New York: McGraw-Hill.

Klein, M. (1975) *Envy and Gratitude and Other Works 1946–1963*. New York: Delacorte Press.

May, R. (1972) *Power and Innocence: A Search for the Sources of Violence*. New York: Norton.

Ogburn, W.F. (1964) *On Culture and Social Change*. Chicago: The University of Chicago Press.

Rayner, E. (1991) *The Independent Mind in British Psychoanalysis*. London: Free Association Books.

Winnicott, D.W. (1958) *Through Paediatrics to Psycho-Analysis*. New York: Basic Books.

Winnicott, D.W. (1974) *Playing and Reality*. Harmondsworth: Penguin.

Winnicott, D.W. (1988) *Human Nature*. London: The Winnicott Trust by arrangement with Mark Paterson, 1988.

3 Psychoanalysis and social change

3.1 The relevance of psychological factors in the explanation of gross economic and social inequalities

From the foregoing discussion emerges the inadequacy of theoretical approaches based on tight disciplinary boundaries to provide a thorough account of the complexity of the factors at play in shaping social evolution. In fact, in these approaches everything must find a necessary and sufficient explanation within their boundaries. In this way, however, many significant elements of social phenomena are left outside. For instance, we can observe[1] in many social situations a more or less marked expression of one or more of the following features:

  i   An uncritical acceptance of the received 'habits of thought and life', which tends to be accompanied by a lack of critical thinking, an excessive fear of social changes, and a lack of interest about everything not directly concerning the personal sphere;

  ii The importance of ceremonial institutions, and of the power and hierarchical system attached to them;

  iii A tendency to establish a rigid dichotomy within 'the good and right' lying inside the group, and 'the bad and mistaken', lying outside; this tendency goes along with the tendency of identification with the group leader, which is a good symbol for the father;

  iv In consequence of these phenomena, throughout history virtually all societies have been based on rigid differences in economic and social status, and on the unequal opportunity for all members to express their potential.

  v   In many cases these inequalities reach the extreme forms of destitution, and are often accompanied by phenomena of imperialism, wars, xenophobia and exploitation at internal and external level.

  vi The limited capacity of populations, and in particular of disadvantaged classes, to react to individual and social injustice: in fact, what we can see, at least until the industrial revolution that came about at the end of the eighteenth century, is the persistence of unfair and despotic regimes over many centuries and the very slow pace at which social change has been realized.

vii After the industrial revolution, true, the world has experienced a much faster rate of change. Much progress has been realized in many fields, but gross problems, injustices and inequalities at all levels of economic and social life still remain. Also in more recent times, people underwent harsh and unfair dictatorships (and also other unsatisfactory economic and social situations) without much reaction, and often showing a passive identification with the dictator.

It seems that, as a result of neurotic conflicts, people seek, more or less unconsciously, some kind of dictatorship as a way to express their 'need of dependency' (see, in particular, Kernberg, 1998). In many cases, there is a kind of cyclical movement in historical evolution, which sees the alternation of periods of progress and conservatism. In several cases, a period of social protest is followed by a harsh dictatorship. But even when the social protest succeeds in obtaining a social change, there is often a regression to previous attitudes (cf. also the next points).

viii There have been, of course, many progressive movements in the history and they have achieved relevant results. However, the impression is that these results, however outstanding in themselves, have not been sufficient to usher in a real new course to social evolution that is more firmly based on sustainable and equitable relations at economic and social level.

ix As a matter of fact, what often (and notoriously) happens after social progress has been realized is: (a) that, in the case of an 'incremental' progress – for instance, an improvement of work conditions – its effects tend to be damped down by a series of direct and indirect counter-reactions; (b) that, in the case of a more widespread change, such as a revolution, the new ruling group will start to show, at least in part, the same negative and predatory traits of the older system.

In this kind of analysis, no single theory can provide a comprehensive explanation, as each theory is likely to grasp only a few aspects of the issues at hand. What seems greatly needed is an interdisciplinary approach which, in maintaining and enhancing the distinctive characteristics of each discipline, will help to identify the complex interchange between them. Such interchange is bound to exist simply because we are addressing, albeit from different perspectives – e.g., economic, sociological, political, psychological and psychoanalytic – the same phenomena.

For instance, in analyzing the social traits mentioned above, an interdisciplinary approach would throw more light on many relevant phenomena. Let us start from a previous remark that, in several cases, a period of social protest is followed by a harsh dictatorship.

This situation can be likened to that of a child that is punished after being 'naughty'. Of course, no mechanical transposition can be made, as each situation carries its own specific economic and social characteristics, which require to be carefully investigated. However, there is also some common ground in psychological and social evolution. In this sense, as already noted, it seems reasonable to assume that people tend to consider society as a kind of 'extended family'.[2] This happens because persons tend to transpose to society their most unconscious psychological conflicts which found their origin in the family sphere.

3.2 The unconscious need for authoritarian relations

This being the case, a fundamental conclusion follows: the relations between oppressing and oppressed (or privileged and disadvantaged, or exploiting and exploited) classes and groups of society can find – along with all the existing economic and social theories – an additional and complementary explanation in the expression of neurotic conflicts at the individual and collective level.

Thus, a hierarchical society tends to reproduce the authoritarian[3] and frustrating relations the child had experienced in its infancy, with all the resulting neurotic conflicts and defence mechanisms. Also for this reason, in societal life, each class or group tends to cling, mostly in an unconscious way, to the role attributed to them by society. In many cases, as well described by Freud in particular in *Totem and Taboo*, enviousness and anger tend to be repressed and overcompensated by a dependent and complaisant attitude.

At this point, however, a person sceptical about this approach can ask, 'even admitting the hierarchical aspects implied in a given society, what is the problem if people are (or, at least, appear) at ease with that situation?' However, a closer scrutiny of real situations would evidence a number of striking features. In many cases, persons talk about their rulers as they actually knew them.

What in general happens is that the rulers tend to be idealized: so, they tend to embody only good qualities – they are respectable, elegant, honest, generous, sensible, charitable. All the negative aspects of these persons tend to be strongly denied. And even when persons note some negative aspects in this picture, these tend to be justified and/or downplayed in one way or another. Besides, even when a more objective (or else exaggeratedly negative) appraisal[4] is present, this does not always lead to a strong quest for social change.

In fact, also as a result of the neurotic conflicts just outlined, feelings of defeatism and resignation can easily become overwhelming: in this case, people tend to think that no social change would be really attainable. This happens because the ruling class is held to be too powerful and/or necessary for economic development. In this regard, some people can say 'better an old enemy than the uncertainty of the new'.

By observing such mental portraits one may well ask if the rulers with their ceremonial setting can constitute for many people a good symbol of the idealized and omnipotent family that the child, and later the adult, would have got in the past. The plausibility of this hypothesis stems also from the circumstance that many psychoanalytic studies have pinpointed the relevance of these phenomena not only in childhood but also in adulthood. Hence, these relations tend to be present, to a greater or lesser extent, in virtually any kind of society and to encompass every province[5] of economic and social life.

This mental construction has a parallel to the child's attitude towards the growth process. It wishes to grow, for its own sake and also perhaps to release the oppressive aspects of its parents, but, at the same time, it is very frightened to accomplish this process. At this point, however, our sceptical interlocutor may remain unconvinced and then can ask again, 'Right, let us suppose your hypothesis be true, so what? If people are happier imagining the rulers as an idealized family, the same could apply for, say, *telenovelas*, so where is the problem? In this light, if we abolished *telenovelas* people will probably become less happy.'

3.3 The need for idealized and imaginary relations

Put in this way, our interlocutor can be right. However, by adopting a more encompassing approach, the analysis becomes much more intriguing. In fact, we can ask, what are the profound reasons which lead us to establish an emotional and imaginary contact with persons whom we do not actually know and who are unaware of our feelings towards them? In everyday life, if a person falls in love with someone who does not even know of these feelings, such behaviour is considered unsound, frustrating, if not a 'bit crazy'.

Hence, why should the same reasoning not hold true for the emotional and imaginary relations of persons with more institutionalised figures? These, of course, may be represented not only by the political rulers, but by other authoritative figures in economic and social spheres, and also by more leisure-time figures such as actors, singers and sports-champions.

In all these instances – which, of course, require a thorough interdisciplinary approach for their full appraisal – psychoanalysis tend to hypothesize that such need for idealization constitutes a kind of defence against frustrating and unsatisfactory relations that persons may have experienced in particular during their childhood.

However, it is not only the feeling of dissatisfaction that urges persons to try to forget their bad experiences and to replace them with idealized parents within an idealized world. Such process, in fact, if it consisted only of these aspects, could be considered as a normal process of putting to the background the bad experiences and to the foreground the good ones.

What makes bad experiences in childhood so troubling and dangerous for the individual's future development is that they involve emotional conflicts which – by involving feelings of abandonment, anger, guilt and inadequacy that have been largely repressed in a kind of primitive defence mechanism – can jeopardize the sound development of the child.

In all this picture, we need to be aware of the intrinsic complexity of these relations, which require to be contextualized in order to grasp their full significance. For instance, let us suppose that in an ordinary family the parents do not pay much attention to the needs of their child. A typical instance is when they buy a lot of toys for the child but spend little time actually playing with it.

The child perceives this aspect and feels itself abandoned and angry at its parents. This process can be greatly reinforced by the *Oedipus* complex which, as noted earlier, constitutes the first 'social relation' of the child. In fact, it is more than likely that the child, in its effort to find an explanation for the parents' attitudes, tends, in a typical infantile reasoning, to attribute everything to its own behaviour. Thus, if the parents overlook the child, this can imply, in its perception, that the mother prefers the father to him, or the father prefers the mother to her. And this happens, because it may perceive itself too 'little and inadequate' in respect of the parent of the same sex.

The anger and rivalry triggered by this process can greatly reinforce these effects: now the child, as the result of its feeling of guilt arising from its desire 'to eliminate' the 'rival parent', feels profoundly unworthy of receiving love and consideration. And, in a kind of vicious circle, the feeling of being too little and inadequate is likely to increase. As deeply investigated by psychoanalytic literature, these painful conflicts need to be repressed and, in their place, neurotic symptoms arise. These can assume different forms and intensities according to the child's basic character,[6] and to the characteristics and conflicts of society and of child's caretakers.

As investigated deeply by Freud (in particular, in *Totem and Taboo, Mass Psychology and the Analysis of the Ego, Civilization and Its Discontents*), both ancient and modern societies are based on a profound feeling of guilt related to the unconscious desire to kill the father. In Freud's view, what takes place in the infancy of the person acquires also a phylogenetic character, in the sense that the person is supposed to embody in his mind a kind of reminiscence of that primordial stage of human history.

Following these insights, many psychoanalysts have investigated the role of these early conflicts in the adult life of the person.

3.4 Freud as a social reformer

The previous discussion highlights the great potential of psychoanalysis in attaining a better understanding of individual and social conflicts and, on that basis, in identifying the ways for their progressive solution. However, the potential of psychoanalysis in this respect has remained largely unexplored. This can be due to a host of reasons, both internal and external to the psychoanalytic domain. In consideration of the importance of these aspects, we deem it important to consider how Freud addressed these issues.[7]

As we have seen, Freud's theory provides relevant insights into the conflicts of individual and collective life and the possibility of social change. However, notwithstanding these contributions, among social scientists Freud is rarely regarded as a social reformer. Rather, social scientists – owing, perhaps, to a rather pessimistic vein present in some of Freud's writings – tend to regard his theory as essentially 'conservative', as it would seem to imply that little can be done to abate human aggressiveness.

Certainly, as we have seen, there is such a vein in Freud's theory. But, at the same time, his theory is more far-reaching than this interpretation would suggest, as it contains aspects which clearly point to the possibility of social change.

For instance, in discussing the 1917 Russian Revolution, he is not against such transformation but underlines the importance for social reformers, in order to build a truly better society, to acquire a deeper understanding of human nature. The following passages effectively express these concepts:

> The communists believe that they have found the path to deliverance from our evils. According to them, man is wholly good and is well-disposed to his neighbour; but the institution of private property has corrupted his nature. The ownership of private wealth gives the individual power, and with it the temptation to ill-treat his neighbour; while the man who is excluded from possession is bound to rebel in hostility against his oppressor. If private property were abolished, all wealth held in common, and everyone allowed to share in the enjoyment of it, ill-will and hostility would disappear among men . . . [Here there is a footnote in which Freud stresses his solidarity, also in relation to his own experience, with the situations of economic deprivation] . . . But I am able to recognize that the psychological premises on which the system is based are an untenable illusion. In abolishing private property we deprive the human love of aggression of one of its instruments, certainly a strong one, though certainly not the strongest; but we have in no way altered the differences in power and influence which are misused by aggressiveness, nor have we altered anything in its nature. Aggressiveness was not created by property. It reigned almost without limit in primitive times, when property was still very scanty.
>
> (Freud, *Civilization and Its Discontents*, 1990: 70–71;
> original edition 1930)

Despite these cautious remarks, when discussing the difficulty of lessening human aggressiveness, he observes that:

> At this point the ethics based on religion introduces its promises of a better after-life. But so long as virtue is not rewarded here on earth, ethics will, I fancy, preach in vain. I too think it quite certain that a real change in the relations of human beings to possessions would be of more help in this direction than any ethical commands; but the recognition of this fact among socialists has been obscured and made useless for practical purposes by a fresh idealistic misconception of human nature.
>
> (Ibid.: 109)

These remarks pinpoint the importance of considering the psychological side of every project of social reform, by centring attention on the characteristics of neurotic conflicts and on the role of psychoanalysis in their understanding. In this sense, collaboration among psychoanalysis, Marxism and other theories of social change would be of particular interest, also for devising policies more effective in attaining the objectives of social reforms. In order to better illustrate these issues, let us quote a number of Freud's passages containing a clear explanation of the links intervening between individual and collective psychology:

What means does civilization employ in order to inhibit the aggressiveness which opposes it, to make it harmless, to get rid of it, perhaps? ... His aggressiveness is introjected, internalized; it is, in point of fact, sent back to where it came from – that is, it is directed towards his own ego. There it is taken over by a portion of the ego, which sets itself against the rest of the ego as super-ego, and which now, in the form of 'conscience', is ready to put into action against the ego the same harsh aggressiveness that the ego would have liked to satisfy upon other, extraneous individuals ... If the development of civilization has such a far-reaching similarity to the development of the individual and if it employs the same methods, may we not be justified in reaching the diagnosis that, under the influence of cultural urges, some civilizations, or some epochs of civilization – possibly the whole of mankind – have become 'neurotic'? An analytic dissection of such neuroses might lead to therapeutic recommendations which could lay claim to great practical interest. I would not say that an attempt of this kind to carry psycho-analysis over to cultural communities was absurd or doomed to be fruitless. But we should have to be very cautious and not forget that, after all, we are only dealing with analogies and that it is dangerous, not only with men but also with concepts, to tear them from the sphere in which they have originated and been evolved ... But in spite of all these difficulties, we may expect that one day someone will venture to embark upon a pathology of cultural communities.

(Ibid.: 83, 84, 85, 91, 92, 109, 110)

These concepts constitute the basis of Freud's enquiry into the psychological processes and conflicts of collective and cultural life, as set out more extensively in *Totem and Taboo*, and *Group Psychology and the Analysis of the Ego*.

Thus, in consequence of the sense of guilt arising from the child's aggressiveness towards its caretakers, a good portion of such aggressiveness is directed towards the child's *ego* in the role of a controlling and punitive instance for its aggressiveness. From this origin stems the severity, rigidity and inflexibility of the *superego*. These characteristics of *superego*, however, as being based on the expression of neurotic conflicts, are able neither to create a better environment for the person nor to solve his or her problems.

As already noted, quite often the severity of *superego* leads – through the so-called paranoid and narcissistic transformation of personality, extensively studied in psychoanalysis – single individuals, groups or societies to do nasty and persecutory actions towards other individuals, groups or societies into which their aggressiveness has been projected, and so to sabotage the objective of establishing sound interpersonal relations.

3.5 The problem of the psychoanalytic *Weltanschauung*

The previous discussion raises an important question: should psychoanalysis possess a *weltanschauung* – defined approximately, due to difficulty of translation, as a vision of the world also implying a kind of ethical system – and, in the affirmative case, of what kind?

Freud addressed this issue especially in the final chapter of the *New Introductory Lectures on Psycho-Analysis*. He underlined that psychoanalysis is a branch of scientific investigation and, as such, its *weltanschauung* should be located in that province. In this sense, psychoanalysis, in the opinion of Freud, cannot acquire a *weltanschauung* as a distinct ethical (or philosophical, religious, political) system of behaviour, just because it is not an ethical discipline. Of course, psychoanalysis, by helping the person to overcome his or her inner conflicts, can also contribute to reduce the neurotic aggressiveness related to such conflicts. In this way, a better behaviour could reasonably be expected. But such outcome does not spring up by following some abstract ethical rules but by a scientifically based process of self-understanding.

In this regard, individual self-understanding is not without consequences for social self-understanding, since psychoanalysis is at the same time an individual and a collective psychology. Therefore, the application of psychoanalysis to the comprehension of social phenomena, although not entailing a direct ethical impact as such, can have important consequences in this respect.

As a matter of fact, a better appraisal of the manifold expressions of the psychological conflicts underlying social structures can open the way for a corresponding reduction of such social patterns of behaviour and for the parallel increase of the real possibilities of expression for the members of society.

On that account, we can also note that psychoanalysis has the great merit of making clear that following ethical rules without a clear self-understanding of the inner individual and social conflicts underlying such behaviour is unlikely to warrant – due, as observed before, to the inner 'sabotage' of these rules on the account of neurotic conflicts – the attainment of the proposed objectives. For this reason, Freud considers paramount a closer collaboration between psychoanalysis and social sciences.

In order to better illustrate Freud's point of view, let us quote some passages from his *The Question of Lay Analysis*, in which he underscores the opportunity of also extending to people holding non-medical degrees (the so-called 'lay psychoanalysts') the possibility of becoming a psychoanalyst. The reason underlying this opinion – which has triggered a lively debate whose analysis is beyond the scope of this work – is that the knowledge necessary for becoming an analyst is different from that required for becoming a medical doctor. As a matter of fact, the crucial knowledge identifying an analyst should cover, in Freud's opinion, not only direct psychoanalytic knowledge and the basics of medicine but should also extend to matters belonging to the field of social sciences, such as history and mythology. In this perspective, Freud thinks that psychoanalysis, in collaboration with other social sciences, can find interesting applications in a host of social issues. As he points out, in a sparkly discussion with an imaginary interlocutor:

> as a 'depth-psychology', a theory of the mental unconscious, [psychoanalysis] can become indispensable to all the sciences which are concerned with

the evolution of human civilization and its major institutions such as art, religion, and the social order. It has already, in my opinion, afforded these sciences considerable help in solving their problems. But these are only small contributions compared with what might be achieved if historians of civilization, psychologists of religion, philologists, and so on would agree themselves to handle the new instrument of research which is at their service. The use of analysis for the treatment of neuroses is only one of its applications; the future will perhaps show that it is not the most important one. . . . Then let me advise you that psycho-analysis has yet another sphere of application. . . . Its application, I mean, to the bringing-up of children. If a child begins to show signs of an undesirable development, if it grows moody, refractory, and inattentive, the paediatrician and even the school doctor can do nothing for it, even if the child produces clear neurotic symptoms, such as nervousness, loss of appetite, vomiting, or insomnia. . . . Our recognition of the importance of these inconspicuous neuroses of children as laying down the disposition for serious illnesses in later life points to these child analyses as an excellent method of prophylaxis. . . . Moreover, to return to our question of the analytic treatment of adult neurotics, even there we have not yet exhausted every line of approach. Our civilization imposes an almost intolerable pressure on us and it calls for a corrective. Is it too fantastic to expect that psycho-analysis in spite of its difficulties may be destined to the task of preparing mankind for such a corrective? Perhaps once more an American may hit on the idea of spending a little money to get the 'social workers' of his country trained analytically and to turn them into a band of helpers for combating the neuroses of civilization.

[and the answer of the interlocutor] 'Aha! A new kind of Salvation Army!'

Why not? Our imagination always follows patterns. The stream of eager learners who will then flow to Europe will be obliged to pass Vienna by, for here the development of analysis may have succumbed to a premature trauma of prohibition. You smile? I am not saying this as a bribe for your support. Not in the least. I know you do not believe me; nor can I guarantee that it will happen.

(Freud, *The Question of Lay Analysis*, 1990: 83, 84, 85, 86; original edition, 1926)

As we can see, this approach constitutes a good agenda for social progress, which is still largely unexplored.

3.6 How can we establish an effective collaboration between psychological and social sciences?

At this stage a central problem arises: once we have acknowledged the great varieties of cultural forms, how can we depart from the excess of cultural relativism discussed before without falling back in the opposite excess, in a kind of psychological determinism? As we can see, answering this problem is paramount in order to establish a sound collaboration between psychological and social sciences.

A first remark coming to the fore is the advisability of improving such collaboration. In fact, when analysing a given context, we can easily note the multiple dimensions through which individual and collective action unfolds: economic, social, legal, political, ethical. Now, as a given set of social sciences tends to correspond to these domains, and considering that the interrelations between these spheres are numerous, the opportunity of a better collaboration between psychological and social sciences appears clearly.

How, then, can this collaboration help explain the variety of cultural forms? With regard to the theme of the book, the relations between heterodox economics and psychoanalysis, we can make the following remarks:

A   As also emerges from the previous discussion, the dichotomy between 'nature' on the one side and culture on the other appears to be groundless. It is in fact a typical aspect of our nature a high level of flexibility and capacity to gear to various circumstances. And, relatedly, another typical aspect of our nature is the capacity and need to establish interpersonal relations within the development of emotional and intellectual faculties.

It is, then, in these characteristics of human nature, and not in some 'exogenous factor', that lie the seeds of an endless typology of cultures and societies. But how can we explain the diversity of cultural patterns? A number of factors are likely to play a relevant role:

i   One relates to the endless differences in character and personality. In this sense, since we never meet two identical persons so we never meet two identical groups. The same applies to the psychological conflicts in the person's mind and within the group, which relate to the complex issue (cf. above), of the 'choice of neurosis'.

ii   In this regard, the dynamics of the person and of the group are cognate but by no means identical. What tends to happen in the group is that some dominant traits of personality of the leading members are spread and assimilated in various ways, by a kind of identification process, by the members of the group. Thus, different cultural patterns can originate and be reinforced over time by a kind of cumulative process, with their distinctive aspects and ways of expressing psychological conflicts.

iii   However, it would be highly unrealistic to suppose that cultural patterns do not display important aspects of similarity. As ethnographic and psychoanalytic observation would show, these common aspects are related to the strong emotional bonds between the members of the group, the identification of the single member with the group and the group leader, the formation of shared beliefs, values, and codes of conduct between the members of the group.

A typical instance in this respect is constituted by eating habits (cf. also above) which, however different they may be across different cultures, are likely to play a relevant role in all of them.

iv   All this should not be interpreted as a monolithic aspect of the group. In fact, the group culture goes in tandem with the unique personality of each member and the mutual influence between them in shaping the articulated expressions of 'group behaviour'.

As we also see in Chapter 6, individual and collective action are not unrelated entities, owing to circumstance that much individual action takes place in institutions and organizations.

B   Of course, it is also true that psychological factors cannot constitute the sole seat of societal evolution. As a matter of fact, other realms of social sciences, in particular, economics, law, politics, are likely to play a relevant role in such evolution, also considered in their interaction.

We need not spend many words in remarking that, say, the phenomenon of scale economies, or the relations between aggregate demand or aggregate supply, or between inflation and exchange rates, require an 'economics-based' explanation.

The same applies to the provinces of law and politics.

In this sense, the dynamics of these fields acquire a distinct logic that necessitates a specific discipline for their understanding. But this does not imply that these disciplines, owing to their own specificity, are self-sufficient.

For instance, if we wish to understand the phenomenon of scale economies, we need to learn their typologies and how they take place in real situations, and how they accord with firms' strategies, values and cultural orientation.

Since these strategies, however, do not depend only on the 'technical factors' but interact in multiple ways with the institutional, social and psychological dimensions of human action, the relevance of interdisciplinary approach appears in a clear way. Thus, such an approach is fully compatible with a progressive specialization of the related fields. In fact, a pattern of specialization which depends on the growing complexity of the system, tends to reinforce the interlink between the different parts and then the need for a comprehensive interpretation of these phenomena.

In this regard, an interdisciplinary approach can make headways towards a better understanding not only of the phenomena under investigation, but also and relatedly, of the psychological reasons which can underlie the formation of theories and the interpretation of social[8] phenomena.

All that said, one can wonder how a collaboration between heterodox economics and psychoanalysis can unfold in practice. A first important task is that of addressing the problem of psychological disturbances. These, of course, express themselves in the individual dimension but the social dimension is never absent.

Every person, in fact, is also a member of a society and the available studies[9] show that the most impairing forms of psychological disturbances tend to be more diffused within the disadvantaged sections of the population.

Another important and related field of enquiry pertains to how persons perceive and interpret economic and social phenomena, with particular attention to the phenomena of crises and imbalances. In this regard, psychoanalysis can help explain, in particular through the role of *superego* addressed before, why so many people remain bound to rigid conceptions of life and so tend to overlook relevant aspects of the economic and social system. As we shall see, these aspects are particularly evident in the failure of both lay people and experts to foreshadow the eruption of the recent economic crisis. However, even in other fundamental domains of economic and social life the situation is not much better.

In the analysis of these aspects, a cognate aspect (cf. also the second part) that can explain the 'sticky' conceptions of many people can be found in the role of habits of thought and action in preserving and transmitting the main aspects of the cultural heritage.

An interdisciplinary analysis would help look into the complex interchange between individual and collective level in the working of institutions and organizations, with particular attention to the implications for policy action.

Notes

1 For more details on these aspects refer to Adorno (1950), Ammon (1971), Bion (1970), Kernberg (1998).
2 Needless to say, the concept of family is a very evolutionary one and is influenced by the complexity of social and psychological development.
3 We can define the adjective 'authoritarian' along with the definition contained in the Webster's Unabridged Dictionary, according to which such aspect pertains to a government or principle in which individual freedom is completely subordinated to the authority of the state, centred in one person or small group not accountable to the population. Such aspects may also characterize smaller organizations and personal relations. In this regard, there can be various forms and degrees of authoritarian relations. Of course, this does not imply that any form of hierarchy should be only or overwhelmingly neurotic-driven. In most cases a set of rules and of corresponding social functions is necessary for guaranteeing the relative stability of the social framework. On the other hand, it seems also true that a social intercourse completely neurotic-free is unlikely to be found. The issue then is to promote the maximum of participation by reducing the unnecessary authoritarianism as described before.
4 It is interesting to note that, as we are strongly tied to our personal and social situation, the process of social judgment tends to be more or less severely biased. See, for instance, in the field of social psychology, the stimulating works of Nisbett and Ross (1980), Ross and Nisbett (1991).
5 For instance, in many countries there has occurred in the last decades a diminution of the authoritarianism of the patriarchal family, even if the social and emotional basis of this kind of family is still far from having being eliminated. The same cannot be said for other kind of relations – for instance, labour relations. As also highlighted by psychoanalytic oriented studies on organizational structure, labour activities within both public and private institutions are still arranged mainly through rigid hierarchical and bureaucratic systems which, by tending to reproduce at social level a child–adult neurotic relation, allow limited room for independence and creativity (cf., in particular, De Board 1990; Gabriel, 1999; Kernberg, 1998; Ketz de Vries and Miller, 1984).

6 These issues are related (see above) to the issues of the severity of neurotic symptoms and of 'the choice of neurosis'. In this regard, the question arises, why, in the presence of the same family and social setting, children can develop different kind of symptoms: for instance, hysterical traits, obsessive behaviour, depressive orientation. These symptoms can go together with a modification of character traits: for instance, a child, in order to keep its parents' affection, can develop a tendency to negate its parents' faults, together with a marked dependency on their opinions and behaviour. Another child, instead, can over-criticize its parents and form character traits and opinions sharply opposed to those of the parents.

7 Needless to say, many psychoanalysts have provided notable contributions on these issues, also from partly different theoretical orientations: among others, we can mention Sandor Ferenczi, Gunner Ammon, Wilfred Bion, Erik Erikson, Otto Fenichel, Reuben Fine, Peter Gay, Karen Horney, Otto Kernberg, Melanie Klein, Harry Stack Sullivan.

8 As noted before, these processes can be more or less severely biased by our unconscious fantasies, emotions and conflicts.

9 Refer, among others, to the data and initiatives of the World Mental Health, http://www. who.int/mental_health/en/, the work of Desjarlais and others, and the initiative of *The Lancet*. These studies evidence that social position has a bearing on the type and frequency of psychological disturbances. As one can expect, the most impairing forms tend to be most diffused among the most disadvantaged sections of the population. However, this does not imply that the other groups of society are neurotic-free. As we will try to show, severe neurotic disturbances do not necessarily carry with them impairing symptoms and may also be compatible with an apparently normal life.

References

Adorno, T.W. et al. (1950) *The Authoritarian Personality*. New York: Harper & Row.

Ammon, G. (1971) *Gruppendynamik der Aggression*. Berlin: Pynel-Publicationen.

Bion, W.R. (1970) *Attention and Interpretation: A Scientific Approach to Insights in Psycho-analysis and Groups*. London: Tavistock Publications.

De Board, R. (1990) *The Psychoanalysis of Organizations: A Psychoanalytic Approach to Behaviour in Groups and Organizations*. Abingdon and New York: Routledge.

Desjarlais, R. et al. (1995) *World Mental Health. Problems and Priorities in Low-Income Countries*. New York and Oxford: Oxford University Press.

Freud, S. (1912–1913) *Totem und Tabu*. Leipzig, Vienna and Zurich: Internationaler Psychoanalytischer Verlag. English version, *Totem and Taboo*. Standard Edition. New York: Norton, 1990.

Freud, S. (1926) *Die Frage der Laienanalyse. Unterredungen mit einem Unparteiischen*. Leipzig, Vienna and Zurich: Internationaler Psychoanalytischer Verlag. English version, *The Question of Lay Analysis*. Standard Edition. New York: Norton, 1990.

Freud, S. (1930) *Das Unbehagen in der Kultur*. Leipzig, Vienna and Zurich: Internationaler Psychoanalytischer Verlag. English version, *Civilization and Its Discontents*. Standard Edition. New York: Norton, 1990.

Freud, S. (1933) *Neue Folge der Vorlesungen zur Einführung in die Psychoanalyse*. Leipzig, Vienna and Zurich: Internationaler Psychoanalytischer Verlag. English version, *New Introductory Lectures on Psycho-Analysis*. Standard Edition. New York: Norton, 1990.

Gabriel, Y. (1999) *Organizations in Depth*. Thousand Oaks, CA: Sage Publications.

Kernberg, O. (1998) *Ideology, Conflict and Leadership in Groups and Organizations*. New Haven, CT: Yale University Press.

Ketz de Vries, M.F.R. and Miller, P. (1984) *The Neurotic Organization*. New York: Jossey Bass Publishers.

Nisbett, R.E. and Ross, L. (1980) *Human Inference: Strategies and Shortcomings of Social Judgement*. New Jersey: Prentice-Hall.

Ross, L. and Nisbett, R.E. (1991) *The Person and the Situation: Perspectives of Social Psychology*. New York: McGraw-Hill.

4 Some controversial aspects of psychoanalysis

4.1 The intrinsic difficulty of a 'scientific' interpretation of feelings

As seen in the previous chapters, psychoanalysis is a highly complex discipline attempting, as it does, to explain psychological processes through an integrated approach. Because of this, psychoanalysis does not move along a smooth pathway. In fact, it is coping with two related sets of problems:

1 The divergences among psychoanalysts regarding certain aspects of Freudian theory.
2 Criticism of the psychoanalytic approach coming from both psychology and other disciplines.

With regard to the first point, we have seen that these divergences do not affect the unitary character of the psychoanalytic domain, but are part of the normal dialectic of every discipline that wishes to be truly scientific. Indeed, psychoanalysis, being above all a method of enquiry, is dynamic in character and consequently, as stressed by Freud and subsequent psychoanalysts (cf. above), its hypotheses are only approximations – which, in their turn, require further verification – of some of the extremely complex processes occurring in the human mind.

With respect to the second point, a thorough analysis would require a lengthy discussion, so we limit ourselves to a short outline. Many criticisms have been levelled at psychoanalysis.[1] The *leitmotif* of the vast majority of them refers to the scientific status of psychoanalysis. According to these criticisms, psychoanalysis has no valid scientific status because its hypotheses cannot undergo the same tests of validation of those applied to the 'truly scientific fields'. In this sense, according to these critics, psychoanalytic hypotheses cannot neither be verified nor falsified.

For instance, how can the existence of the unconscious or of the *Oedipus* complex be demonstrated? Or, to take another important Freudian concept, how can we measure the 'quantitative aspects of the instincts'?

True, the problem of 'demonstrating' the scientific validity of psychoanalytic theories cannot find univocal and straightforward solutions. In fact, as is well known, the unconscious – by its very nature – cannot be seen, heard, touched, or 'measured', so we can only 'prove' its existence by analysing our feelings in their interaction with those of others. For the unconscious is a dynamic concept – elaborated from a great number of observations mainly related to psychoanalytic experience – which can help explain and synthesize some aspects of the structure of mental processes.

But it is one thing to acknowledge these difficulties, quite another to maintain that psychoanalytic hypotheses do not allow any kind of scientific verification. In this regard, the methodological approach underlying these criticisms does not seem convincing. In fact, by carrying such a line of reasoning to its logical consequences, we would find that all feelings involved in human relations should be considered as groundless entities.

For instance, in a romantic relationship, a person could not dare to say to his or her partner 'I love you', because the logical answer would be 'how can you scientifically prove it?'; and, certainly, there are neither mathematical theorems, nor econometric estimates, nor laboratory experiments for validating such a statement. On the same grounds, no one could formulate any reasoned opinion regarding personal feelings and attributes.

The same applies to the sciences dealing with human creativity, like arts and literature. For instance, no one could say with any claim of objectivity 'what a beautiful poem this is' because there is no way to corroborate this statement by means of a 'truly scientific methodology'.

Furthermore, even the so-called pure sciences would be badly affected by this reasoning. Indeed, as shown by many institutionalist, pragmatist and psychoanalytic contributions, much of what we call 'pure science' is interpreted through the experiences, feelings and perceptions of those dealing with it. The following passage of Freud is interesting, as it relates not only to psychoanalysis but also to other scientific domains:

> We have often heard the demand that a science be built on clear and precisely defined basic concepts. In reality, no science, not even the most exact, starts out with such definitions. The true beginnings of scientific activity consist, rather, in the description of phenomena, which are then grouped, classified, and brought into relation with each other. Even when simply describing the material, we cannot avoid applying to it certain abstract ideas, acquired from somewhere or other but certainly not just from the new observations alone. . . . Strictly speaking, then, they are in the nature of conventions – although everything actually depends on their being not chosen arbitrarily, but determined by meaningful connections with the empirical material, connections that, ostensibly, we surmise before we can properly identify and substantiate them. Only after a more thorough investigation of the relevant empirical field can we formulate its basic scientific concepts more precisely, progressively revising them to widen their applicability while keeping them completely free of contradictions. Then the time may also have come to try and pin them down in definitions. But the advance of knowledge will brook no rigidity here.

As the example of physics strikingly demonstrates, even those 'basic concepts' firmly established in the form of definitions are constantly being substantially revised.
    One such conventional, and at the present still rather obscure, basic con-
cept, which is none the less indispensable to us in psychology, is that of *drive*.
Let us to try to flesh it out by considering it from a variety of angles.

(Freud, 2005: 13–14; original edition 1915)

In this sense, psychoanalysis – as well as social sciences, philosophy and
literature – is no less scientific than 'pure sciences', the only difference being that
it deals with issues that require a different scientific approach and which cannot
be simplified to fit a classical laboratory experiment.

For these reasons, we cannot agree with those who consider psychoanalysis,
especially in the practical work of psychoanalysts, as an 'intuitive art' well distinguished from science. As we have seen, this opinion runs against Freud's view
of the scientific character of psychoanalysis: a character which cannot be reduced
to any positivistic conception of scientific phenomena; and that, for this reason,
has its focus on the elaboration of tentative explanations of the multiple aspects of
psychological phenomena.

Certainly, psychoanalysts work with the inner nature and conflicts of the person, and their main goal is to aid the person to attain a better self-understanding of
such conflicts and, in this way, to bring out his or her true personality. This task
is achieved by applying a scientific method that is tested and revised as psychoanalytic experiences progress. In this process, the 'inner artistic intuition' of the
psychoanalyst in understanding a person's problems constitutes a crucial factor,
which, however, is not separate from scientific investigation, but, rather, is reinforced and refined by the coextensive increase of his or her scientific knowledge
and experience. Furthermore, the significant links existing between art, culture
and science should not be overlooked. The same reasoning can be applied to the
interdisciplinary study of economic and social phenomena.

These remarks highlight the fact that psychoanalysis faces many of the typical
problems of the social sciences. Of course, this is not to say that all criticisms are
groundless and that, as a consequence, psychoanalysis represents the world of
soundness, perfection and truth.

In particular, we believe to be well founded the claim that psychoanalysis, in
its main developments, has not sufficiently considered the contributions of other
disciplines for a deeper understanding of the complex interactions between individual and society.

4.2 Some controversial aspects of Freud's theory

In this section, we will try to foreground the most controversial aspects of the
debate about Freud's theory, since they impinge upon the basic concepts of psychoanalysis and the development thereof. As observed before, two different interpretations of Freud's work can be identified:

A   According to one interpretation, Freud tends to see psychic life as the arena for the perennial struggle between opposite instincts: for instance, in his continual elaboration – which we do not need for our purpose to follow in its complex evolution – between sexuality and self-preservation, or later on, between life (or *eros*) and death (or aggressiveness). According to this view, these instincts mainly depend on the innate individual biological constitution and, therefore, tend to be regarded as deterministic in their unfolding. Psychic life is considered to be the result of the 'kneading' of these instincts, but there appears to be no real dialectic or interchange between them: they stand, in a *Faustian* spirit,[2] in an irreducible opposition, and little can be done to improve such a situation.

Take, for instance, the concept of sexuality. According to this view, sexuality is an instinct which lies basically in bodily needs – like hunger and thirst – and therefore is supposed to be driven only by the principle of pleasure. Furthermore, this instinct is considered as lacking any self-regulating or integrating process as it would strive for an uncontrollable satisfaction regardless of any other human need or feeling. Such an instinct, of course, would render any social life impossible, and, for this reason, must be repressed. However, this repression entails neurosis and – owing to the strength and pre-determined 'biological' mould of these instincts – little could be done to reduce the trade-off between neurosis and civilization.

In this view, neurosis is seen as the necessary price to pay for moving from the principle of pleasure to the principle of reality – that is, through the education process, from the uncontrolled instincts of the child to the repressed, neurotic and 'civilized' behaviour of the adult.[3]

B   However, this view seems too simplistic. In this regard, a key point is that Freud, although he tends to construct his theory on the basis of conflicting instincts, does not seem to assert that these instincts should display a deterministic development. As already noted, he expressly acknowledges the importance in the development of a person of the joint action of the following factors: (i) a person's 'innate' constitution, including the entire set of his or her biological and intellectual traits; (ii) the influence of 'accidental events', by which he chiefly means the role played by the family and socio-cultural contexts.

Considering these relations, outlined above, between neurosis and civilization, Freud's position is far more complex than the simple statement that neurosis, as being based on the repression of instincts, is a necessary ingredient of social life. Certainly, in some passages he makes these kinds of statements, but, very importantly, he also stresses that neurosis[4] is likely to sabotage the attainment of the objectives of civilization, because it is allied – most often, in a subtle and disguised way – with the forces hostile to civilization that have been (only apparently) repressed.

C   The previous remarks lead us to underscore another relevant point: even when Freud seems to adhere to a 'hedonistic' view of human conduct – in the meaning of an unrestrained search for 'pleasure', regardless of any affective and social link – this does not seem to imply that he considers such orientation as an expression of natural and immutable laws but, rather, as an expression of neurotic conflicts which are, at least in part, specific to any given ISEF. Indeed, in these cases, as also elucidated by subsequent psychoanalysts, the obsessive search for 'pleasure' acts – like, as observed before, any other neurotic symptom – as a defence from 'incompatible representations', having their roots in the infantile story of the person.

This point is extremely important and has been addressed in particular by the authors belonging to the field of 'object and interpersonal relations' theories. The supposed contrast between 'instincts' and 'reality' – to which should correspond a conflict between an uncontrolled unconscious and an *ego* conceived as a necessary controlling and 'repressing' factor for the existence of society – is to be interpreted not as an expression of 'human nature' but as a distinctive trait of a neurotic disturbance. Indeed, in these situations what is repressed (e.g., made unconscious) refers to all the aspects of personality that, owing to neurotic conflicts, assume an infantile and anti-social character. It is also interesting to observe that these conflicts do not develop in isolation but encompass both the individual and social dimension.

In this regard, the more damaging expressions of the neurotic-driven aggressiveness, like nuclear wars and mass-destruction, do not take place out of bursts of 'instinctual behaviour', apart from and in opposition to social life, but are deeply ingrained in ISEF that can even be supposed to act as a repressing instance for the 'instinctual behaviour' of the person. As observed before, society may also act as a key carrier for the expression of aggressive behaviour – in particular, through the development of cultural forms and models that tend to be internalized in the *ego* and *super-ego* of the person.

Of course, society also tries to curb aggressive behaviour but in the presence of relevant neurotic conflicts these attempts are not always successful, especially for abating the more 'institutionalised' (e.g., more rooted in the structure of collective action) forms of aggressive behaviour.

D   Perhaps, one key element that could bring a degree of unclarity to Freud's theory is his employment of the concept of sexuality. As a matter of fact, although Freud has always underlined the manifold character of sexuality, in his writings he speaks of 'sexual instinct' and 'repression and satisfaction of instincts' in a way that sometimes may seem to refer only to the biological and 'bodily' side of that instinct: however, as we have seen, according to his theory, sexual instinct reaches out not only to the normal biological sexual activity but also to the affective involvement related to such activity: and, relatedly, to the so-called 'sublimated' activities of the person, which are linked, in a complex interplay, with all the social, intellectual and artistic creations upon which society is based.

In this sense, sexuality, in non-neurotic situations, constitutes an important aspect of the *eros* or love, and, in this respect, lies at the heart of interpersonal and social relations. The interpretative problem rests in the fact that the term 'sublimation' carries two meanings, which, though highly blurred in most of our psychological experience, are neatly different at conceptual level: (a) a means for the expression of neurotic conflicts in a disguised way, and (b) a means for the expression of the normal motivations and orientations of human personality.

In this sense, the *eros* can be considered as a manifold entity which can express itself in various ways. Thus, it is normal for the person to establish different kinds of relations, more or less sublimated but all based on the *eros*, with his or her fellows.

These different concepts of sublimation are outlined but not always clearly singled out in Freud's analysis, and this constitutes perhaps one of the reasons for some entangled aspects of his analysis of society.

E   This unclarity emerges in particular in *Civilization and Its Discontents* – the work where (apparently) Freud has more extensively laid down his thesis about the necessity of repression of sexuality and aggressiveness for the preservation of society – but, in our view, it could be sorted out relatively easily. Here, in the first chapters, he speaks of sexuality and aggressiveness in broad terms, without specifying whether he considers these psychological instances as a normal or a neurotic expression of individual and social life.

Nevertheless, even without such specification, his description of these instances is all alike to a neurotic disturbance and, in fact, later in his paper, he makes evident that this is the case. He stresses that, in this respect, society acts like a neurotic individual who, through the instance of the *superego* – which, as observed before, constitutes the 'moral conscience' as emerging out of a feeling of guilt related to the child's aggressive feelings[5] towards its parents – tries to repress the *neurotic* expressions of sexual and aggressive 'instincts'. Having discovered the existence of neurotic societies, Freud wonders (cf. above) about the interesting possibility of employing psychoanalysis for interpreting and reducing the psychological disturbances at societal level. In this regard, Freud considers this kind of intervention quite possible but is rather pessimistic about its viability in contemporary societies. There are, in fact, on the one hand, the difficulties in identifying the complex relations between individual and collective neuroses, and on the other hand, the problem of devising policies aimed at improving the social understanding of these conflicts.

4.3 Synthesis and conclusions

We can conclude this chapter by noting that in Freud's theory the concepts of instincts and, within this ambit, of psycho-sexuality (the *eros* or *libido*) are very complex and far-reaching as they embrace all the aspects of human personality, including the affective and intellectual. Far from saying that the mind – e.g., the spheres of feelings and intellect – is severed from 'instincts' and, on that account, substantially powerless against these, Freud seems only to posit that the study of the 'mind' should be considered in all its complex interchanges with the 'body', simply because we do not live apart from our body. If, as effectively expressed by Rollo May (1972), a person can safely say, 'Certainly, I am my body, but am also my mind', also the symmetric relation holds true, and then it would be appropriate to say 'Certainly, I am my mind, but am also my body.'

One of the main aims of Freud's instincts theory is to provide a framework for the elaboration of his psycho-sexual theory of human development which, as observed by many authors, represents one of his major contributions to psychoanalysis.

In this regard, Freud has made clear the many components of the concepts of instinct and, within this domain, of the role of libidinal links between the members of society, which include affection and emotions and the possible neurotic conflicts related to them, in maintaining social cohesion.

In this sense, one of the most important insights of psychoanalytic theory is that the intellectual, affective and biological aspects of instincts are intertwined in the complexity of each person and unfold in every aspect of individual and collective life. Even when the expression of one of these aspects is more pronounced, this does not mean that the other aspects cease to operate, but only that they operate in the background, in a partly unconscious and indirect way that may nonetheless heavily impinge on the aspects appearing in the foreground. In this process, the role of symbolic meaning is of special importance in the expression of these aspects.

For instance, as noted before, the act of feeding assumes importance for the child not only because it satisfies a biological need but also because it tends to be interpreted by the child as an expression of affection; and the child, in making this and other connections, also expresses and develops its cognitive and intellectual faculties.

The same complexity emerges if we follow how these early experiences progressively harden into a distinctive social nature. In this regard, we can easily observe that the need to eat and drink and the pleasure associated with these activities are a universal feature of human beings. Indeed, if we consider the social contexts of eating habits, the surprising element is that, whereas cultures vary widely in the characteristics of their eating habits, virtually all seem to attribute to such habits a pre-eminent role in many family and social situations. Eating habits – for instance, in the form of typical dishes and restaurants – often help to identify the distinguishing features of many cultures.

One explanation of these phenomena may be that eating habits can express, partly at a symbolic and unconscious level, many individual and collective feelings having their origin in the oral stage of development. In this regard, many factors may intervene in the explanation of the significance of eating habits: for example, practical reasons, in the sense that eating activities often come about during break or leisure time, and the fact that these activities are in many cases a source of experience and knowledge.

However, it is true that in Freud's work these concepts are often implicit and sometimes, especially in his later theory of the death instinct, he tends to assume a pessimistic view of human development, in that he seems to infer from his theory that little can be done to reduce human aggressiveness.

In this respect, we believe that Freud's theory of the death instinct – which, however, it is important to remember, Freud conceived only as a tentative interpretation of human behaviour – hindered him from carrying out a deeper analysis of neurotic aggressiveness, which was carried out later on by other authors.

Notwithstanding these shortcomings, it should not be overlooked that one of the central aspects of Freud's theory is the discovery of a new method for the analysis of psychological disturbances, through which the person can reach a better self-understanding of his/her neurotic conflicts. This means that the abatement of neurotic conflicts is associated with a decrease in the neurotic aggressiveness related to them, and Freud explains the dynamics of this process in depth. Therefore, as already observed, even when he endorses the view that life has the character of an irreducible struggle between life and death instincts, he does not assume either that these are given, for every concerned individual, in any 'fixed and immutable proportions', or that there is any systematic tendency across individuals for the prevalence of one or the other of these instincts. Consequently, little determinism is allowed in his theory, which, on the contrary, throws light on the complexity of the factors at play in determining human behaviour.

These conflicts are likely to assume different expressions in different societies and, thus, take on a distinctive evolutionary character. Hence, if the child seems to behave only out of its instinct-based needs, this does not happen only because it neurotically refuses to adapt to the principle of reality but also because it does not know enough about the requirements of the external world. In fact, for the effective working of the principle of reality, the child needs to grow and develop its cognitive and intellectual faculties. In this respect, education (at least a sound one) plays not only the role of showing the limits of individual behaviour but also that of helping the child to learn how to bring out its potential. These concepts are closely related. Indeed, for a child learning the needs of other people is not only a necessary limitation of its behaviour but, more importantly, may lead, by helping it establish adequate relations with them, to a better expression of its personality. Furthermore, as highlighted by Freud and many others, intellectual faculties play a critical role from the very beginning of individual life. These findings have been confirmed by many important contributions. A pioneering contribution was carried out by R. Spitz (1945), who pointed out in a field-based enquiry that children brought up in foundling hospitals tend to be affected by severe neurotic disturbances, even when their biological needs have been fully satisfied.

In this sense, the role of society is much more complex than simply that of 'repressing instincts': society also represents the irreplaceable setting for the development and *expression* of the complex and conflicting aspects of human personality. In fact, as we have seen, human instincts constitute a manifold entity where the affective, intellectual and biological aspects combine to make up the individual personality. Since these aspects cannot unfold in isolation, a society needs to be built in order to afford their expression, with, of course, all the complexities, conflicts[6] and feed-back effects associated with such evolutionary patterns. Therefore, the ability of society to create an adequate environment for a full development of its members depends crucially on the characteristics of every culture considered. These, in turn, depend on the complex interplay of the individual and collective conflicts and orientations, also in their relation to the 'materialistic' aspects of society.

In that connection, the consideration, especially by the 'independent psychoanalysts', of the emotional orientations of a person as 'evaluation states' and the importance attributed to the environment for the development of the 'true self' (Rayner, 1991) have a striking parallel with important institutional concepts: in particular, Commons's theory of social valuing and of institutions as a means for controlling, liberating and expanding individual action. In this regard, an interdisciplinary use of these concepts can shed a deeper light on the characteristics of many social phenomena.

In this sense, the repression of instincts – intended as the whole set of familiar and social limitations not conducive to the full expression of individual feelings and abilities – is not only unnecessary for the existence of society but may also be a cause of its destabilization. In fact, as we have seen, the repression of instincts can trigger more neurotic conflicts which, by entailing further neurotic aggressiveness, constitutes one of the main causes of the impairment of the social fabric.

Needless to say, Freud's theory is neither 'complete' nor free from contradictions but, given the complexity and the evolutionary nature of the issues at hand, it would have been very difficult for him to provide a 'perfect theory'. In the light of this fact, our remarks have not tried to identify 'what Freud really said' but, rather, to stress a number of aspects along a new avenue of research.

It is also worth noting that, as emerges from the previous discussion, psychoanalysis is completely at odds with a conception of human nature as an expression of universal natural laws.

Certainly, psychoanalysis adopts a set of 'basic hypotheses', but, as noted earlier, these stem from the observation of a number of common human characteristics and are continually developed, refined and revised as a result of subsequent research.

Examples of these basic hypotheses include the trauma of birth, the child's need to be fed, cared for and loved by its caretakers, and the emotional conflicts associated with the process of growing. By assuming these and other hypotheses, psychoanalysis has developed an articulated theoretical framework which takes into account the familiar and social contexts in which the child's development takes place.

Notes

1 For an in-depth treatment of these issues refer to, among others, Elliott (1994), Fine (1979), Greenberg and Mitchell (1983), Tyson and Tyson (1990).
2 In Freud's work there are many references to Goethe's *Faust* as an example of the symbolic expression of the never-ending opposition between instincts.

52   *The psychoanalytic approach, its potential*

3 In this regard, it is important to stress that, as we shall see in the next points, this interpretation represents only a part of a much more articulated theory. Even where this interpretation seems to prevail, as in *Civilization and Its Discontents*, Freud stresses that the repression of sexual instincts has gone too far in our society, thus causing an increase in neurotic conflicts which end up impairing the attainment of social goals. This implies, however, that the types of neurotic conflicts existing in any given society are not deterministic in nature but depend on the dynamic interplay of the individual in his or her ISEF. In this interaction, a crucial role is played by the way in which individuals and institutions confront their problems.

4 As we shall see later, neurosis, as a consequence of the interplay of these factors, presents itself as having an evolutionary character, the study of which would be particularly intriguing. In this sense, it is interesting to observe that the 'institutional' transmission of the typical forms of neurosis is generally far from complete, owing to the complexity of the factors at stake in determining the evolution of social, economic and cultural forms. In this regard, psychoanalysis stresses that neurotic conflicts convey complex meanings, and, hence, also constitute for the person an imperfect but important way to overcome his or her developmental difficulties.

5 As already observed, Freud suggests that in the child aggressiveness could be reinforced, in particular within the *Oedipus* complex experience, by the anger experienced towards the 'rival' parent because of his or her real (or supposed) role in repressing the satisfaction of its desires. This theory introduces an important qualification as to the supposedly ineluctable nature of human aggressiveness implied in the death instinct theory and opens up the way for a more complete analysis of the neurotic reasons underlying such aggressiveness.

6 It is important to note that conflicts need not necessarily be driven by neurosis. As also shown by institutional economics, conflicts tend in a sense to be always present in collective action owing to the difficulty for its members to reach a common agreement on economic and social issues.

References

Elliott, A. (1994) *Psychoanalytic Theory*. Oxford: Blackwell.

Fine, R. (1979) *A History of Psychoanalysis*. New York: Columbia University Press.

Freud, S. (1915) Das Unbewusste. *Internationale Zeitschrift für ärztliche Psychoanalyse*. English version, *The Unconscious*. London: Penguin, 2005.

Freud, S. (1930) *Das Unbehagen in der Kultur*, Leipzig, Vienna and Zurich, Internationaler Psychoanalytischer Verlag. English version, *Civilization and Its Discontents*. Standard Edition. New York: Norton, 1990.

Greenberg, J.R. and Mitchell, S.A. (1983) *Object Relations in Psychoanalytic Theory*, Cambridge, MA: Harvard University Press.

May, R. (1972) *Power and Innocence: A Search for the Sources of Violence*. New York: Norton.

Rayner, E. (1991) *The Independent Mind in British Psychoanalysis*. London: Free Association Books.

Spitz, R. (1945) Hospitalism: An Inquiry into the Genesis of Psychiatric Condition in Early Childhood. *Psychoanalytic Study of the Child*, 1: 53–74.

Tyson, P. and Tyson, R.L. (1990) *Psychoanalytic Theories of Development*. New Haven, CT and London: Yale University Press.

Part II

The perspective of institutional economics and its potential for a better understanding of economic and social phenomena

As noted in the introduction, several chapters of the book deal with heterodox contributions: this part is dedicated to the analysis of institutional economics (IE), in its 'old' tradition. In the next chapter we sketch the main characteristics of the school within its historical setting.

Then, Chapters 6 and 7 address Veblen's and Commons's contributions, with a focus on the aspects more useful for a better appraisal of economic crisis.

Finally, in Chapter 8 we investigate the reasons for the decline of institutional economics in the post Second World War period and the perspectives of today.

5 Institutional economics
The historical and theoretical framework

In this chapter we outline the many contributions institutional economics has provided to the understanding of the complex factors underlying individual-society dynamics.

5.1 The main concepts

As is known, institutional economics[1] originated in the United States in the first decades of the twentieth century. Its cultural roots can be identified in the philosophy and psychology of Pragmatism – in particular in the theories of Charles Sanders Peirce, John Dewey and William James – and in the German historical school, whose principles were developed by a scholar, Richard T. Ely, who had a considerable influence on the formation of the first generation of institutionalists.

The principal founders of institutional economics are Thorstein Veblen, John Rogers Commons, Walton Hale Hamilton, Wesley Mitchell and Clarence Ayres. Relevant contributions were also provided by L. Ardzooni, A.A. Berle, J.C. Bonbright, J.M. Clark, M.A. Copeland, J. Fagg Foster, I. Lubin, Gardiner C. Means, Walter Stewart and many others.

Significant contributions with important connections to institutional economics were provided by, among others, John Kenneth Galbraith, Fred Hirsch, Albert Hirschman, Gunnar Myrdal, Karl Polanyi and Michael Polanyi.

Within institutional economics, two main strands can be identified: (i) the old institutional economics (OIE), constituted by the first institutionalists and by subsequent scholars who shared their main concepts; and (ii) the new institutional economics (NIE), composed of later scholars adopting principles having important references in the Neoclassical and Austrian schools.[2] In our work, we focus chiefly on the *old institutional economics*, and in particular on Veblen's and Commons's contributions, but we are aware that many other authors would deserve more attention, and we will address some of them throughout this work.

In this regard, it is interesting to observe the significant links[3] between the OIE and, among others, the following theories: (i) various strands of sociology and social psychology, including the 'Sociological or Ecological School of Chicago', the social psychology of William James and of William Ogburn; (ii) a number of theories of technological innovation, often referred to as neo-Schumpeterians, which share important concepts with the OIE: for instance, the importance of path-dependency processes in explaining the characteristics of science, technology and innovation in any given context.

The pivotal concepts characterizing the *old institutional economics* can be summarized as follows: ceremonial/instrumental behaviour, instincts, culture, evolution, habits, path-dependency, tacit knowledge, power, technology, collective action, social provisioning, market imperfections, social planning, working rules and social valuing. As noted by numerous authors, the OIE does not present a completely unitary framework. Within this ambit, two main strands can be identified:

1   An approach first expounded by Veblen, stressing the dichotomy between ceremonial and instrumental institutions; the role of habits of thought and action; the cumulative character of technology in its relations with the propensities of workmanship and parental bent.
2   An approach initiated by Commons, which focuses attention on the evolutionary relations between economy, law and institutions; the nature of transactions, institutions and collective action; the role of conflicts of interest and the social valuing associated with them; the nature and evolution of ownership, from a material notion of possession to one of relations, duties and opportunities; the role of negotiational psychology for understanding economic and social phenomena.

Notwithstanding a number of differences between these approaches, the elements of convergence are remarkable: for instance, between the concepts of ceremonial and instrumental institution, on the one side, and the process of social valuing, on the other. In this sense, the observed differences tend to concern more the issues addressed than the basic aspects of the OIE.

Within this conceptual framework, institutional economics stresses that the presence of an institutional context – with its values, norms, conflicts, organizations, routines, habits and customs – constitutes a necessary factor for the human activity of social provisioning. In other words, every economic action embodies, at the same time, also a social, institutional, historical and psychological dimension. Thus, an understanding of economic actions demands a joint analysis of all these dimensions which, for this reason, necessitates the adoption of an interdisciplinary approach.

5.2 The driving sentiments and ideals of the early institutional economists

In the analysis of the early period of institutionalism, it is not exaggerated to speak of it as a unique and exceptional experience of an alternative economics perspective. The beginning of this period can be traced to Veblen's article 'Why Is Economics Not an Evolutionary Science?' in 1898. From that time until the outbreak of the First World War, institutional economics grew steadily but not impressively. It was with the urgency of meeting the needs of the war that the matter of fact approach of institutionalism rose to its full prominence.

In this respect, the very term 'institutional economics' was coined by Walton Hale Hamilton's article of 1917. This article marks the point in which OIE acquires a fuller awareness of its distinctive approach within economics.

In this regard, the role of Hamilton was particularly influential in spreading out the new perspective. His approach, by centring attention on the nature of market imperfections and their influences on economic and social systems, seemed particularly fit for analysing the inefficiencies and maladjustments of American economy. By carrying out detailed studies of particular industries, it was shown, by his and many other contributions, that inefficiency can be found not only in monopoly positions but also in situations of excessive[4] competition. For, in the latter cases, excessive competition easily ends up in industrial structures characterized by duplication, disorder, inefficiency, lack of innovation, incapacity to attain economies of scale.

Also in connection with these aspects, a set of contributions was centred on the analysis of industrial relations and labour organization, with particular attention to the process of wage fixation, safety provisions and unemployment compensation. Another important and related issue was the analysis of business cycles. It was developed chiefly by Wesley Mitchell[5] through an extensive use of statistical analysis.

In this way, fresh light was shed on a phenomenon that had been hitherto the object of much theoretical speculation but that was actually largely unknown in its real contours. And, in turn, the availability of new data made possible a more effective comparative appraisal of the theories trying to interpret these data.

On these issues, there were in that period scores of contributions[6] by institutional economists. This aspect reflects not only their academic interest but also their involvement in institutions and projects devoted to the study of these problems. In these fields, they performed successfully the role of researchers, professors, research directors and advisers of policy-makers.

In this period it can safely be maintained (for instance, Rutherford, 2011) that OIE came to assume a relevant, perhaps even slightly mainstream, role in the economics profession, in policy action and in the general sentiment of the intellectual life of the time. It was a period of great intellectual ferment, characterized by an enthusiasm for exploring new avenues of research and of new courses of policy action for the solution of economic and social problems.

The leading ideas of the institutional economists appear to be the following: (i) the belief in the complex and interactive character of 'human nature', and the consequent importance of the social and institutional framework for its amelioration; (ii) the refusal of any abstract and deductive theorizing detached from the observation of reality, and the consequent emphasis on inductive methodology based on case studies and statistical analysis; (iii) the importance attributed to the notion of 'social control', by which was meant a proactive role of institutions and policies in addressing economic and social problems; (iv) an interdisciplinary orientation – in particular with the philosophy and psychology of pragmatism and other related contributions of social psychology – in order to achieve a more realistic account of the characteristics of human nature in its individual and social unfolding.

This new wave had its seats in a number of important universities – in particular, Amherst, Chicago, Columbia, Wisconsin – which became the springboard, through their institutional economists, of important collaborations with numerous research institutions and governmental bodies.[7] The general sentiment pervading these initiatives was one of optimism about the possibilities of social progress and was by no means confined only to institutional economists as it involved the philosophy and psychology of pragmatism, and various strands of psychology, sociology and political science.[8]

These contributions are fairly related to institutional economics and constitute an important aspect in the construction of a new conceptual framework in social sciences. The driving ideas of these contributions are the interdisciplinary orientation, the focus on the historical evolution, the analysis of real situations through case-studies and context-specific enquiries. These ideas, together with their most distinctive concepts, can complement in interesting ways the perspective of institutional economics. We can mention the concepts developed by the 'Ecological[9] School of Chicago' such as the processes of social disorganization and social reorganization and the corresponding processes of integration/marginalization of individuals and groups. And, within these dynamics, the role of a balanced development of cities, of primary groups and of participation in collective action for the development of the person.

Within sociology, an over-arching concept that can be applied to a host of social situations is William Ogburn's cultural lag (1957), which occurs when 'one of two parts of culture which are correlated changes before or in greater degree than the other part does, thereby causing less adjustment between the two parts than existed previously'.

As can be seen, this concept embodies – also on account of the psychoanalytic background[10] of Ogburn – an interdisciplinary orientation, and can then easily by extended to the study of the interaction between the psychological and social dimensions of the 'cultural lag'.

Also in this case, a stream of optimism permeates these studies, which has its roots in the notion that 'human nature' and the social context are mutually interdependent and that the latter can exert a great influence, through an appropriate system of policies and of 'social control', on the improvement of 'human nature'. For all these reasons, the approach of institutional economics is particularly relevant for the analysis of structural problems and economic crises.

5.3 Relations with the philosophy and psychology of Pragmatism

As just noted, institutional economics was influenced by the philosophy and psychology of Pragmatism. But also the other way round applies, in the sense that the new concepts and issues of institutional economics were employed by

Pragmatist thinkers. In particular, this is true for John Dewey, who lived in the same period (1859–1952) as the two major exponents of institutional economics – Thorstein Veblen (1857–1929), and John Rogers Commons (1862–1945) – and who, approximately in the same period as Veblen and Commons (1890–1940), produced his most significant contributions.

The Principles of Psychology *of William James and the role of habits*

The concept of habit has played a key role within the Pragmatist approach, also for its influence on institutional economics. In this regard, important contributions were provided by William James, who, in his *Principles of Psychology*, investigated the role of habits in both the individual and the collective dimension. In the individual dimension, the disposition of the person to form habits is explained by James as a result of the circumstance that:

> Man is born with a tendency to do more things than he has ready-made arrangements for in his nerve centres . . . If practice did not make perfect, nor habit economize the expense of nervous and muscular energy, he would therefore be in a sorry plight.
>
> (James, 1890: 113)

In this sense, the set of personal habits performs the important function of reducing conscious attention upon them. This entails the apparent paradoxical result that the person, although routinely performing a number of actions, is largely unable to know *how* he or she has performed them.[11] This concept is expressed in the following passage:

> We all of us have a definite routine manner of performing certain daily offices connected with the toilet, with the opening and shutting of familiar cupboards, and the like. Our lower centres know the order of these movements, and show their knowledge by their 'surprise' if the objects are altered so as to oblige the movement to be made in a different way. But our higher thought-centres know hardly anything about the matter. Few men can tell off-hand which sock, shoe, or trousers-leg they put on first. They must first mentally rehearse the act; and even that is often insufficient – the act must be *performed*.
>
> (James, 1890: 115)

The interesting aspect of this analysis is that, in describing some important features of personal habits, it also casts light on the role of collective habits in social dynamics. As a matter of fact, habits constitute the normal way of working not only of personal life but also, in a complex interplay of reciprocal influences, of collective life. The following passages convey these concepts vividly:

> Habit is thus the enormous fly-wheel of society, its most precious conservative agent. It alone is what keeps us all within the bounds of ordinance, and

saves the children of fortune from the envious uprisings of the poor. It alone prevents the hardest and most repulsive walks of life from being deserted by those brought up to tread therein. It keeps the fisherman and the deck-hand at sea through the winter; it holds the miner in his darkness, and nails the countryman to his log-cabin and his lonely farm through all the months of snow; it protects us from invasion by the natives of the desert and frozen zones . . . It keeps different social strata from mixing.

(James, 1890: 121)

This analysis of habits is significantly linked to the role that the continual flux of actions plays on their formation. In fact, habits are acquired or eliminated cumulatively and are intimately connected with the system of values of the person. This is related to an important concept of Pragmatism, namely, that individuals do not unfold their personalities in abstract terms but out of their actions in both the individual and collective spheres. In this light, the person is considered as an active agent seeking to attain his or her goals which, however, cannot be reduced to a simple hedonistic principle. These goals, in fact, embrace all the complex set of values and motivations of the person in his or her interaction with the social structure and, for this reason, should be studied in their evolutionary patterns.

Consequently, habits are not 'neutral' and 'automatic' instances, as they carry with them, partly at an unconscious level, all the complex, often conflicting, aspects making up the individual personality. In this sense, habits constitute the 'psychological procedures' through which the emotions, motivations and values of the person find their concrete expression. Thus, it is necessary to continually improve personal behaviour through the acquisition of 'sound habits' and the elimination of bad ones:

No matter how full a reservoir of *maxims* one may possess, and no matter how good one's *sentiments* may be, if one have not taken advantage of every concrete opportunity to *act*, one's character may remain entirely unaffected for the better . . . There is no more contemptible type of human character than that of the nerveless sentimentalist and dreamer, who spends his life in a weltering sea of sensibility and emotion, but who never does a manly concrete deed . . . Every smallest stroke of virtue or of vice leaves its never so little scar. The drunken Rip Van Winkle, in Jefferson's play, excuses himself for every fresh dereliction by saying, 'I won't count this time!' Well! He may not count it, and a kind Heaven may not count it; but it is being counted none the less. Down among his nerve-cells and fibres the molecules are counting it, registering and storing it up to be used against him when the next temptation comes. Nothing we ever do is, in strict scientific literalness, wiped out. Of course, this has its good side as well as its bad one. As we become permanent drunkards by so many separate drinks, so we become saints in the moral, and authorities and experts in the practical and scientific spheres, by so many separate acts and hours of work.

(James, 1890: 125, 127)

By developing these insights, pragmatist thinkers and institutional economists have stressed in many contributions the twofold nature of habits. Indeed, habits embody and synthesize, in an evolutionary way, all the principles, values and knowledge accumulated over time. In this sense, they exhibit in every context both the ceremonial and instrumental aspects pointed out by institutional economists. As described effectively by Veblen, ceremonial behaviour is rigid, past-binding and based on a passive acceptance of the norms followed. In contrast, instrumental behaviour possesses a matter-of-fact quality aimed at problem-solving activities. Within this ambit, technology-based activities are considered, especially in Veblen's and Ayres's analyses, the best example of instrumental behaviour. From these insights, it follows that habits constitute a necessary factor for accumulating knowledge within institutions and, at the same time, an element which may hinder this process. Nevertheless, as we will see in the next chapter, the role of technology in fostering economic and social progress is very complex as it requires the analysis of many interrelated aspects.

Notes

1 For a detailed analysis of these issues refer, among others, to Hodgson, Samuels and Tool (1994), Rutherford (1994, 2011).

2 For an analysis of the potentialities and problems of collaboration between the OIE and NIE refer to the previous quotations. In Chapter 11 we will show the usefulness of employing some concepts more addressed in NIE – in particular, informational asymmetries and principal/agent relations, developed in particular by the *new regulatory economics* – in conjunction with important concepts of the OIE (in particular, habits, social valuing, path-dependency, culture and evolution) – in order to obtain a deeper understanding of the problems underlying policy action.

3 Refer, among others, to Arthur (2009); Bastide (1950); Dosi, Nelson and Winter (2000); Etzioni (1988); Etzioni and Lawrence (1991); Hodgson, Samuels and Tool (1994); Nelson and Winter (1982).

4 As can be seen, the interesting aspect of this analysis is that competition is not considered as an abstract mechanism amenable automatically to optimization but as an institution which requires a continual definition of what is in any circumstance its optimal or acceptable level (cf. also Chapter 9 on the institutional analysis of the market).

5 In promoting these issues, Mitchell also played a relevant institutional role; suffice it to remember his activity as founder and promoter of the National Bureau of Economic Research (NBER).

6 In the heyday of institutional economics, relevant contributions on the above mentioned issues were provided by, among others, Ayres (1936, 1944); Berle and Means (1932); Bonbright (1937, 1961); Bonbright and Means (1932); Burns (1936); Clark (1924, 1948, 1958); Copeland (1924); Douglas (1924); Edie (1922); Glaeser (1957); Goodrich (1925); Hamilton (1917, 1940, 1957); Hamilton and Wright (1928); Hansen (1927); Hobson (1917, 1923); Hoxie (1915, 1917); Kapp (1950, 1961); Levin et al. (1934); Lubin and Everett (1927); Marshall (1918); Mills (1936); Mitchell (1924, 1925, 1927); Moulton (1935, 1943, 1949); Nourse (1944); Nourse and others (1934); Stewart (1917); Taussig (1915); Tawney (1921); Taylor (1928); Thorp (1928); Tugwell (1922, 1924); Tugwell and Hill (1934); Witte (1932).

7   We can mention the Brookings Institution, the Committee for Economic Development, the Committee on Government Statistics and Information Services, the National Bureau of Economic Research (NBER), the Federal Trade Commission, the Bureau of Industrial Research, the National Planning Board and many others.
8   Cf. on these issues, among others, Cooley (1909, 1913); Lynd (1939); Ross (1901); Wallas (1908, 1914).
9   The word 'ecological' comes from the stress put by their exponents on the need to realize a balanced development of the cities. In this way, the school anticipated many future developments of urban and environmental economics. For significant contributions related to this 'school' refer, among others, to Park and Burgess (1921); Parker (1920); Smith and White (1929); Thomas (1966); Wirth (1928).
10 Cf. Ogburn (1919, 1922, 1957, 1964), Ogburn and Goldenweiser (1927).
11 In this sense, the process of habit formation has many parallels with the characteristics of tacit knowledge, which was studied in particular by M. Polanyi (1958).

References

Arthur, W.B. (2009) *The Nature of Technology: What It Is and How It Evolves*. London: Penguin.

Ayres, C.E. (March 1936) Fifty Years Developments in Ideas of Human Nature and Motivation. *American Economic Review*, 26: 224–236.

Ayres, C.E. (1944) *The Theory of Economic Progress*. Chapel Hill, NC: University of North Carolina Press.

Bastide, R. (1950) *Sociologie et Psychoanalyse*. Paris: P.U.F.

Berle, A.A. and Means, G.C. (1932) *The Modern Corporation and Private Property*. New York: Macmillan.

Bonbright, J.C. (1937) *The Valuation of Property*. New York: McGraw Hill.

Bonbright, J.C. (1961) *Principles of Public Utilities Rates*. New York: Columbia University Press.

Bonbright, J.C. and Means, G.C. (1932) *The Holding Company*. New York: McGraw Hill.

Burns, A.R. (1936) *The Decline of Competition: A Study of the Evolution of American Industry*. Westport, CT: Greenwood Press.

Clark, J.M., 'The Socializing of Theoretical Economics', in Tugwell (1924), quoted.

Clark. J.M. (1948) *Alternative to Serfdom*. New York: Knopf.

Clark, J.M. (1958) *Social Control of Business*. New York: Kelly.

Cooley, C.H. (1909) *Social Organization*. New York: Schoken.

Cooley, C.H. (1913) The Institutional Character of Pecuniary Valuation. *American Journal of Sociology*, 18 (January): 543–555.

Copeland, M.A., 'Communities of Economic Interest and the Price System', in Tugwell (1924), quoted.

Dosi, G., Nelson, R.R. and Winter, S.G. (eds.) (2000) *The Nature and Dynamics of Organizational Capabilities*. Oxford: Oxford University Press.

Douglas, P.H., 'The Reality of Non-Commercial Incentives in Economic Life', in Tugwell (1924), quoted.

Edie, L.D. (1922) *Principles of New Economics*. New York: Crowell.

Etzioni, A. (1988) *The Moral Dimension*. New York: Free Press.

Etzioni, A. and Lawrence, P.R. (eds.) (1991) *Socio-Economics*. New York: Sharpe.

Glaeser, M. (1957) *Public Utilities in American Capitalism*. New York: Macmillan.

Goodrich, C.L. (1925) *The Miner's Freedom: A Study of British Workshop Politics.* Boston, MA: Marshall Jones.

Hamilton, W.H. (1917) Problems of Economic Instruction. *Journal of Political Economy,* 25 (January): 1–13.

Hamilton, W.H. (1940) *The Pattern of Competition.* New York: Columbia University Press.

Hamilton, W.H. (1957) *The Politics of Industry.* New York: Knopf.

Hamilton, W.H. and Wright, H.R. (1928) *A Way of Order for Bituminous Coal.* New York: Macmillan.

Hansen, A.H. (1927) *Business Cycles Theory, Its Development and Present Status.* Boston, MA: Ginn.

Hobson, J.A. (1917) *The Evolution of Modern Capitalism.* New York: Scribner.

Hobson, J.A. (1923) *Incentives in the New Industrial Order.* New York: Seltze.

Hodgson, G.M., Samuels, W.J. and Tool, M. (eds.) (1994) *The Elgar Companion to Institutional and Evolutionary Economics.* Aldershot: Edward Elgar.

Hoxie, R.F. (1915) *Scientific Management and Labor.* New York: Appleton.

Hoxie, R.F. (1917) *Trade Unionism in the United States.* New York: Appleton.

James, W. (1950) *The Principles of Psychology.* New York: Dover Publications. First published in New York by Holt and Company, 1890.

Kapp, K.W. (1950) *The Social Costs of Private Enterprise.* Cambridge, MA: Harvard University Press.

Kapp, K.W. (1961) *Toward a Science of Man in Society.* The Hague: Martinus Nijoff.

Levin, M., Moulton, H. and Warburton, C. (1934) *America's Capacity To Consume.* Washington, DC: Brookings Institution.

Lubin, I. and Everett, H. (1927) *The British Coal Dilemma.* London: Allen and Unwin.

Lynd, R. (1939) *Knowledge for What?* Princeton, NJ: Princeton University Press.

Marshall, L. (1918) *Readings in Industrial Society.* Chicago: University of Chicago Press.

Mills, F.C. (1936) *Prices in Recession and Recovery.* New York: National Bureau of Economic Research.

Mitchell, W.C. (1925) Quantitative Analysis in Economic Theory. *American Economic Review,* 15 (March): 1–12.

Mitchell, W.C. (1927) *Business Cycles: The Problem and Its Setting.* New York: National Bureau of Economic Research.

Mitchell, W.C. 'The Prospects of Economics', in Tugwell (1924), quoted.

Moulton, H.G. (1935) *Income and Economic Progress.* Washington, DC: Brookings Institution.

Moulton, H.G. (1943) *The New Philosophy of Public Debt.* Washington, DC: Brookings Institution.

Moulton, H.G. (1949) *Controlling Factors in Economic Development.* Washington, DC: Brookings Institution.

Nelson, R. and Winter, S.G. (1982) *An Evolutionary Theory of Economic Change.* Cambridge, MA: Harvard University Press.

Nourse, E.G. (1944) *Price Making in a Democracy.* Washington, DC: Brookings Institution.

Nourse, E.G. et al. (1934) *America's Capacity To Produce.* Washington, DC: Brookings Institution.

Ogburn, W.F. (1919) The Psychological Basis for the Economic Interpretation of History. *American Economic Review,* 9 (March): 291–308.

Ogburn, W.F. (1922) 'Bias, Psychoanalysis, and the Subjective in Relation to Social Sciences'. Reprinted in Ogburn (1964), quoted.

Ogburn, W.F. (1957) 'Cultural Lag as Theory'. Reprinted in Ogburn (1964), quoted.

Ogburn, W.F. (1964) *On Culture and Social Change*. Chicago: The University of Chicago Press.

Ogburn, W.F. and Goldenweiser, A. (eds.) (1927) *The Social Sciences and Their Interrelations*. Boston: Houghton Mifflin.

Park, R.E. and Burgess, E.W. (1921) *Introduction to the Science of Sociology*. Chicago: The University of Chicago Press.

Parker, C.H. (1920) *The Casual Laborer and Other Essays*. New York: Harcourt, Brace and Howe.

Polanyi, M. (1958) *Personal Knowledge. Towards a Post-Critical Philosophy*. London: Routledge and Kegan Paul.

Ross, E.A. (1901) *Social Control*. New York: Macmillan.

Rutherford, M. (1994) *Institutions in Economics: The Old and the New Institutionalism*. Cambridge: Cambridge University Press.

Rutherford, M. (2011) *The Institutional Movement in American Economics, 1918–1947: Science and Social Control*. Cambridge, UK and New York: Cambridge University Press.

Smith, T.V. and White, L.D. (eds.) (1929), *The City as a Social Laboratory*. Chicago: The University of Chicago Press.

Stewart, W.W. (1917) Social value and the Theory of Money. *Journal of Political Economy*, 25 (December): 984–1002.

Taussig, F.W. (1915) *Inventors and Moneymakers*. London: Macmillan.

Tawney, R.H. (1921) *The Acquisitive Society*. London: Bell.

Taylor, H. (1928) *Making Goods and Making Money*. New York: Columbia University Press.

Thomas, W.I. (1966) *On Social Disorganization and Social Personality* (selected papers edited by Morris Janowitz). Chicago: The University of Chicago Press.

Thorp, W.L. (1928) *Economic Institutions*. New York: Macmillan.

Tugwell, R.G. (1922) *The Economic Basis of Public Interest*. Menasha, WI: The Collegiate Press.

Tugwell, R.G. (ed.) (1924) *The Trend of Economics*. New York: Knopf.

Tugwell, R.G. and Hill, H.C. (1934) *Our Economic Society and Its Problems*. New York: Harcourt, Brace.

Veblen, T. (1898) Why Is Economics Not an Evolutionary Science? *Quarterly Journal of Economics*, XII (July).

Wallas, G. (1908) *Human Nature in Politics*. London: Archibald Constable.

Wallas, G. (1914) *The Great Society*. London: Macmillan.

Wirth, L. (1928) *The Ghetto: A Study in Isolation*. Chicago: The University of Chicago Press.

Witte, E.E. (1932) *The Government in Labor Disputes*. New York: McGraw-Hill.

6 Veblen's evolutionary perspective

In this chapter we outline[1] the main aspects of Veblen's theory. In the first paragraphs we analyse the central concepts of his theory – in particular, habits, instincts, evolution and technology – also by pointing out their strong interdisciplinary orientation. Then, in the next paragraphs we consider some important insights of his *The Theory of Business Enterprise*, with particular attention to its relevance for the interpretation of the economic crisis.

6.1 Habits

As is known, Thorstein Veblen was the first founder of institutional economics. In his famous article[2] 'Why Is Economics Not an Evolutionary Science?', he stresses that mainstream economics, owing to the adoption of simplistic hypotheses and a basically static approach, has great difficulty in analysing the complexity of economic phenomena.

In order to grasp the nature of such complexity, it becomes necessary to adopt an evolutionary approach to the study of these phenomena. In particular, it is necessary to enquire into the evolutionary links between, on the one hand, the individual propensities and orientations and, on the other hand, the transformations of the economic, social and technological aspects of the related contexts.

It can be observed that the characteristics of previous historical stages are eliminated only gradually and that many features continue to inform the new institutional fabric and its related habits of thought and life. This continuity – which implies also a conflict between different orientations and cultural values – is transmitted and perpetuated through habits of thought and life. In this regard, also drawing on the theories of James, Peirce and other scholars, Veblen remarks that:

> The later psychology, reinforced by modern anthropological research, gives a different conception of human nature. According to this conception, it is the characteristic of man to do something, not simply to suffer pleasures and pains through the impact of suitable forces. He is not simply a bundle of desires that are to be saturated by being placed in the path of the forces of the environment, but rather a coherent structure of propensities and habits which seeks realisation and expression in an unfolding activity . . . The economic

life history of the individual is a cumulative process of adaptation of means
to ends that cumulatively change as the process goes on, both the agent and
his environment being at any point the outcome of the last process . . . What
is true of the individual in this respect is true of the group in which he lives.
All economic change is a change in the economic community, – a change in
the community's methods of turning material things to account. The change
is always in the last resort a change in habits of thought. This is true even of
changes in the mechanical processes of industry.

(Veblen, 1990b: 74, 74–75; original edition 1919)

The existence of habits of thought and life that arise and change slowly and cumulatively implies, in Veblen's analysis, that people do not behave out of a supposed
'rational' decision-making process aimed at maximizing their 'hedonism': thus, they
do not react instantly to different economic circumstances as assumed within the utility function framework. In fact, as also highlighted by the notion of super-ego, following norms may constitute a goal in itself since norms reflect the values and criteria through which society classifies and appraises human conduct. Hence, norms can
suggest to the person the appropriate behaviour, and, consequently, the adequacy of
individual behaviour is assessed through the criteria indicated in the norms.

Indeed, the internalization of norms forms a part – often very important – of
the individual's personality, and, therefore, the decision-making process partly
assumes an unconscious nature, in the sense that the person is not fully aware of
the inner motivations driving his or her behaviour.

The emergence and consolidation of habits and norms are appraised, in
Veblen's analysis, as the outcome of a complex interaction between individual
characteristics – interpreted mainly through his concept of instincts – and the features of economic and social systems. This interaction is considered explicitly
within an evolutionary perspective. Any society, with its distinguishing characteristics, is the unique product of its economic and cultural evolution; in brief, it
is embedded in its past:

Under the discipline of habituation this logic and apparatus of ways and
means falls into conventional lines, acquires the consistency of custom and
prescription, and so takes on institutional character and force . . . In human
conduct the effects of habit in this respect are particularly far-reaching. In
man the instincts appoint less of a determinate sequence of action, and so
leave a more open field for adaptation of behaviour to the circumstances of
the case . . . Cumulatively, therefore, habit creates usages, customs, conven-
tions, preconceptions, composite principles of conduct that run back only
indirectly to the native predispositions of the race, but that may affect the
working-out of any given line of endeavour in much the same way as if these
habitual elements were of the nature of a native bias. Along with this body
of derivative standards and canons of conduct, and handed on by the same
discipline of habituation, goes a cumulative body of knowledge, made up
in part of matter-of-fact acquaintance with phenomena and in greater part

of conventional wisdom embodying certain acquired predilections and preconceptions current in the community.

(Veblen, 1990a: 7, 38, 39; original edition 1914).

In studying the evolutionary nature of habits, it is important to note their conflicting and somewhat contradictory nature; typical, in this regard, is the case of ceremonial and instrumental behaviour which, though being typically antithetical, is likely to be present, in various forms, in the same persons and institutions.

Thus, the study of habits raises a number of important questions: what are the social factors that determine the evolution of habits and how they interlace with persons' propensities? In the following sections we will address a number of important concepts developed by Veblen which are significantly related to these issues.

6.2 Instincts and evolution

Veblen's focus on habits draws attention to important aspects of the nature of human development and the role played by instincts (or propensities). This enquiry is of special interest for our discussion. In fact, it brings into a unitary interpretative framework the complexity of the aspects making up human personality – biological, intellectual, affective – by considering them within their evolutionary pattern. The following passages express these concepts neatly:

> The instincts are to be defined or described neither in mechanical terms of those anatomical or physiological aptitudes that causally underlie them or that come into action in the functioning of any given instinct ... 'Instinct', as contra-distinguished from tropismatic action, involves consciousness and adaptation to an end aimed at ... The ends of life, then, the purposes to be achieved, are assigned by man's instinctive proclivities; but the ways and means of accomplishing those things which the instinctive proclivities so make worth while are a matter of intelligence ... All instinctive action is intelligent in some degree. This is what marks it off from the tropism and takes it out of the category of automatism.
> Hence all instinctive action is teleological. It involves holding to a purpose.
> (Ibid.: 4, 5–6, 31)

Veblen's analysis cannot be considered as a complete theory of instincts. As we have seen in the analysis of Freudian theory, this circumstance is typical of any theory of instincts. Notwithstanding this difficulty, we think that Veblen was able to grasp a point which we deem central for a better understanding of human behaviour: namely, that instincts constitute multifarious entities expressing the complex interplay between the biological, affective and intellectual aspects of personality.

In Veblen's analysis, workmanship[3] and parental bent[4] are held to be the most important human instincts. They are likely to prevail in a situation where other instincts that can act at cross-purposes with them – for instance, predatory instincts which may be expressed through a framework of ceremonial and 'acquisitive' institutions based on invidious distinctions – have little social grounds to express themselves.

Veblen seems to suppose that the first stage of human life was of this kind but, since then, a number of disturbing factors[5] have caused a progressive deviation, which was reinforced by a process of cumulative habituation. This idea is expressed in the following passage:

> The selective control exercised over custom and usage by these instincts of serviceability is neither too close nor too insistent . . . It appears, then, that so long as the parental solicitude and the sense of workmanship do not lead men to take thought and correct the otherwise unguarded drift of things, the growth of institutions – usage, customs, canons of conduct, principles of right and propriety, the course of cumulative habituation as it goes forward under the driving force of the several instincts native to man,– will commonly run at cross purposes with serviceability and the sense of workmanship.
>
> (Ibid.: 49, 49–50)

6.3 Technology

In this evolutionary process, technological progress is deemed to play an important role in social change. Technological progress, in turn, depends on the characteristics of the capitalistic system which tends, although through a far from straightforward pattern, to substitute new systems of production for older ones. Technological progress modifies not only the material world but also, through a process of learning, adaptation and habituation, the ways of thinking and acting. This process, depending on the interplay of many factors which are mostly uncertain and path-dependent, is not considered in Veblen's enquiry as having a teleological character.

The reason why Veblen considers technological progress so crucial for changing individual behaviour arises from his observation that, along with the instincts of workmanship and parental bent, people may also develop tendencies at cross-purposes with them.

The extent to which workmanship and efficiency prevail on these tendencies depends largely on the characteristics and intensity of technological progress. In fact, by inducing individuals to adapt themselves to new methods of production, technological progress brings out, through a process of habituation to new habits of thought and life, the workmanship instinct. For this reason, technological progress is considered paramount in order for people to eliminate habits of thought based on more primitive stages of life – mainly based on ceremonial and 'acquisitive' institutions – and to develop a scientific and matter-of-fact mentality, which represents the essence of instrumental behaviour.

In Veblen's view – although it is not very clear in many aspects – the pivotal element of technological progress able to induce such profound social transformations can be summarized as follows: technology, in becoming more and more 'colourless and impersonal', makes it increasingly difficult for the person to impute to his or her work instruments aspects of magical workmanship that go beyond their objective characteristics.

For instance, the ancient handicraftsman, who used simple instruments with great ability, could more easily attribute to his instruments anthropomorphic characteristics than could the worker operating in a big and impersonal factory. Through this process of imputation, according to Veblen, the rational and objective aspects of technology tend to be overlooked in favour of a magical and 'ceremonial' vision of the world.

This process of imputation, in his view, while not impinging upon the acquired ability of the workers, is likely to impair future technological advances by instilling in the workers habits of thought and life not conducive to the progressive 'rationalization' of technology.

The tendency to 'personify' the world never completely disappears with the development of technological progress, since it is considered by him a sort of congenital weakness of human nature.

In this regard, we wish to observe that, although in Veblen's analysis technological progress tends to acquire, in some respects, the character of an ineluctable drive, this does not imply that he considered human development in a deterministic way.

In fact, whenever confronted with the possibility of foreseeing a situation, Veblen was extremely aware of the difficulty involved in this task. In particular, at the end of his book – *The Instinct of Workmanship and the State of the Industrial Arts* – Veblen was quite aware that technological progress, *per se*, was not sufficient to induce a more rational behaviour (in substantive terms), due to the complex and interrelated role played by psychological, social, economic and technological factors in determining the dynamics between individuals and institutions. This complexity emerges clearly when he speaks of the 'revulsion' against technology:

> Nor is it by any means a grateful work of spontaneous predilection, all this mechanistic mutilation of objective reality into mere inert dimensions and resistance to pressure; as witness the widely prevalent revulsion, chronic or intermittent, against its acceptance as a final term of knowledge. Laymen seek respite in the fog of occult and esoteric faiths and cults, and so fall back on the will to believe things of which the senses transmit no evidence; while the learned and the studios are, by stress of the same 'aching void', drawn into speculative tenets of ostensible knowledge that purport to go nearer to the heart of reality, and that elude all mechanistic proof or disproof . . . Neither the manner of life imposed by the machine process, nor the manner of thought inculcated by habituation to its logic, will fall in with the free movement of human spirit, born, as it is, to fit the conditions of savage life. So there comes an irrepressible – in a sense, congenital – recrudescence of magic, occult science, telepathy, spiritualism, vitalism, pragmatism.
>
> (Ibid.: 333–334, 334)

From these passages it appears that Veblen regarded technological progress only as a useful way to acquire more science-based habits of thought and not as a goal in itself. He believed that people, by acquiring these more technology-based habits of thought, would become more able to develop an improved assessment of all the matters regarding their lives. In this respect, Veblen's theory appears to be very different from any positivistic position although, as we are going to see, these issues are nor clearly settled in Veblen's theory.

6.4 The evolution of business enterprise

As is known, Veblen has set up a far-reaching evolutionary theory in economics, whose main aspects are instincts (or propensities), habits, institutions, technology. One central aspect of Veblen's analysis is the dichotomy between production oriented to the profit and production oriented to the satisfaction of the needs of society. To this corresponds the distinction between engineers and business men, on the individual level, and between ceremonial and instrumental institutions, at the collective level.

In this picture, the institution of business enterprise includes both engineers and business men. Also for this reason, such theory – as expounded in particular in *The Theory of Business Enterprise* – plays a central role in Veblen's theory. In Veblen's opinion, the evolution of technological progress applied to the industry will tend, in the absence of counter forces, to sweep away the system of business enterprise. The reason for this is that the system of business enterprise is considered to rest – although not completely – on more primitive, predatory and acquisitive habits of thoughts.

Therefore, in his words, 'Broadly, the machine technology acts to disintegrate the institutional heritage, of all degrees of antiquity and authenticity . . . It thereby cuts away that ground of law and order on which business enterprise is founded' (Veblen, 2012: 374; original edition 1904).

For these reasons, the system of business enterprise is considered by Veblen as intrinsically unstable. This happens because the two tendencies underlying it – technological progress and ceremonial-acquisitive tendencies – are not only incompatible between themselves, but also with the system of business enterprise. In fact, technological progress tends to push the system towards a society based on serviceability whereas the ceremonial-acquisitive tendencies towards archaic and predatory pre-industrial societies. These concepts are expressed in the following passage:

> Modern business principles and the modern scheme of civil rights and constitutional government rest on natural-rights ground. But the system of natural rights is a halfway house . . . The quests of profits leads to a predatory national policy . . . If national (that is to say dynastic) ambitions and warlike aims, achievements, spectacles, and discipline be given a large place in community's life, together with the concomitant coercive police surveillance, then there is a fair hope that the disintegrating trend of the machine discipline may be corrected. The régime of status, fealty, prerogative, and arbitrary command would guide the institutional growth back into the archaic conventional ways and give

the cultural structure something of that secure dignity and stability it had before the times, not only of socialistic vapors, but of natural rights as well.

(Ibid.: 394, 398–399)

In this analysis it remains an open question which of the two tendencies will prevail in the long run, and the book closes in the following way:

> Which of the two antagonistic factors may prove the stronger in the long run is something of a blind guess; but the calculable future seems to belong to one or the other. It seems possible to say this much, that the full dominion of business enterprise is necessarily a transitory dominion. It stands to lose in the end whether the one or the other of the two divergent cultural tendencies [technological progress or ceremonial-acquisitive tendencies] wins, because it is incompatible with the ascendancy of either.

(Ibid.: 400)

This conclusion, which can undoubtedly be considered as one of the most brilliant of Veblen's intuitions, tends to be too dichotomic (cf. also below). In fact, such conclusion is based on the idea that technological progress, in its supposed rationalizing role, cannot modify from within the basic principles of business enterprise, as identified in the natural rights and in the notion of perfect competition associated with them.

The role of credit and the rise of the modern corporation

In this context of a profit oriented character of the business enterprise, the role of credit is of central relevance. Veblen identifies two typologies of credit: (a) loans related to the operation of buying and selling: for instance, dilations in payments, and sales discounts; (b) credits aimed at increasing the financial resources of the firm (the so-called credit extension), in particular through the issue of shares and securities. But what is the inner reason which pushes firms to incur in debt? The main reason consists in shortening the turnover of production.

> The business man's object is to get the largest aggregate gain from his business. It is manifestly for his interest, as far as may be, to shorten the process out of which his earnings are drawn, or, in other words, to shorten the period in which he turns over his capital.

(Ibid.: 93)

This process acquires a 'necessary' character because, once a firm acquires a credit-based differential advantage, the others are bound to follow the same path in order to keep pace with competition. However, according to Veblen, the aggregate gain coming from their debt exposure is negligible or null. This conviction is based[6] on the belief that the process of credit creation does not contribute to increase effective demand. In his words:

To a very considerable extent the funds involved in these loans, therefore, have only a pecuniary (business) existence, not a material (industrial) one; and, so far as that is true, they represent, in the aggregate, only fictitious industrial equipment . . . Money as such, whether metallic or promissory, is of no direct industrial effect . . . *Nummus nummum non parit* [money does not create money – however, we will see later on that the working of modern economies is quite different].

(Ibid.: 103)

In these circumstances, the process of credit creation takes a cumulative tendency which tends to give rise to a cycle of expansion and inflation followed by depression and liquidation of the existing activities. The phase of depression is promptly utilized by creditors for acquiring at low price the ownership of firms. This process constitutes a relevant aspect of a general process of restructuring and concentration of economic activities aimed at realizing economies of scale and at obtaining the control of strategic elements of the value chain.

Economic crises, competition and monopoly

As we have seen, one pivotal aspect of the business enterprise pertains to its intrinsically speculative nature. This tendency is nurtured by the process of credit extension, which easily ends up in what we call today 'speculative bubbles', followed by periods of depression. However, this is not the end of story, as two other factors enter the picture: the over-investment (in respect of 'what the traffic will bear') and the growing efficiency of the productive system, which tends to reduce the capital per unit of product. We can see what happens in the two cases:

A   In the absence of technical progress, the process of liquidation which follows the over-investment makes possible a new expansive period. This happens because the liquidation process tends to cause a sharp reduction of the supply of novel investment. This entails a situation of under-investment in respect of what the market can absorb, which triggers a new wave of investment.

B   In the presence of technical progress, the liquidation process tends to weaken or eliminate the successive period of expansion. In this case, in fact, if the liquidation process is accompanied by a restructuring of economic activities based on higher productivity, this means that there will be less need of capital per unit of product.

As a consequence, there will be less (or no more) scarcity of capital as in the previous case, and then there will be an attenuated (or zero) expansion related to the new investments. In this case, then, from a period of depression does not follow a period of expansion to the same extent, and then the economic system tends to stick around a situation of chronic depression.

In this picture, Veblen identifies two factors that may counteract this tendency: (a) the increase of 'unproductive consumption' and (b) the tendency towards the elimination of competition and the parallel rise of forms of monopoly and oligopoly.

With regard to the first point, he believes that so-called unproductive consumption – which Veblen locates in the near totality of public spending – would impede the insurgence of economic depression not owing to its effect on the effective demand but because this consumption, by diverting the effective demand by productive activities, will reduce the rate of saving and investment.

In this more 'traditional' vision (cf. Note 6), in fact, the basic idea is that investments are financed by savings but, as we shall see later in the paper, this is not the case in modern economies. In any case, Veblen tends to believe that the increase of productivity is likely to outrun the negative effect of public spending.

With regard to the second point, Veblen holds that, up to a certain point, a monopoly arrangement (including also the cartels) constitutes the best antidote to economic crises. This happens because in this way (i) it becomes possible to reach out to scale economies in production and organization; (ii) it makes it easier to obtain more favourable conditions in the market for labour and investments; and, last but not least, it constitutes, within the objective of profit maximization, an effective means of regulating prices and quantities on the basis of 'what the traffic will bear'.

6.5 Some problematic aspects of Veblen's theory

Veblen's analysis raises many important questions which, due to their complexity, demand a more in-depth examination. As we have seen, in his vision technological progress cannot modify the essence of natural rights but can only supplant them through a construction of society based on serviceability.

However, this account does not consider that economic reality, even at the inception of the industrial revolution, has always been much more complex than conveyed by too sharp simplifications. In particular, (a) the markets are not abstract mechanisms but institutions created and maintained by a complex legal and institutional framework.[7] Furthermore, markets tended, as they grew more complex, to depart from the simple models of perfect competition and perfect monopoly. (b) The objectives of firms have become more and more articulated, also as a result of the growing complexity of the firms and of the various stakeholders involved. (c) Also for these reasons, public intervention has played an increased strategic role for economic development, including that of ensuring an adequate level of effective demand. These remarks lead us to critically analyse a number of crucial aspects of Veblen's theory of technological progress.

A   One element of modern technology which Veblen considers paramount for reducing magic and ceremonial habits of thought is its supposed mechanical and 'colourless' nature. In presence of these characteristics, it is more difficult for individuals to impute magical and animistic traits to modern technology than to simpler instruments. Nevertheless, we can observe that this mechanical character – which reminds us of the working rules of physical laws – is typical of any kind of technology. In fact, even in the use of the simplest instrument man has to consider its physical properties if he wants to employ it effectively. And, with regard to the 'colourless' character of modern technology, this does not constitute an absolute trait, but, rather, a matter of human attribution that does not depend on the mechanical characteristics of the technology employed, but rests, at least in part, on the economic, social and cultural aspects of the context in which it is 'embedded'. As a matter of fact, modern-day technology can be 'colourful' and creative – for example, in the case of information and communications technology – whereas an old technology can be quite 'colourless' and plain, as for an exploited worker in a poor agricultural setting. The 'colour' we attribute to technology depends on what technology represents for us, which, in turn, depends on the complex interplay between individual and collective values, conflicts and motivations: namely, it depends on the 'colour' of our spiritual life and on the characteristics of the ISEF considered. Furthermore, we can observe – in accordance with important psychological and psychoanalytic research – that to the person, imputing a symbolic meaning to his/her work instruments does not necessarily imply an 'irrational and primitive' psychological process, since it constitutes an expression of his or her relational and affective spheres. Thus, the imputation process represents a symbolic and important expression of a person's inclinations and social links. Of course, the typical contents of these imputations are likely to vary across different cultures and may also be the expression of psychological conflicts, but such differences concern only the contents of these attributions and not the process of imputation as such.

B   Veblen seems to regard the spiritual life or 'the free movement of human spirit' at odds with the logic of the machine process. However, this supposed dichotomy raises many problems: what is the meaning of spiritual life? In Veblen's view, spiritual life appears sometimes to be synonymous with 'irrational and primitive behaviour'. For instance, in the passage quoted above, he lumps under the same heading of 'spiritual life' concepts as diverse as magic, occult science, telepathy, spiritualism, vitalism, pragmatism. These concepts are in some cases not only different but – we believe – quite antithetical, as for instance between magic, occult science and telepathy on the one hand, and spiritualism, vitalism,[8] pragmatism on the other.

C   But now, let us assume that, following Veblen's reasoning, the machine process would fully exert its effect and thus the more primitive habits of thought and life will be gradually displaced. In this case, will individuals lose their spiritual life in the sense that they would act in a 'rational', machine-like way? In Veblen's analysis these fundamental questions are left unanswered, even though they assume great importance for understanding his theory. In fact, if we suppose that, following Veblen's analysis, in our society the main purposes of the operation of the machine process are mainly related to the principles of 'conspicuous consumption' (1899) and 'pecuniary gain' (1904) – that is, in his view, principles chiefly resting on habits of thought and life coming from primitive stages of life, having their roots in propensities at cross-purposes with workmanship and parental bent – the logical consequence of a successful functioning, in Veblen's terms, of the machine process would be the following: a progressive abatement of conspicuous consumption, accompanied by a parallel substitution of the 'productive' objective, related to 'material serviceability', for the 'pecuniary gain' objective, related to the dynamics of 'exchange value'.[9] However, since in Veblen's analysis conspicuous consumption is supposed to cover a substantial share of consumption in contemporary society, the possible outcomes of a full operation of the machine process would be – skipping, for the sake of simplicity, the intermediate hypotheses – the following alternatives: (i) an in-depth reorganization of the production process oriented to matching the 'true' needs of society. This entails a widespread social valuing process on problems which are intrinsically multifarious and controversial, as witnessed by the intense debate on the various typologies of capitalism, socialism and the related concepts of market, competition, enterprise, labour, value, democracy, participation and public action. As a matter of fact, these questions involve, on the part of persons and groups, not only the 'materialistic' aspects of life but also and pre-eminently the spheres of motivations, values and visions of the world. There arises a problem, then, to build an adequate institutional set-up through which, at the various social and institutional levels, an agreement can be reached upon questions that, owing to their level of complexity, need continually be defined and re-defined over time. (ii) Otherwise, if such re-organization does not occur (or if it occurs with insufficient strength), this means that the 'rationalizing effect' of the machine process has not worked strongly enough. Hence, such a result suggests that the unfolding of the machine process has failed to instil more rational habits of thought and life.

D   Each of these two alternatives opens up a beehive of questions: (i) in the first case, what are the implications of a sharp decrease of conspicuous consumption? Will man live in an industrious and peaceable society of the kind Veblen envisaged existing in the past, in which the only difference would be the widespread application of the machine process to the production of the truly necessary items? Which criteria will be adopted to make this selection and, hence, to identify what are the real needs of society? For instance, the items, other than the necessaries, to be produced, the ways and criteria for rewarding the labour, the time and resources to devote, for instance, to scientific and technological research, the fields worth following and the social goals associated with them? (ii) In the second alternative, why do people need to pursue conspicuous consumption and the related 'pecuniary objective' of economic action which, as we have seen, have their roots in instincts that are at cross-purposes with workmanship and parental bent? If modern society is considered as a deviation from an early peaceable and natural stage of life, why have workmanship and parental bent instincts failed to assert themselves neatly in our society?

E   Veblen does not address these problems directly. He tends to assume that, once upon a time, man lived in a pacific stage based on the full operation of workmanship and parental bent instincts. But, at a certain point, owing to the presence of external pressures (not clearly specified) related to the expansion of society – and, later on, of capitalistic institutions – there occurred a progressive deviation from such a stage towards increasingly less genuine ways of thought and life which, by way of progressive habituation, asserted themselves as the ordinary way of living. However, this interpretation of human development meets with a problem: if people deviate increasingly from a pacific stage, this implies, as also asserted by Veblen, that the workmanship and parental bent instincts do not work strongly enough, perhaps because of the presence of instincts at cross-purposes with them which can develop – through the process labelled by Veblen as 'contamination of instincts' – as a response to external pressures. Now, considering that 'external pressures' – whatever they might be – are likely to carry, at least in part, a significant endogenous component, the consequence seems to be that this early stage was far less peaceable and smooth than assumed by Veblen, resting as it did on an unstable equilibrium made up of conflicting propensities.

F   Owing to this complexity, in Veblen's reconstruction of human development the role of technology is far from clear: in fact if, in Veblen's analysis, the evolution of capitalism[10] (and the technological progress associated with) is deemed to be the main cause of deviation from a pacific stage of life, why from just now onwards should such progress begin to exert the opposite effect? For instance, considering our present-day stage of internet technology, it does seem that – after a century of massive technological progress since Veblen's time – the problems pointed out by Veblen are still remarkably in the foreground. In particular, considering all the problems of our time – among others, uneven development, environmental decay, economic and cultural (sometimes even armed) conflicts – there emerges the impression that technological progress has not induced a parallel shift of human action from the pecuniary objective (more egoistic) to one of serviceability (more altruistic). This may have happened because, as observed before, workmanship and parental bent instincts are more complex than usually assumed and, furthermore, present an evolutionary character; they are, at least in part, endogenously determined.

G   One explanation for these problems can be that the rationalizing role Veblen attributes to technology seems to derive from his implicit assimilation of 'instrumental rationality' to 'substantive rationality'. Thus, more rational ways of producing (e.g., how to produce) are supposed to entail more 'rational' or adequate ways of life (e.g., what to produce). One reason for this belief could be found in the role Veblen attributed to the instinct of workmanship and to its link, outlined before, with the instinct of parental bent. In this sense – as far as we understand Veblen's reasoning – technological progress, by fostering the instinct of workmanship, would reinforce the instinct of parental bent as well. This is a very acute intuition. However, in order to get such synergic effect, we do need something more than mere technological progress. As a matter of fact, as shown by many studies, the point is that instrumental and substantive rationality are related but different concepts, and so an increase in the former cannot be simply considered as a proxy for the increase in the latter. In particular, one reason why reality is so complex may depend on the circumstance that the instinct of workmanship is a more over-arching concept than explicitly supposed by Veblen. In fact, if we conceive of such an instinct – as seems to be implied in Veblen's analysis, also for his reference to the propensity of the 'idle curiosity' – not only as a set of technical capabilities but also as a general propensity to intellectual and cognitive constructive activities; and, furthermore, following Veblen, posit a significant relation with parental bent instinct, it becomes evident that technological progress constitutes only an aspect of the manifold expressions of the instinct of workmanship. In this regard, our impression is that advances made in this direction are not due to an abstract 'rationalizing' role of technology *per se* but to the kind of links that technological progress establishes with social and economic objectives and the related process of social valuing. This implies that technological progress is far from 'neutral' as regards the attainment of these objectives and, therefore, does not follow a deterministic pattern out of its 'immanent rationality', but is partly moulded by the characteristics of any given context, being, as it is, deeply embedded therein. In this regard, an increased capacity for analysing social problems – a capacity which can also benefit from progress in psychological and social sciences – could well be regarded as a genuine expression of the instinct of workmanship which can play a relevant role in social evolution.

H   As also observed by Commons, one difficulty in Veblen's analysis resides in the lack of the concepts of reasonable value: that is, the criteria to assess the difference between 'what is going on' and 'what ought to go on' (M. Tool, in Hodgson, Samuels and Tool, 1994, vol. I, p. 406).

Veblen tends to reduce this problem to the dichotomy between prejudices and genuine behaviour, which is at the basis of his distinction between the objectives of 'pecuniary gain' and 'serviceability' of human action. But this distinction already requires an implicit social assessment of what a prejudice is and what a genuine behaviour is: and what are the foundations of such assessments? Ethical, psychological, economic, juridical, social? And what interrelations may intervene between them? In particular, considering that, for good or bad, our economic activity is rewarded in pecuniary terms, it becomes still more difficult to distinguish precisely in any economic action between the objectives of 'pecuniary gain' and 'serviceability'. This happens because it is likely that these objectives are blended in the complexity of the (partly unconscious) motivations, values and conflicts of each person involved (see also Chapter 9). As a matter of fact, even if we act only out of our workmanship propensity – for instance, by working as an independent professional – we do need to be rewarded in pecuniary terms in order to get a living. So, in order to single out, from any given economic action, the two main objectives – 'pecuniary gain' and 'serviceability' – we need to employ other criteria which require a careful social valuing process.

These rather unclear aspects of Veblen's theory comport with a corresponding difficulty of assessing the role of institutions in social reforms. One reason for this problem lies in the circumstance that Veblen (and the Ayres tradition of institutional economics) tends to appraise institutions chiefly in their negative role of hindering the full course of the 'rationalizing effects' of technological progress on social life. In this way, the only hope for social change would rest on the operation of some exogenous-conceived phenomenon – in particular, technological progress. But we have seen that technological progress, *per se*, does not eliminate the social value problems inherent in its complex development.

Conclusion

At the end of this outline we can note that Veblen has provided fundamental insights into the comprehension of the links existing between the economic, social and psychological aspects of society by analysing the pivotal concepts that describe these relations – that is habits, instincts, evolution and technology.

In this regard, we wish to observe that some of our previous remarks, which highlighted a number of unclear aspects in Veblen's theory, do not reduce the validity of this theory but, rather, point out its great potential. In fact, one of the main sources of these difficulties resides in the lack of any clear reference to psychological theories for developing his main arguments.

Indeed, in Veblen's analysis many important psychological concepts are implicit, and in this respect Veblen had great psychological intuitions. Examples can be found: (i) in his analysis of habits of thought and life, which he tended to regard as the result of the internalization (mostly at an unconscious level) of shared norms and values; (ii) in his concept of instinct, in which he grasps the importance of considering both emotions and intellect as the entities making up human personality; (iii) in his study of human development, by pointing out the importance of symbols and fantasies.

As we have seen, these concepts present a striking parallel with many psychological and psychoanalytic concepts: for instance, the role of internalization of norms and models of behaviour in child development, the complexity of instincts (or propensities), the role of Freud's notion of 'compulsion to repeat' and the importance of symbols and fantasies in individual and collective action.

In this respect, we believe that there are significant synergies between psychoanalytic concepts and Veblen's theory which can help illuminate relevant aspects of social evolution.

Notes

1 We have addressed these aspects, in a partly different way, also in Hermann (2005, 2013).
2 Reprinted in Veblen, (1990b (1919)). In the quotation of passages we will refer to this edition.
3 In Veblen's analysis the instinct of 'idle curiosity' also plays an important role in social evolution, especially through its effects upon scientific and technological progress. Such instinct can be considered as the more 'unconditioned' and intellectual aspect of the instinct of workmanship.

4 In Veblen's analysis the instinct of parental bent is conceived as a general sense of solicitude extending itself beyond the family sphere.

5 Veblen's discussion on this point is not very clear: he seems to impute these disturbing factors to the changes related to the expansion of societies. However, as we will see later on, this hypothesis runs into some difficulties.

6 We can note here (and later in the work as well) an aspect that is rather typical of the first generation of institutionalists: namely, the circumstance that their theories, while highly innovative and 'heterodox' in many respects, tend, on the macroeconomic side, to accept some tenets of the neoclassical approach. In particular, they tended to overlook the importance of aggregate demand, its possible divergence with effective supply, and the role played by public spending and credit creation in increasing such demand.

7 These aspects have been developed in particular by J.R. Commons (cf. also below). In this regard we think that Commons's and Veblen's analysis, notwithstanding their differences, can be jointly employed in the analysis of a host of economic and social phenomena.

8 As observed before, Veblen employs important concepts from the philosophy and psychology of Pragmatism. The reason why he includes Pragmatism in the list of the 'anti-technological' tendencies may lie in the fact that there are two main versions of Pragmatism – the first, set forth by the founder of Pragmatism, C.S. Peirce, meant as a theory of knowledge and a method of scientific investigation, and the second, developed later on by, among others, W. James and J. Dewey, intended as a theory of the truth, experience and values – and that Veblen considered the latter version as antithetical to the 'immanent rationality' of technological progress. Later we shall discuss some difficulties of Veblen's analysis regarding these aspects. For an analysis of the different conceptions of Pragmatism refer, among others, to the volume edited by L. Menand, *Pragmatism: a Reader*, New York, Vintage Books, 1997. With reference to these issues, of particular interest are Commons's remarks: 'We are compelled, therefore, to distinguish and use two meanings of pragmatism: Peirce's meaning of purely a method of scientific investigation, derived by him from the physical sciences but applicable also to our economic transactions and concerns; and the meaning of the various social-philosophies assumed by the parties themselves who participate in these transactions. We therefore, under the latter meaning, follow most closely the social pragmatism of Dewey; while in our method of investigation we follow the pragmatism of Peirce. One is scientific pragmatism – a method of investigation – the other is the pragmatism of human beings – the subject-matter of the science of economics . . . Not until we reach John Dewey do we find Peirce expanded to ethics, and not until we reach institutional economics do we find it expanded to transactions, going concerns, and Reasonable Value' (Commons, 1990: 150–151, 155; original edition 1934).

9 As we have seen, this dichotomy is at the basis of Veblen's famous distinction between the role of the engineers, acting under the workmanship propensity and therefore directing their action toward the objective of serviceability, as contrasted with the role of capitalists, acting under the influx of propensities at cross-purposes with workmanship, based on acquisitive and aggressive traits, and finalized, through the applications of various restrictions on production, to increase their pecuniary gains.

10 In this regard, Veblen considers the role of capitalism in fostering technological progress far from straightforward, since the contradiction between the 'pecuniary gain' and 'material serviceability' objectives of economic action entails a similar, and even more complex, contradiction at firms' level as whether to speed up or retard the pace of technological progress. For a more detailed analysis refer to Veblen, in particular (1904), (1919) and (1921).

References

Commons, J.R. (1990) *Institutional Economics: Its Place in Political Economy*. New Brunswick, NJ: Transaction Publishers. Originally published by Macmillan in 1934.

Hermann, A. (2005) Evoluzione, istituzioni e tecnologia nell'opera di Thorstein Veblen. *Studi Economici e Sociali*, 41 (2–3): 63–91.

Hermann, A. (2013) La *Theory of Business Enterprise* di Thorstein Veblen e la sua rilevanza per i problemi attuali. *Nuova Economia e Storia*, 19(3): 33–61.

Hodgson, G.M., Samuels, W.J. and Tool, M. (eds.) (1994) *The Elgar Companion to Institutional and Evolutionary Economics*. Aldershot: Edward Elgar.

Menand, L. (ed.) (1997) *Pragmatism: A Reader*. New York: Vintage Books.

Veblen, T. (1898) Why Is Economics Not an Evolutionary Science? *Quarterly Journal of Economics*, XII: July.

Veblen, T. (1899) *The Theory of Leisure Class*. New York: Penguin.

Veblen, T. (1921) *The Engineers and the Price System*. New York: Huebsch.

Veblen, T. (1990a) *The Instinct of Workmanship and the State of the Industrial Arts*. New Brunswick, NJ: Transaction Publishers. Originally published by Macmillan in 1914.

Veblen, T. (1990b) *The Place of Science in Modern Civilization*. New Brunswick, NJ: Transaction Publishers. Originally published by Viking Press in 1919.

Veblen, T. (2012) *The Theory of Business Enterprise*. Forgotten Books. Originally published by Scribners in 1904.

7 Commons's theory of collective action

Other important contributions to the understanding of the dynamics of individual and collective action were provided by John Rogers Commons. We will organize our discussion[1] around a number of his key concepts, by pinpointing their relevance for the analysis of the problems of today.

7.1 Institutions and transactions

One of Commons's most important insights[2] is that collective action constitutes a necessary element for an adequate performance of individual action. The dialectic and dynamic relations intervening between individual and collective action are effectively expressed in this passage:

> Thus, the ultimate unit of activity, which correlates law, economics and ethics, must contain in itself the three principles of *conflict, dependence,* and *order*. This unit is a Transaction. A transaction, with its participants, is the smallest unit of institutional economics.
>
> (Commons, 1990: 58; original edition 1934)

Transactions are classified into three categories – Bargaining, Managerial and Rationing – according to the relationship intervening between the parties involved. The first concerns the relation between individuals with equal rights – which does not necessarily correspond to equal economic power – for instance, between buyer and seller. The second regards the relations between people organized within an institution, for instance between a manager and his or her collaborators. And the third refers to the relations between the person and a kind of collective action where there is less direct involvement. This happens, in particular, with the policy action of Government and Parliament, but also with the collective action of the most important economic and social associations of society (for instance, political parties, unions, consumers' associations).

These transactions are quite diverse according to the degree of direct intervention of collective action but, at the same time, are extremely intertwined. In their various combinations, they make up the tangled weft of collective action. It is interesting to observe the complex, conflicting and evolutionary role that institutions assume in Commons's analysis, as expressed in the following passage:

Thus conflict, dependence, and order become the field of institutional economics, builded upon the principles of scarcity, efficiency, futurity, working rules, and strategic factors; but correlated under the modern notions of collective action controlling, liberating, and expanding individual action.

(Ibid.: 92)

The importance of this concept of institution lies in the fact that it does not consider individual and collective action as opposite entities, but as different but complementary aspects of the 'human will-in-action'. The importance attributed by Commons to the human will does not mean, however, the adoption of a mere 'contractual' view of institutions that overlooks the role of coercion and unexpected consequences of human action. As a matter of fact, Commons takes these aspects explicitly into account, but, instead of treating them as exogenously determined by some dusky and impersonal 'structural factor' or 'natural law', considers them as the outcome of the joint action of all the 'human wills-in-action' in any given context.

Of course, collective action is something more than the mere sum of individual actions. In fact, in many ways collective action has a bearing on individual behaviour and, furthermore, can generate effects which do not lie in the intentions of the individuals promoting it. However, if collective action and its related institutional structure arise out of conflicts, it could hardly be the case that collective action is not influenced by the characteristics of individual action. But, and this constitutes one of Commons's most significant insights, such individual actions tend increasingly to unfold within institutions – e.g., within a framework of collective action – rather than being the expression of a series of self-contained acts.

In particular, his definition of transactions and institutions makes it easier to analyse the various forms of collective action in their economic, social, cultural and psychological domains, and in their interrelations with political economy.[3] In his words:

> So it is with every operation of the human will. It is always directing itself to investigating, explaining and controlling the limiting factors that obstruct its purposes at the moment and under the circumstances. It is always injecting an 'artificial' element into the forces of nature, and that artificial element is its own ultimate purpose accompanied by an intermediate or immediate instrumental purpose of obtaining control of the limiting factor, through control of the mechanism.
>
> Thus it is, also, with all of the phenomena of political economy. They are the present outcome of rights of property and powers of governments which have been fashioned and refashioned in the past by courts, legislatures and executives through control of human behavior by means of working rules, directed towards purposes deemed useful or just by the law-givers and law interpreters.
>
> (Commons, 1995: 378; original edition 1924)

Even when the action seems utterly individualistic – for instance, in the case of a bargaining transaction where the buyer and the seller seem to act exclusively out of their personal interest – there is the presence, often implicitly, of a significant collective element. Indeed, even that transaction is defined and regulated by a set of norms, institutions and transactions which are the expression of a number of collective interests – for instance, in the sphere of consumption, these can be expressed by antitrust bodies, justice and arbitration courts, consumers and environmental associations, and, of course, by all the related institutions, legislations and regulations.

The emergence of concerted capitalism

Commons identifies three stages in the development of capitalism: (i) the period of scarcity, in which there was 'the minimum of individual liberty and the maximum of communistic, feudalistic or governmental control through physical coercion'; (ii) the period of abundance, characterized by 'a maximum of individual liberty, the minimum of coercive control through government, and individual bargaining takes the place of rationing'; (iii) the third period is that of 'stabilization' whose main features are:

> new restraints on individual liberty, enforced in part by governmental sanctions . . . but mainly by economic sanctions through concerted action, whether secret, semi-open, open, or arbitrational, of associations, corporations, unions, and other collective movements of manufacturers, merchants, labourers, farmers, and bankers.
>
> (Commons, 1990: 774; original edition 1934)

As we shall see later, this classification is of particular significance for the institutional analysis of the market.

7.2 Negotiational psychology, will-in-action and the process of choice

In his analysis of institutions Commons sets forth the concept of 'negotiational psychology' in order to attain a better understanding of the role of collective action in individual behaviour and, relatedly, the role of individual behaviour in collective action. Indeed, negotiational psychology involves the idea of conflict between different feelings and values, which finds their expression in the dynamics of individual and collective action. Within this process, the importance attributed to social psychology appears in the following passages:

> Every choice, on analysis, turns out to be a three-dimensional act, which – as may be observed in the issues brought out in disputes – is at one and the same time, a performance, an avoidance, and a forbearance . . . The psychology of transactions is the social psychology of negotiations and the transfers of ownership . . . Thus each endeavors to change the dimensions of the economic values to be transferred . . . This negotiational psychology takes three forms according to the three kinds of transactions: the psychology of persuasion, coercion, or duress in bargaining transactions; the psychology of

command and obedience in managerial transactions; and the psychology of pleading and argument in rationing transactions. . . . Negotiational psychology approaches more nearly to the 'Gestalt' psychology, which, however, is distinctly an individualistic psychology, concerned with the mental growth of the individual from infancy. The resemblance consists in the fact that the Gestalt psychology is a part-whole psychology, wherein each particular act is connected with the whole configuration of all acts of the individual.

(Ibid.: 73–74, 88, 91, 106)

One consequence of this view, relevant also for our subsequent discussion, is that the difference between individual and social psychology tends to be blurred, in the sense that the one is considered the complement – a kind of *alter ego* – of the other. In fact, the interesting aspect of Commons's concepts of transactions and institutions is the joint consideration of the individual and collective element as two necessary aspects of collective action. This entails a shift of the analysis from a person-to-nature to person-to-person relations,[4] with the related importance of an interdisciplinary approach for their understanding; this appears from the following passage:

Transactions have become the meeting place of economics, physics, psychology, ethics, jurisprudence and politics. A single transaction is a unit of observation which involves explicitly all of them . . . Like the modern physicist or chemist, its ultimate unit is not an atom but an electron, always in motion – not an individual but two or more individuals in action. It never catches them except in motion. Their motion is a transaction.

(Commons, 1995: 5, 7–8; original edition 1924)

With regard to psychoanalysis, Commons agrees with its methodology although he considers it, along with all other psychological theories, a kind of individual psychology. This appears in the following passage:

Yet opinion and action cannot be separated in scientific investigation, for action is opinion-in-action and science measures the action while inferring the opinion. Habitual and customary assumptions are read into habitual and customary acts. Here the process of investigation is similar to psychoanalysis, but, instead of an individualistic science which investigates nerves or dreams as an explanation of individual behavior, social science investigates habitual and customary assumptions as an explanation of transactions.

(Commons, 1990: 698; original edition 1934)

Now we can observe that, as we have seen before, psychoanalysis, especially in its recent developments, draws attention to the biological component of human psychology not as a way of disregarding the emotional, intellectual and collective dimensions of the personal life but, conversely, for addressing all the complex interactions between the psychological and biological components of personality.

7.3 Social value and policy action

A notable aspect of Commons's analysis is that his definition of transaction considers, in their interaction, all kinds of social and economic relations – from the more individualistic to the more collective. A crucial element in these dynamics concerns the role played by all these transactions in making up policy action.

In fact, also in relation to his institutional involvement in many reform projects on labour and regulatory policies[5] he highlights that policy action takes place not only within the boundary of rationing transactions, but also within the domains of the other two types of transactions (bargaining and managerial) which seem to regard more individualistic spheres of action. Even in these cases individuals seek to attain their objectives through the aid of collective action, and then their actions tend in one way or another to influence policy domain.

This view of a dialectic and dynamic interaction between individual and collective action brings to the fore the multiplicity of factors underlying economic structures and the paramount role played by past and future. In this sense, Commons's analysis takes into account the evolutionary character of economic systems, which he regards not as deterministic in nature but, as stressed before, as complex systems in which many forces are at play and where uncertainty is the rule. These aspects show the importance of the process of social valuing in the dynamics of collective action. Within this context, the concept of reasonable value is employed by Commons in order to draw attention to the conflicting, imperfect and evolutionary nature of the process of social value. These concepts are effectively set forth in the following passage:

> Each economic transaction is a process of joint valuation by participants, wherein each is moved by diversity of interests, by dependence upon the others, and by the working rules which, for the time being, require conformity of transactions to collective action. Hence, reasonable values are reasonable transactions, reasonable practices, and social utility, equivalent to public purpose . . . Reasonable Value is the evolutionary collective determination of what is reasonable in view of all the changing political, moral, and economic circumstances and the personalities that arise therefrom to the Supreme bench.
>
> (Commons, 1990: 681, 683–684; original edition 1934)

Reasonable value is by definition an imperfect process whose characteristics can be interpreted as the synthesis of the conflicting and evolutionary components of collective action. In these situations, it is important that every component of society finds adequate expression through the forms of collective action. The imperfection of social valuing is also caused by its partly unconscious and conflicting character, often embodied in well-ingrained habits of thought and life. In fact, social value process goes to the heart of the nature of political economy, which is considered not as an activity stemming from the application of abstract laws but as a collective and evolutionary decision-making process involving many institutions. In this sense, political economy has a close-knit relation with law and ethics.

7.4 What kind of policy action?

At this stage, it can be interesting to wonder what political economy it is that Commons advocates. One central aspect lies in his analysis of concerted capitalism and in the role played by different institutions in defining the 'reasonable value' of the various transactions involved. As we have seen, one distinctive aspect of his contribution rests in his far-reaching meaning of transactions, which run all the way up from the seemingly atomistic bargaining transaction, to the hierarchical levels of managerial transactions to the more overt policy dimension of rationing transactions.

The most relevant implication of this theory for policy action is the need to improve the institutional process of collaboration between the actors involved. This can be realized – and this was also an important intuition of J.M. Keynes[6] – through the strengthening of a wide range of 'intermediate institutions' lying between the 'Individual' and the 'State'. Typical examples are unions, associations of consumers and producers, and the various kinds of 'authorities' and 'agencies'. The fields covered by this action are likely to be what we call today competition, industrial and labour policies.

Conversely, as regards macroeconomic policies, Commons's prescriptions – following, as we have noted, a trend typical of many institutional economists – are consonant with various aspects with those of neoclassical economists.

He devoted to these issues – and in particular the role of monetary and banking policies – a lengthy discussion in the later parts of the volume I of his *Institutional Economics*. He draws attention to the role of credit economy in the modern economy and the role of the banking system in this respect. The banks have the prerogative, in his view, to create at their discretion purchasing power in the hands of the borrowers.

This analysis, however interesting, remains in many respects confined to the realm of neoclassical economics. In fact, the purchasing power of the borrowers is considered to originate mainly from previous savings, which are deposited in the banks and then lent to the borrowers. In this way, the role of credit creation in providing additional purchasing power – and, hence, aggregate demand – is largely overlooked. And, by a similar reasoning, the role of public spending in creating aggregate demand is also overlooked.

In this regard, Commons's chief policy prescription is to stabilize the purchasing power of money at full employment level in order to prevent an inflationary over-expansion of economic activities.

This goal is fine, of course, but how to realize it in real economies? In his proposal, Commons makes reference to the largely neoclassically oriented theory of Knut Wicksell, according to which the long-term interest rate of equilibrium should be approximately equal to the marginal productivity of capital. In this way, full employment at zero inflation could be guaranteed, whereas any higher or lower level would trigger a depressive or inflationary cycle.

This theory – as well the overall work of Wicksell – contains interesting aspects, but it can be considered more as an ideal condition than an actual description of the functioning of the modern economy. Here, the main problem is that firms operate in a large competitive system and are compelled to sell their products in order to survive. Moreover, for a number of reasons (cf. also the fourth and fifth parts), there is at the macroeconomic level a structural tendency for effective demand to lag behind effective supply.

As we know, this aspect marks a fundamental difference between neoclassical and Keynesian economics, a difference which contributes to explaining the notion of the relative independence of effective demand from effective supply. According to Keynesian theory (in particular, 1936), the causation tends to run in the opposite direction: it is credit creation that generates additional demand which, in turn, is transformed into new income, and, hence, according to the marginal propensity to consume, into new saving.

In this situation, the analysis of the nature of money and interest rate runs in a completely different direction. Now, as credit creation does not depend anymore on previous saving, the interest rate cannot be considered as a reward for 'abstinence' but, as highlighted by Keynes, as the price for renouncing liquidity.

For this reason, the level of interest rate, however important, loses its centrality in the process of credit creation. The latter will depend on a number of factors like the expected level of effective demand and of firms' profitability, the banking policies of favouring productive or speculative investments, and the characteristics of fiscal policies.

For these reasons, a sensible monetary policy would not try to keep the interest rate at some abstractly conceived 'optimal level' but would aim to reduce it as much as possible in order to stimulate economic activity through an increase of the 'marginal efficiency of capital', which broadly corresponds to the expected profitability of firms.

However, all that said, it would be misleading to describe Commons's position as a simplistic adherence to the neoclassical position. True, he largely endorses Wicksell's theory, but, we can suppose, from an institutional viewpoint.

Although Commons's position on these issues remains largely implicit, what one can infer from his overall treatment is that measures aimed at stabilizing the purchasing power of money can work only in a proper institutional setting: one in which due attention is given to the process of institutional collaboration between different actors, institutions and policies.

From our perspective, we believe more promising a synergy between the concepts expounded by Commons[7] and the insights of Keynesian economics. As we will try to show, the novelty of Keynes's perspective is not confined to the 'technicalities' of economic models but reaches out to the whole view of considering the role of institutions in economic progress. For this reason, there is a growing convergence between institutional and Keynesian economics.

Conclusion

As we have seen, Commons has expounded a rich theoretical framework for the analysis of the evolution of capitalistic institutions. In this regard, his far-reaching conception of institutions and transactions allows us to consider the multiple and interdisciplinary dimensions of collective action, with particular attention to their bearing on policy action.

Needless to say, Commons's theory also contains aspects which demand further investigation. For instance, his concepts of transactions and institutions have the great advantage of embodying all economic and social relations within a unitary interpretative framework. In his view, an ideal society would be one in which all transactions would warrant a fair distribution of duties and opportunities between all participants. However, there is not always a close scrutiny of the imbalances occurring in many transactions, nor of how they might impinge on economic and social development.

For instance, what happens when there are considerable and persistent market imperfections – in particular, public goods, monopoly and oligopoly positions, asymmetric information, transaction costs, externalities – often related to significant differences of contractual power between the parties? And which policies and institutional set-ups can re-balance that situation?

In this regard, Commons focuses attention on important aspects of policy-making: in particular, the evolution of 'reasonable value' in decisions by courts of justice and in significant case-studies of labour legislation – where most often he also played a relevant institutional role (cf. in particular 1964; and 1990, second volume). However, considering that reasonable value related to these activities is, by its very definition, an imperfect and evolving entity, the evolution of this process still remains rather unclear in regard to the following aspects: (i) what factors determine the evolution of the 'reasonable value' and (ii) at what extent such evolution matches up with the profound needs and orientations of society.

These issues, of course, do matter also from a psychological standpoint. In this respect, Commons's negotiational psychology provides a powerful theoretical framework for an interdisciplinary analysis of social life. However, the limitation of this approach is that it does not provide clear hypotheses about the needs and orientations of the individual and the way they can interact with the social context. One reason for this shortcoming is that Commons's negotiational psychology, by emphasizing chiefly the social dimension of psychological dynamics, attained a limited collaboration with psychological theories because they are chiefly regarded as individualistic (cf. also above).

In this respect, Veblen's theory of instincts (1914) goes deeper in providing an explanatory framework of the inner motivations of the person. However, also in this case there was little collaboration with other psychological theories. And this is one of the reasons, as we have seen, why Veblen's theory does not provide a clear explanation of the conflicts between different instincts (or propensities) in their individual and social expression.

Notes

1 We have dealt with these issues, in a partly different way, also in Hermann, 2004.
2 In particular Commons, 1990 (1934) and Commons, 1995 (1924).

3 It is also important to note that the role attributed by Commons to the objectives and values of collective action does not imply that the related outcomes should always be the intentional ones. In fact Commons, in his dealing with the notions of uncertainty and 'futurity', explicitly takes into account the unintentional effects of collective action.
4 It can be interesting to note that these concepts allow Commons to pinpoint the similarities and differences between institutional economics and Darwin's theory which, as is known, has had many influences on social sciences; in this regard, Commons observes that, 'Natural selection, which is natural survival of the "fit," produces wolves, snakes, poisons, destructive microbes; but artificial selection converts wolves into dogs, nature's poisons into medicines, eliminates the wicked microbes, and multiplies the good microbes . . . And these transactions, since the principle of scarcity runs through them, have curious analogies to the factors which Darwin discovered in organisms. Custom, the repetition of transactions, is analogous to heredity; the duplication and multiplication of transactions arise from pressure of population; their variability is evident, and out of the variabilities come changes in customs and survival. But here the survival is the "artificial selection" of good customs and punishment of bad customs, and it is this artificiality, which is merely the human will in action, that converts mechanisms into machines, living organisms into institutionalized minds, and unorganized custom or habit into orderly transactions and going concerns' (Commons, 1990: 636, 638).
5 Refer, in particular, to the essays collected in the volume *Labor and Administration*, 1913.
6 Refer in particular to the 'The End of Laissez-Faire', contained in the fourth part of the *Essays in Persuasion*.
7 As regards the relations between Commons and Keynes, it is interesting to note that Keynes made reference in his *Essays in Persuasion* to Commons's theory of capitalistic evolution. On the other hand, in Commons's *Institutional Economics* he mentions Keynes, also in relation to the debate with Hayek and Hawtrey on monetary policies, without, however, any kind of appraisal of Keynes's positions.

References

Commons, J.R. (1964) *Labor and Administration*. New York: Kelley. First edition 1913.
Commons, J.R. (1995) *Legal Foundations of Capitalism*. New Brunswick, NJ: Transaction Publishers. Originally published by Macmillan in 1924.
Commons, J.R. (1990) *Institutional Economics: Its Place in Political Economy*. New Brunswick, NJ: Transaction Publishers. Originally published by Macmillan in 1934.
Hermann, A. (2004) Economia, diritto e istituzioni nell'opera di John Rogers Commons. *Il Pensiero Economico Moderno*, 24(3): 45–71.
Keynes, J.M. [1963 (1931)] *Essays in Persuasion*. New York: Norton.
Keynes, J.M. (1936) *The General Theory of Employment, Interest and Money*. London: Macmillan.
Veblen, T. (1990) *The Instinct of Workmanship and the State of the Industrial Arts*. New Brunswick, NJ: Transaction Publishers. Originally published by Macmillan in 1914.

8 The decline of institutional economics in the post Second World War period and the new developments of today

Introduction

As we have seen, institutional economics played a relevant role in its first stage, and it can safely be said that it came to be, although perhaps by a slight margin, the 'mainstream economics' of the time. That period ran approximately from Veblen's first important contributions in 1898 – the article 'Why Is Economics Not an Evolutionary Science?' and the book *The Theory of Leisure Class* – to the implementation of the *New Deal* in the early 1930s, where many institutionalists played a significant role.

However, even in the years of institutionalism's heyday, the mainstream economics reaction against institutional economics was never absent. Furthermore, as already noted, some neoclassical aspects were present even in the institutional domain, with some shading-off among institutionalists towards more mainstream positions. The most common criticisms levelled at institutional economics were its supposed descriptive character and the absence of any clear and unifying theoretical framework. To these criticisms, institutionalists responded by highlighting their matter-of-fact approach, which, contrary to the abstractness of neoclassical constructions, could facilitate the solution of the most important economic problems. Up to a certain time, then, neoclassical criticisms, albeit never absent and weak, did not succeed in really affecting the relative supremacy of institutional economics.

As noted by various commentators[1] (cf. for instance, Myrdal, 1972), what triggered the crisis and decline of institutional economics was the eruption of the Great Crisis of 1929. Why did this crisis of institutionalism occur? The answer is two-fold: (i) institutionalists were (relatively) unable to forecast the eruption of the crisis; (ii) the proposed remedies for the crisis were (or, at least, seemed) not so path-breaking as those advocated by the Keynesian exponents.

As regards the first point, it is true that in the period before the crisis, no economist (neoclassical, institutionalist, or otherwise) was either able to predict the crisis or, at least, to pinpoint the unsustainability of the economic growth that preceded the crisis. As regards the second point, the situation changed in the period of the great crisis, where many institutional economists provided significant theoretical and applied contributions.[2] Among other relevant issues, these contributions centred on the role of sticky prices in creating a high margin of profits and an unfavourable income distribution for working classes which, in its turn, led to the working classes having insufficient capacity to consume. This situation was not counteracted by new investments, as a large part of the profits was saved or invested in financial activities.

Also in the making up of the *New Deal*, institutionalists played an active part in drafting the related programme. Their proposals centred on realizing some forms of economic planning, with a view to reducing mark-ups and so obtain prices more oriented to costs. In this way, a more equitable distribution of income could ensue, which would steer a parallel increase of the capacity to consume on the part of the citizens. Also a programme of public works was considered useful, but the general feeling was that a large budget deficit would 'crowd out' private initiative in the middle to long run.

This aspect is partly true – and, on that account, Keynes, too, remarked that large deficits cannot be considered a permanent solution for economic imbalances – but, as the arguments employed by institutionalists partly resonate with neoclassical theory, they conveyed the impression, no matter how well founded, that their policy proposals were not sufficiently innovative to really lift the economy out of the crisis. This impression was reinforced, as we will see presently, by the rather sceptical attitude of institutionalists towards Keynes's theory.

For this reason, since the economic planning advocated by institutionalists was applied but to a limited extent and as a significant part of the *New Deal*[3] was centred on public spending – and as the theory of public spending was considered eminently a Keynesian creature – the main merit of this programme was due to Keynesian theory.

In this respect, the crisis[4] of institutional economics can be traced to the circumstance that such discipline set an over-arching agenda, one that would have required for its unfolding a systematic interaction with other fields and disciplines. This, however, did not occur at sufficient level. What happened most of the time was that, when confronted with other disciplines, not much interchange took place.

The typical reaction of institutionalists was one of self-defence and insulation, and was based on the reaffirmation of the 'distinctiveness and autonomy' of their theoretical framework. As we shall see later, this reaction is by no means confined only to institutional economics, but tends to be the 'normal' attitude of social and psychological sciences. For these and other reasons, institutional economics underwent a period of marked decline, that spanned, approximately, from the mid-1930s to the late 1980s, when a new season for institutional economics was set in motion.

The aspects we consider in more detail in explaining such a decline are the relations of institutional economics with Keynesian theories, the links between theoretical and empirical analysis, and the interdisciplinary orientation.

8.1 Institutional economics and Keynesian economics

In this regard, it can safely be said that, in the main and with a number of exceptions, institutional economics has never been very enthusiastic about Keynes's theory (1936) of aggregated demand. In fact, the main message – although, as we shall see, very far from the complexity of Keynes's theory – that this theory seemed to convey was that the only way to push the economy was through deficit spending. And, furthermore, that such deficit could be maintained or increased over time without much damage to the economic system.

In relation to this interpretation, many institutional economists were rather critical and suspicious of Keynesian theories. They remained unconvinced of Keynes's macroeconomic approach which, in their view, did not consider adequately the variety of microeconomic aspects; and, in particular, they underscored the danger of a policy of deficit spending on the inflation rate and on the crowding out of the private sector. As can be easily seen, these arguments are true up to a point, but they also resonate with more mainstream ones,[5] even though, of course, the overall stance and policy prescription of institutionalists were very different, and often more in accordance with Keynesian oriented policy prescriptions.

However, the weak aspect of the institutionalist attitude does not lie in pointing out the possible limitations of Keynes's theory but in not fully grasping the challenge posed by that theory, which goes well beyond a simple advocacy of deficit spending. In fact, such a theory does nothing less than building anew, and virtually from scratch, the modern macroeconomic theory. As a matter of fact, before that time, no real macroeconomics existed at all. As is known, both classic and neoclassic economics strictly adhered to the so-called 'Say's law', according to which aggregate supply 'automatically creates' its own demand. Should economic systems work like this, no macroeconomics would be needed, since the sum of individual behaviour (in particular, consumers and firms considered in severalty) would explain everything.[6] In this world, optimization and economic progress would proceed in tandem, provided only that market would be allowed to work free from interferences on the part of the public sector.

This picture was completely reversed by Keynes's theory. Here, while a reasonable 'perfection' – or, at least, no major imperfections – of markets at microeconomic level is assumed, the thesis is expounded that the macroeconomic outcome can easily be at variance with an optimal allocation of resources. This is due to the structural tendency of aggregate demand to lag behind aggregate supply.

This, in turn, depends on the tendency of aggregate saving to exceed aggregate investment. The main causes of this phenomenon are (a) a relative low level of the propensity to consume, which is to be traced back to the wide differences in income, since the propensity to consume for higher incomes is likely to be less; and (b) the effects of technological progress which, by tending to make redundant many jobs, require[7] an increasing aggregate supply in order to secure the full employment level (cf. also the fifth part).

This is, however, not the end of the story, as at the least three other factors should be added in order to 'close' a macroeconomic system like this: (i) the tendency of nominal wages to lag behind inflation rate, with a consequent diminution of real wages; (ii) the dynamics of the real interest rate, its dependence upon monetary policies and its effects on the expected profits of firms (or marginal efficiency of capital, MEC); (iii) the role of 'animal spirits', namely, the tendency of persons to embark on economic initiatives not so much on account of the prospective returns but owing to an instinctive proclivity to action.

To these aspects, which mainly pertain to the short-term dimension, should be added Keynes's analysis of the long-term perspectives in economy and society, which was developed in particular in the *Essays in Persuasion*. As we shall see in Chapter 14, for Keynes, focusing attention also on short-term problems constitutes only a part of more profound awareness of the structural transformations of society. The full unfolding of these tendencies can open up new avenues of progress, in which the 'economic motive' associated with the more negative traits of capitalism – selfishness, greediness, avarice – can gradually become unimportant and be replaced by social and cooperative relations.

In all this account, Keynes is fully aware – also by making explicit reference[8] to Commons's taxonomy – of the transformation of individual capitalism into a concerted capitalism in which the role of public action, also in the form of semi-autonomous agencies, would play a pivotal role.

Turning to our theme, this forward-looking and articulated theory was largely overlooked by institutional economists, as they tended to consider a simplified version of it. On the other hand, the same holds true for Keynesian economists, who paid little attention to institutional theories.

The result of the gulf so created has been a delay in better clarifying fundamental aspects of the economic systems that would have much benefited from a more systematic collaboration between these theories. We can mention, in particular, the role of the legal and institutional framework in promoting a balanced economic and social development.

As we shall also see later, this kind of enquiry can cast more light on the following aspects: (i) the role of public spending and credit creation in the formation of aggregate demand, which can help explain their massive increase in the post Second World War period both in absolute and relative terms; (ii) the effects of macroeconomic and structural policies; (iii) the nature of expectations; (iv) the manifold expression of market imperfections.

8.2 The relations between theoretical and empirical analysis

As we have seen, one motive of the ascendance of institutional economics lies in its claim to be more empirical, more concerned with the investigation of the facts and data of the real world. This world, and in particular the economic domain, was becoming more and more complex and was characterized, along with with the emergence of the modern corporation, by the growing importance of market imperfections.

In this situation, neoclassical economics, with its abstract[9] and deductive theorizing, was considered unfit to adequately address these new phenomena. Hence, a novel approach was urgently needed, and institutional economics seemed ready to take up the challenge. As noted above, institutional economists became heavily involved in many relevant issues, such as labour legislation, structure of costs and prices, business cycles, antitrust policies, public utilities regulation, public works and other areas of public intervention. As noted by Rutherford:

All of this [activity] seems to indicate the strength of the institutionalist movement. Well established at leading universities and research institutes, with excellent access to external funding sources, involved with important government legislation and programs, and linked to recent developments in related disciplines. In all of these respects, institutionalism had as much or more strength than neoclassical economics . . . Nevertheless, when Wisconsin and Columbia resumed hiring in 1946–1947, it was not institutionalists who were hired, but Keynesians and neoclassical economists, indicating that some very significant shifts in the academic environment must have taken place between the 1930s and 1946–1947 when hiring resumed.

(Rutherford, 2011: 350)

Thus, the question poses itself, why did this decline occur, in spite of the empirical orientation of institutional economics? One reason, as we have just seen, is constituted by the affirmation of Keynesian economics. But this is by no means the sole reason. In fact, another and related reason for such decline rests in the unclear and often contradictory way in which institutional economics addressed the central issue of empirical analysis.

In order to better develop this issue, let's have a closer look at the methodological underpinnings of empirical work carried out by institutional economists. This work went under three main headings: (i) Statistical analysis of the main economic categories (consumption, investments, profits, prices) at various levels of disaggregation, in order to enquire into the dynamics of business cycles and the characteristics of industrial sectors; (ii) analysis of the legislation and court decisions, with particular reference to the issues of industrial and competition policies, and of public utility regulation; (iii) case studies related to particular firms, industrial sectors and other economic realities.

These activities were flourishing and produced significant results, but something stood in the way of hindering their full unfolding. This factor can be located in the massive development of mathematical and econometric analysis on the part of both neoclassical economics and various strands of the new Keynesian theory. Of course, mathematical models and econometric models are quite different things – a mathematical model might not be amenable to econometric analysis and we can perform econometric estimates without a clear model, mathematic or otherwise, underlying them – but in the common perception both were considered as a step towards a more 'scientific and objective way' of investigating economic phenomena. In fact, mathematical models, whether or not allowing econometric estimates, were constructed as 'a piece of theory' amenable, actually or at least potentially, to empirical verification. The philosophical basis of this development was positivism, which found a development also in a narrow conception of behaviourism.

The institutionalists' reaction to these events was largely ineffectual, because they partly shared (at a higher or lesser degree) a kind of positivist attitude. In this regard, their philosophical background oscillated between pragmatism and positivism, and was never sufficiently clarified. In fact, they adopted John Dewey's notion of behaviourism, but this was often intermingled with a positivist notion of behaviourism. However, these notions are very different and cannot be mixed up, as they refer to the following aspects:

A   The pragmatist conception of behaviourism refers to the importance of analysing the 'experience' of a person in its entirety. Hence, we should consider not only the more directly observable and 'measurable' behaviour, but the whole set of feelings and orientations in their individual and collective dimension.

B   In the positivistic conception only directly observable behaviour is considered 'scientific', because, it is claimed, only this kind of behaviour can be 'measured' in a more neutral and objective way.

These notions carry very different implications for social analysis. We can see this with a simple example: let's suppose we are investigating children's behaviour at the school. Following a positivist orientation, the researchers will try to find a set of factors which identify the 'normal' or 'optimal' behaviour at the school – for instance, rate of attendance and level of proficiency – and then they will proceed to estimate, by a variety of statistical and econometric techniques, the degree of fulfilment of these objectives. Conversely, pragmatist oriented researchers would probably carry out the same kind of analysis, but would not stop there. From that perspective, the results obtained would not be the end of the story but would constitute only the basis of further investigation of the individual and social factors leading to a certain behaviour.

In fact, if we are studying children's behaviour, we should not forget that we are dealing with persons living in a social context. Hence, in order to get a more complete assessment of the 'normality' of their behaviour, we should ideally get a profile for each child of its personal life, with the related emotions and conflicts. This study would also involve the main characteristics of its family and social relations, and of the social and institutional framework surrounding each child. For instance, social classes and groups and the organization of education, with all their values and conflicts.

Needless to say, we are aware of the difficulty of such analysis and of the expediency of identifying single parts in a complex problem. Within this ambit, it can be useful to look for correlations between aggregate phenomena, namely, between phenomena involving a collective dimension.

However, we should be aware that every generalization involves a simplification, in the sense that many others factors are left out of the door. This applies especially when we try to establish a causality between factors in order 'to demonstrate' the validity of a theory.

In this regard, what seems important to remark is that aggregate analysis, however important, cannot become a substitute for the study of each person considered. For this reason, as we shall presently see, a plurality of methodologies is needed in order to carry out a comprehensive empirical analysis.

In facing these issues, institutionalists did not clearly identify and confront the various meanings of empirical analysis. They swung between a (relatively) uncritical endorsement of positivist methodology and an advocacy of the importance of the holistic approach which, however, remained mostly a kind of 'petition principle'.

If we consider that this came about when neoclassical and Keynesian economics – and, later on, other branches significantly related to neoclassical economics such as public choice, new institutional economics and new regulatory economics – were investigating a number of important phenomena – in particular, macroeconomic imbalances, market imperfections, the role of public action and of interest groups – the reasons for the crisis of institutionalism appear clearly.

A good strategy for institutionalism to cope with this challenge would have been to chart an open and thorough confrontation with the various theories dealing with these issues.

For instance, in the case of market imperfections (cf., also, the third part), by recognizing the importance of incentives, transaction costs and informational asymmetries but, at the same time, also pointing out that the positivistic methodology underlying these advances, even if useful in rendering the issues more treatable, tend to produce too narrow a picture of these phenomena.

In this context, institutional economists can point out that, certainly, incentives are important but they cannot be reduced to the maximization behaviour implied in the neoclassical conception of *homo oeconomicus*. In fact, many other psychological and cultural factors are likely to enter the picture.

In order to address these aspects thoroughly, the empirical analysis would require a plurality of methodologies. In this sense, statistical and econometric analysis should be coupled with case studies, historical analysis of larger contexts, focus groups on particular problems, also with a view to obtaining a more active involvement of the actors implied.

One relevant consequence of this broadened enquiry is that it would lead to a more pluralistic interpretation of the phenomena examined. In fact, considering these phenomena in their real complexity would make easier a comprehensive confrontation of different explicative theories.

A possible drawback of this methodology – pointed out in particular by mainstream economists – is that putting too many factors into the basket would engender uncertainty and confusion. These aspects can be true to a degree but, at the same time, they are largely overstated. In fact, complexity does exist, and trying implicitly to overlook relevant factors in order to simplify the picture would run a double risk: not only the risk of leaving out of sight a number of relevant factors but also of not making clear the underlying criteria and values of the researcher.

From this perspective, what is needed in order to overcome these problems is a thorough process of social valuing, as a way of clarifying the criteria and values employed in the analysis. An important aspect of this more comprehensive approach relates to the interdisciplinary orientation of institutional economics, which we also consider in the next paragraph in relation to the issue of 'empirical analysis'.

8.3 The need for an interdisciplinary approach

As we have seen, one distinctive aspect of institutional economics is its interdisciplinary orientation. This applies in particular to psychology, where institutionalists explicitly set out on their research agenda a close collaboration with such discipline. This can be seen, for instance, in the following passage by Wesley Mitchell:

> As soon as an economist has assimilated this idea that he is dealing with one aspect of human behaviour, he faces his share in that problem so conspicuous in current psychology, nature and nurture, the propensities with which men are born and their modifications in experience. I do not imply that the economist must read all the literature upon instincts and repressions which the psychologists publish. Doubtless acquaintance with that literature is helpful; it suggests a wide variety of hypotheses, and it makes one critical of the naïve theories about human mind which each mind proffers in profusion.
>
> (Mitchell, 'The Prospects of Economics', in Tugwell,
> 1924: 23)

However, despite this far-sighted agenda, institutionalism did not fully realise its promises. In fact, as also noted by Rutherford (2011), not much work was produced which made explicit and creative use of concepts coming from institutional economics and psychology. There are several reasons for this outcome:

1   The psychological sciences were still, in the first decades of the twentieth century, in a preliminary stage of development. This made it difficult to employ a number of relevant psychological concepts – for instance, cognitive limits and biases, the role of emotions, and the interrelations between cognitive and emotional sphere, which only later on reached a more full-fledged development – to the study of economic and social phenomena.

2   Also psychoanalysis was in an early stage of development. Furthermore, what made difficult its collaboration with social sciences was its supposed exclusive emphasis on the bodily aspects of 'instincts'. For this reason (cf. also Part I) institutionalists and other social scientists have established little collaboration with psychoanalysis. The same applies to collaboration with 'cultural psychoanalysis', with one notable exception being constituted by Schneider's book (1948) *Freudian Psychology and Veblen's Social Theory*.[10]

3   At the same time, and in parallel with the relatively slow progress of other fields of psychology, there was during that period a quick affirmation of behaviouristic psychology, defined as in the positivistic meaning referred to above, according to which the only relevant behaviour is the one which can be observed and 'measured' through a number of proxies.

In this situation, as already noted, institutionalists did not get a clear stance and tended to shift towards a narrow conception of behaviourism. This can be seen in

Mitchell's contributions mentioned before. In fact, after the quoted passage, he remarks that:

> 'Institutions' is merely a convenient term for the more important among the widely prevalent, highly standardized social habits. And so it seems that the behavioristic viewpoint will make economics theory more and more a study of economic institutions . . . The extension and improvement of statistical compilations is therefore a factor of the first consequence for the progress of economic theory. Gradually economics will become a quantitative science. It will be less concerned with puzzles about economic motives and more concerned about the objective validity of the account it gives of economic processes.
>
> (Mitchell, in Tugwell, 1924: 25, 27)

The rationale underlying Mitchell's position was, however, at that time, quite innovative: in fact, it rested on the purpose of getting more precise data in order to go beyond a mere theoretical speculation not in contact with facts. This was particularly the case for the analysis of business cycles, where he clearly recognized their complexity, their relations with the characteristics of the context, and the specificity and common aspects of the various cycles.

In this sense, we believe that Mitchell's position on the importance of data is quite appropriate, with its limitation resting on considering as reliable data only those based on statistical aggregates.

In this context laying stress on the quantitative side of phenomena became quite common in that period, and was emphatically expressed by the following passages of F.C. Mills:

> The modern economist enumerates, measures, weighs . . . 'When you cannot measure what are you speaking about, when you cannot express it in numbers', said Lord Kelvin, 'your knowledge is of a meager and unsatisfactory kind; it may be the beginning of knowledge, but you have scarcely in your thoughts advanced to the stage of a *science*, whatever the matter may be' . . . In summary: Our useful knowledge of events in the world about us is essentially statistical in character; that is, it is not concerned fundamentally with unique, individual events, but with aggregates of events which may be described in terms of averages, of typical characteristics. In generalizing about such aggregates we are of necessity precluded from speaking in terms of invariant laws.
>
> (Mills, 'On Measurement in Economics', in Tugwell, 1924: 37, 46)

Now, it is beyond question that we acknowledge the importance of statistical analysis for gathering a better knowledge of economic and social phenomena. The aspect with which we cannot agree is that the relevant data can be obtained only from statistical enquiry. For instance, in the example above of children's behaviour at school, it is extremely useful to collect statistics on attendance, performance and satisfaction, as well as on the characteristics of the school system and of the family and social structure of the children. But these data are neither the only relevant ones nor the only obtainable ones.

As a matter of fact, it is important to remember that, when we elaborate statistics on, say, school attendance, or consumers' behaviour or firms' behaviour, the related procedure consists in comparing one or more measurable data pertaining to entities which are composed of many other dimensions. One solution to this problem, which lies at the bottom of the positivist attitude, is to broaden and refine statistical procedure by including more variables, by rendering the proxies more precise, and by devising more effective indicators. This pathway is fine, of course, but it is also true that statistical analysis cannot capture all the complexity of the phenomena under examination. The reason for this is simple enough, and consists in the fact that statistical data are always derived data which are obtained by comparing the population under investigation along some measurable dimension. As such, these data, however important, can never touch directly 'the soul and the heart' of the members of the population. In fact, when we deal with, say, children's behaviour, consumers' behaviour and firms' behaviour, we are dealing with the behaviour of people, in their individual and collective dimensions, which is highly specific for each situation. For this reason – and in order to avoid the well-known dangers of simplification and reductionism – statistical analysis should always be coupled with case studies and other methods for acquiring more 'direct and qualitative' data on the phenomena under investigation: in our example, the behaviour of children, consumers and firms. As can be seen, these two conceptions of scientific analysis carry very different perspectives on the scope of institutional economics, also in its relation with psychological sciences.

In the case of positivist attitude, the only aspects deemed to be scientific are those amenable to statistical analysis whereas, in the case of pragmatist and humanistic perspectives, the analysis tries to consider all the relevant aspects – both direct and more 'qualitative' and indirect and more 'quantitative' – which concur to identify economic and social phenomena at individual and collective level (cf. also Chapter 4).

In this regard, the failure of institutionalists to single out the two different conceptions of empirical analysis have impaired their potential for a critique of the positivistic conception and for a more comprehensive investigation of economic and social phenomena. Also for this reason, economics in its main developments (in particular, neoclassical and neo-Keynesians) in the post Second World War period has become more and more 'quantitative' by relying almost exclusively on econometric analysis.

We can see this weakness of institutional economics in the rather unsuccessful attempt by Mitchell[11] to assert, against the 'pure theory' of neoclassical economics, the necessity that theories should be inductively constructed on the basis of quantitative analysis. The neoclassical answer was that theory should guide quantitative analysis. Mitchell's rejoinder was rather brittle and partly agreed with his critics by maintaining his emphasis on quantitative analysis but claiming that some passages of his first address had been misunderstood. Of course, an obvious rejoinder would have been that every theory should find verification and development in the empirical evidence writ large, and then including also the whole set of 'qualitative' phenomena.

In fact, by relying only on 'quantitative phenomena', the argument about 'empirical evidence' opens the flank to the supremacy of the basic tenets of neoclassical theory, based on deductive analysis. In fact, as quantitative enquiry alone cannot reach the 'soul and the heart' of the phenomena, the implicit philosophical and psychological foundations underpinning the 'basic principles of a theory' can never be really questioned. In this sense, even if the quantitative data – which, for instance, evidence gross market imperfections – run against the theory of perfect competition, it can easily be claimed by neoclassical exponents that these phenomena are 'exceptions'.

In some way, a similar story took place in psychology, where the progressive affirmation of a narrow conception of behaviourism was not effectively questioned by more humanistic fields of psychology. However, this rather gloomy picture requires a corrective. First, despite the limitations mentioned, some interdisciplinary synergy has always occurred in the institutionalist domain. This applies especially to the philosophy and psychology of pragmatism, with the use of the concepts of habits, social norms, social identity, cognitive faculties, and purposive action for the interpretation of economic and social phenomena.

Second, and relatedly, two important institutional economists, Thorstein Veblen and John Rogers Commons, developed an economic theory which makes explicit use of psychological concepts.

Significantly enough for our theme, these theories (cf. the previous chapters) were chiefly humanistic and pragmatist in their orientation. In this regard, both Veblen and Commons had great psychological intuitions by developing important psychological concepts, which complemented in relevant ways – also by considering the social dimension of psychological phenomena – the theories being developed in psychology and psychoanalysis.

However, these insights remained largely undeveloped for many years. The reason for this is, once again, the fragmentation occurring in social and psychological sciences. In fact, the collaboration between Veblen's and Commons's theories, on the one side, and psychology and psychoanalysis on the other, had been scant in both directions. And, on top of that, there was minimal collaboration, too, in the institutional field. In fact, not only did other institutionalists make little use of Veblen's and Commons's theories, but also the relations between the two theories were virtually nonexistent.

As we shall see presently, nowadays the situation is different and significant developments are taking place.

8.4 Recent developments

As a consequence of the limitations outlined above and of more 'exogenous factors' as well, institutional economics has become progressively marginalized in the profession and in society at large in the post Second World War period. In fact, from the more orthodox perspective, it was all too easy to dismiss institutionalism as 'a narrative without a theory'. But, and perhaps even worse, institutional economics largely failed to make waves even in the field of heterodox oriented theories. We have seen before its problematic relation with Keynesian theories.

But, also, the interchange with Marxism and other theories of social justice was not a smooth one. Here, however, the situation seems better. In fact, contrary to Keynesian economics, institutionalism has established a more systematic collaboration with Marxism, in particular as regards the concept of power, and the character and evolution of capitalistic institutions. However, and despite this interchange, in Marxism and other more 'radical fields' of social sciences institutionalism has not gained a great appeal – it was not even very well known within the progressive field – as it was considered 'too moderate, too gradualist' to fit the impatience of revolutionary aspirations.

In this very difficult situation, institutionalists were nonetheless able to survive and produce notable contributions on a wide range of theoretical and applied issues. In the vast majority of cases, these contributions were heavily based on the elaboration of the IE typical concepts. This was accompanied, as noted before, by a lack of systematic confrontation with other fields of economics.

However, despite this insulation and fragmentation which characterized IE, and as well the whole realm of social sciences, some useful reciprocal influence did occur in the economics field. This influence occurred in both directions and, for this reason, it would be mistaken to infer that the contributions by institutionalists – owing to their relative marginalized position – went unnoticed among the economics profession at large.

In this respect, concepts such as the importance of the institutions in economic and social life, the role of habits, the structure of power, the distinction between the instrumental and ceremonial aspects of institutions, the role of social valuing, the relevance of the formal and informal rules, the characteristics of cultures, and the overall evolutionary perspective pervading all these aspects, have exerted an enduring influence, although often implicit and unacknowledged, on the way of reasoning of economists and other social scientists.

This situation characterised the post Second World War period until, approximately, the late 1980s. After that period, there has been a kind of new wave of institutionalism and other heterodox perspectives, which – even if it has not pushed them to their best times – is notable and still in the ascendant. In this phenomenon we can see the probable influence of the following factors: (i) the crisis following the oil shocks of the 1970s made evident the insufficiency of the simplest versions of Keynesian policies (cf., also, Part IV); (ii) the growing awareness of the inadequacy of the more extreme versions of both central planning and neoliberalism to address the growing imbalances of economic and social phenomena: in particular, the highly uneven distribution of income and wealth, unemployment and deterioration of working conditions, environmental decay, political and social (often armed) conflicts. These imbalances culminated in the recent economic crisis, which has triggered a kind of a general reshuffle of all the received economic and social theories.

This has happened also within the mainstream domain. True, even in this period neoclassical oriented theories are still in a 'mainstream position' but their leading role is much more blurred and problematic than before. Under the pressure of events, this paradigm has become more flexible and, also on that account, there is a growing differentiation of opinions on many important issues.

With regard to heterodox economics, there has been a flourishing of new initiatives. New associations have been created – for instance, the Association for Heterodox Economics (AHE) and the European Association for Evolutionary Political Economy (EAEPE) – and the existing ones (in particular, AFIT, AFEE) have become more active and influential. They organize an annual conference and other initiatives, in particular for younger students. They also promote, or are involved in, the activities of a number of scientific journals.

There is growing attention to heterodox issues and there is a steady, even if not spectacular, increase in the number of people involved in these activities. The *spectrum* of subject-matters covered by heterodox contributions is very ample and continually widening. There are also many contributions which apply these theories to the study of economic and social problems, often considered in their cultural and historical perspective.

Despite this progress, the situation for heterodox economics remains troublesome. One reason is that this germination of ideas and contributions does not succeed in securing for heterodox economists an adequate foothold as regards financing and academic positions. This situation is particularly dangerous for the future of heterodox economics because it does not offer an adequate prospect of tenure and career for the younger generation of economists. A detailed analysis of this side of the problem[12] is beyond the scope of the book.

Perhaps what is needed for the advancement of heterodox economics is a more systematic attention to policy issues. As a matter of fact, if we present our activities as a forum for pluralism, this looks fine, but risks being perceived by both the more informed audience and by lay people as an interesting intellectual venture with, however, no tangible results in terms of better policies. And this in a period where there is a high, explicit and latent, demand for new policy solutions for major economic and social problems. Thus, in order to improve heterodox influence, we can more clearly state the relevance of our perspective for policy action.

Conclusion: what interaction between institutional economics and psychoanalysis?

As we have seen, one distinctive aspect of institutional economics is its interdisciplinary orientation. In this regard, Veblen and Commons went far in this direction by providing an elaborate psychological foundation to their institutional theories.

Within this ambit, many of Veblen's and Commons's concepts could be – without overlooking the differences existing between their theories and their overall vision of the world – jointly used in the study of society. For instance, Commons's concepts of institution, transaction, collective action, working rules, going concerns, reasonable value and negotiational psychology could make more clear the interrelated and conflicting aspects of collective action, in particular in the sphere of the complex propensities and motivations of the individual addressed by Veblen. And, relatedly, Veblen's concepts of habits, instincts, evolution and technology could help to bring into better focus the inner motivations and conflicts underlying human action within the complex framework of transactions, institutions and policy action highlighted by Commons.

Building on these concepts, subsequent contributions have developed the key concepts of institutional economics in many directions. In this regard, an issue which we consider paramount is the process of the formulation of economic and social policies in their relations with institutional dynamics. The relationship between institutions and policies was first pointed out by Commons and then developed by later institutionalists.

In this analysis a central role is played by the process of social valuing, which constitutes, as we have seen, the very core of policy-making. The following passage effectively expresses this concept:

> To conceive of a problem requires the perception of a difference between 'what is going on' and 'what ought to go on'. Social value theory is logically and inescapably required to distinguish what ought to be from what is . . . In the real world, the provisioning process in all societies is organized through prescriptive and proscriptive institutional arrangements that correlate behaviour in the many facets and dimensions of the economic process. Fashioning, choosing among and assessing such institutional structure is the 'stuff and substance' of continuing discussions in deliberative bodies and in the community generally. The role of social value theory is to provide analyses of criteria in terms of which such choices are made.
>
> (Tool, in Hodgson, Samuels and Tool, 1994: 406–407)

A more systematic collaboration between institutional economics and psychoanalysis can help locate the multiple levels of collective action, and in particular: (i) the complexity of individual motivations and systems of values, where the relational and social dimensions play a paramount role; (ii) the complexity of policy action, which involves not only governmental institutions but also every other level of collective action; (iii) consequently, the fact that dynamics of institutions and dynamics of policies represent complementary aspects of collective action, where, in the first (the institutions) the stress is on structure, decision-making process and cultural evolution, while in the second (the policies) the focus is on action and results.

This suggests that a collaboration of this kind, by involving a process of understanding of the characteristics of any given ISEF, can provide better answers to questions which are central for institutional economics, such as:

A   Why do habits of thought depend heavily on the characteristics of the ISEF and tend to change very slowly?
B   Why don't institutions, in some cases, attain their established goals?
C   What is the role of economic, social and cultural conflicts in shaping individual and collective behaviour?

D   What is the role of institutions and policies in fostering economic progress and social justice, in particular in developing countries?

E   What are the characteristics of social valuing in a given context, and how can they be improved?

In the analysis of these problems, by clarifying the needs and conflicts existing between people in their individual and collective expression, institutionalism in collaboration with psychoanalysis can help formulate policies more based on the motivations and experiences of people involved in collective action.

Notes

1   In this respect, the authors more critical with these interpretations (see, for instance, Rutherford, 2011) also agree with the basic periods of ascendance and decline of institutionalism.

2   See the references of Chapter 5 and, in particular, Berle and Means (1932); Levin, Moulton and Warburton (1934); Mills (1936); Moulton (1935, 1943); Nourse (1944); Nourse and others (1934); Rutherford (2011); Tugwell and Hill (1934).

3   For more details on these issues and on the relations between institutional economists with Keynesian theory refer to Rutherford (2011).

4   Of course, besides these 'endogenous' factors, there are other more 'exogenous' elements which have concurred to trigger such a crisis. These can refer to the overall progressive stance of institutional economics, which implied a clear advocacy of public intervention, economic planning, participation and democracy. These aspects were likely to be considered 'too dangerous for the principle of economic freedom' and hence were opposed by a number of political and economic exponents and by the majority of neoclassical economists. However, we are more interested in the 'endogenous factors' which have led to the institutional crisis.

5   As we have seen, also, Veblen's and Commons's theories did not fully recognize the role of aggregate demand and, on fiscal and monetary policy adhered more to a neoclassical standard, even if, of course, they were critical of the overall stance of that theory.

6   It can be interesting to note that it has been the adherence to such 'law' that has permitted 'the logical shift' from classical to neoclassical economics. In fact, classic economics, although relying on the hypothesis of the perfect market, is still constructed through the identification of neat social classes (in particular, workers and capitalists), whereas in neoclassical there exist only economic agents.

7   We will address these aspects in more detail in Part IV.

8   In his essay 'Am I a Liberal?', included in the *Essays in Persuasion* (1931).

9   As noted before, in that period neoclassical economics did not claim to be 'empirical' and did not establish a systematic collaboration with econometrics.

10 In the book there is an interesting attempt to analyse the parallels between Freud's and Veblen's theories. Although this work provides many useful insights – for instance, an in-depth discussion about the possibility of linking cultural forms and psychological traits – it does not succeed, at least in our view, in clearly identifying the aspects where the collaboration between institutional economics and psychoanalysis could better unfold. The reasons for these limitations are to be found in the author's interpretation of Freud's and Veblen's theories. It is assumed that Freud attributes

all the importance in human behaviour to the 'instincts', which are supposed to be mainly driven by the 'principle of pleasure'. This interpretation leads the author to identify an 'anarchistic' strain in Freudian theory, which would have led Freud to the conclusion that the repression of 'instincts' is necessary for the existence of society. As a consequence of this view, the author considers Freud's theory inadequate for the analysis of human behaviour and turns his attention to the contributions of the 'neo-Freudians', who have, in his opinion, the merit of having lessened the role of 'instincts' and brought to the fore the importance of social aspects of life. The same line of reasoning is applied to Veblen's analysis, though, in the author's view, Veblen's workmanship instinct makes his 'anarchism' less definitive than Freud's. Needless to say, we find these conclusions, for the reasons set forth in the previous chapters, highly unconvincing.

11 The debate started with Mitchell's Presidential Address before the American Economic Association (see in particular Mitchell, 1925, 1928).
12 For more details see Elsner and Lee (2008), Lee (2009), Lee et al. (2010), Reardon (2009).

References

Berle, A.A. and Means, G.C. (1932) *The Modern Corporation and Private Property*. New York: Macmillan.
Elsner, W. and Lee, F. (eds.) (2008) Publishing, refereeing, rankings, and the future of heterodox economics. *On the Horizon*, Special issue, 16(4).
Hodgson, G.M., Samuels, W.J. and Tool, M. (eds.) (1994) *The Elgar Companion to Institutional and Evolutionary Economics*. Aldershot: Edward Elgar.
Keynes, J.M. (1963) *Essays in Persuasion*. New York: Norton. Originally published by Macmillan in 1931.
Keynes, J.M. (1936) *The General Theory of Employment, Interest and Money*. London: Macmillan.
Lee, F. (2009) *A History of Heterodox Economics: Challenging the Mainstream in the Twentieth Century*. Abingdon and New York: Routledge.
Lee, F., Cronin, C., McConnell, S. and Dean, E. (2010) Research quality rankings of heterodox economic journals in a contested discipline. *American Journal of Economics and Sociology*, 69(5): 1409–1452.
Levin, M., Moulton, H. and Warburton, C. (1934) *America's Capacity To Consume*. Washington, DC: Brookings Institution.
Mills, F.C. (1924) 'On Measurement in Economics', in Tugwell, R.G. (ed.) *The Trend of Economics*. New York: Knopf.
Mills, F.C. (1936) *Prices in Recession and Recovery*. New York: National Bureau of Economic Research.
Mitchell, W.C. 'The Prospects of Economics', in Tugwell (1924), quoted.
Mitchell, W.C. (1925) Quantitative Analysis in Economic Theory. *American Economic Review*, 15 (March): 1–12.
Mitchell, W.C. (1928) The Present Status and Future Prospects of Quantitative Economics. *American Economic Review*, Supplement, 18 (March): 39–41.
Moulton, H.G. (1935) *Income and Economic Progress*. Washington, DC: Brookings Institution.
Moulton, H.G. (1943) *The New Philosophy of Public Debt*. Washington, DC: Brookings Institution.

Myrdal, G. (1972) *Against the Stream: Critical Essays in Economics*. New York: Pantheon Books.

Nourse, E.G. (1944) *Price Making in a Democracy*. Washington, DC: Brookings Institution.

Nourse, E.G. et al. (1934) *America's Capacity To Produce*. Washington, DC: Brookings Institution.

Reardon, J. (ed.) (2009) *Handbook of Pluralist Economics Education*. Abingdon: Routledge.

Rutherford, M. (2011) *The Institutional Movement in American Economics, 1918–1947: Science and Social Control*. Cambridge, UK and New York: Cambridge University Press.

Schneider, L. (1948) *The Freudian Psychology and Veblen's Social Theory*. New York: King's Crown Press.

Tugwell, R.G. (ed.) (1924) *The Trend of Economics*. New York: Knopf.

Tugwell, R.G. and Hill, H.C. (1934) *Our Economic Society and Its Problems*. New York: Harcourt, Brace.

Veblen, T. (1898) Why Is Economics Not an Evolutionary Science? *Quarterly Journal of Economics*, XII: July.

Veblen, T. (1899) *The Theory of Leisure Class*. New York: Penguin.

Part III

The institutional analysis of the market and the interdisciplinary approach to social evolution

In this part we will employ this pluralistic and interdisciplinary perspective in order to analyse some controversial elements of (i) the definition and analysis of the market; (ii) the theory of historical materialism and the importance of also bringing to the fore the cultural and psychological factors; (iii) the links connecting these issues with the debate between holism and methodological individualism; (iv) the importance of an interdisciplinary approach in reaching out to the manifold aspects of these concepts and, on this basis, in identifying suitable policies for our most urgent economic and social problems; (v) the role of psychoanalytic perspective in elucidating many aspects of person–society dynamics, with particular attention to how it can help improve the process of policy action.

9 The market in the heterodox perspective

Introduction

As is known, the analysis of the market constitutes perhaps one of the most conflicting aspects in the analysis of the various forms of economic organization. For instance, the long-standing debate[1] on 'market socialism' has triggered diametrically opposed positions as regards the role of the market in economic and social development.

On the one hand, the supporters of this system note that the market existed before capitalism and, as a consequence, can also exist in a socialist society. On the other hand, the opponents think that the market constitutes an economic device for the exploitation of workers and, as such, can be present in its most developed form only in a capitalistic economy. Even among non-socialist economists ideas differ widely with respect to the role of the market in many structural, and related, issues – for instance, scientific and technological progress, economic development, unemployment and environmental protection.

As a matter of fact, the analysis of the market is the crux of many important aspects of economic structure and of the corresponding forms of policy action: in particular, public action and private initiative, forms of competition, and the correlated concepts of capitalism, socialism, sustainable development, participation and democracy.

In order to enquire into these complex relations, we employ, in an interdisciplinary and pluralistic perspective, a number of contributions from institutional economics and other important social and psychological theories. In the analysis of such issues, these theories can contribute to cast a stronger light on the following interrelated aspects: (i) the structure of collective action; (ii) the relations between market and non-market arrangements; (iii) the nature of market failures and imperfections; (iv) the problems of co-ordination between the various policies bearing on the market structure, also considered in their supranational dimension.

9.1 The complex meaning of 'market economy'

As is known, mainstream economics places a special emphasis on the virtues of the market economy. And, although there can be different opinions among mainstream economists as regards competition policies in a particular context – for instance, the effects of free trade policies for the economic development of backward economies – their central belief is not open to any real discussion: namely, that a market economy and the competition process associated with it constitute, at least in theory, the most efficient way for resource allocation.

Of course, it can be sometimes approximately true that, for instance, in sports, institutions, the political arena or certain economic situations, a more competitive setting may constitute a kind of incentive for striving to attain better performances. In these instances, the competition process is likened to a 'natural process' à la Darwin, which has the effect of rendering the 'struggle for life' harder.

For example, if we have to start from scratch a new life on a desert island, we have to strive hard in order to survive and, as a result of a successful struggle (sink or swim), we can transform ourselves into much more resistant people. Hence, if the benefits of competition appear to be so evident, what is missing in endorsing such a theory? The answer is that this line of reasoning chiefly describes a process going on, as it can, in the natural world of animals and plants. Here, a kind of Darwinian mechanism of selection of the 'fittest' is certainly at work, even if it is likely that even in that case the phenomena are much more complex than they appear at first sight.

This description, however, transposed to human society, becomes extremely vague: here, we have much more freedom in organizing our environment according to our values and motivations and we can also modify, up to a certain degree, the natural environment. Hence, the discourse on market and competition traverses all our ways and dimensions of life – in particular, social, economic, political, cultural and psychological in their historical evolution.

In this sense, competition is not 'a natural and ineluctable process' handed down by a Divine Providence, in respect to which we can do nothing but respond with an unconditioned adaptation. Conversely, in human society the forms and degrees of competition are highly psychological and cultural phenomena, which are heavily interlinked with the values, motivations and conflict at the individual and collective level.

In this regard, mainstream economics and, more generally, the various versions[2] of liberalism can hardly go beyond the very vague statement that establishing political and economic liberty, and the competition process associated with it, is the most effective way of ensuring economic progress. Of course, this does not imply overlooking the articulation and contributions of the various strands[3] of liberalism. As a matter of fact, the basic principles of liberalism are also being employed by a number of progressive strands of social sciences which are trying to look for a viable 'third way' of social evolution: for instance, the social market economy of 'ordoliberalism' and the many versions of market socialism.

Being aware of these different meanings of liberalism, our main criticisms are directed towards so-called neo-liberalism. As for the 'milder' strands of liberalism, we agree that they highlight the importance of individual freedom but believe that only a careful analysis of the characteristics of any given context can provide a more precise content of the notion of individual freedom. As underscored by institutional economics, individual freedom is not an abstract and 'exogenous' notion which unfolds itself in a *vacuum* but is endogenously created and maintained by collective action: namely, by the characteristics of the institutional and legal framework, with all its set of right and duties, and the economic, social, cultural and psychological aspects associated with them.

These more heterodox theories indicate, each in its own way, the importance of the ties between economic, social and political freedom, on the one hand, and with social justice, on the other. This could be (and has, in part, been) realized by a public intervention aimed at (i) providing public goods; (ii) ensuring as much as possible the equality of the 'starting points'; (iii) avoiding the abuse of economic power in the private realm.

After 1945, these policies were fairly successful until the coming of the oil crisis of the early 1970s. After that, and in conjunction with the silent but progressive emergence of 'the fiscal crisis of the State', this system of 'social market economy (meant in a broad sense)' fell into disrepute. By shaking the psychological and cultural foundations upon which that model was based this situation has given rise to the widespread belief that the main cause of such crisis is 'too much public spending and public intervention'.

In fact (see also the next chapters), since the most evident 'symptoms' of that crisis are a stagflationary situation accompanied by a growing ratio of public spending and public debt to GDP, the opinion has gained a widespread foothold, including among several exponents of the progressive domain, that public intervention is inefficient and no longer sustainable. Hence, the only solution is a drastic cut in public spending in order to restore as much as possible the benefits of a private system.

In this regard, the general opinion, also within the progressive field, is that – short of triggering an (unlikely) revolutionary process and/or (not clearly identified) radical changes – the present situation of 'unfettered capitalism' allows little room for progressive policies. Of course, progressive exponents would try to mitigate the worst effects of neo-liberalistic policies, but the general feeling is one of disenchantment and disillusionment. In light of these remarks, we try to make evident the manifold meanings of the market.

9.2 The juridical articulation of transactions and the 'double' definition of the market

As we have seen, an interesting aspect of Commons's analysis resides in the joint consideration of the individual and collective element as two necessary aspects of collective action. This entails a shift of the analysis from a 'man-to-nature' to a 'person-to-person' relation. Even when the action seems utterly individualistic – for instance in the case of a bargaining transaction where the buyer and the seller seem to act exclusively out of their personal interests – there is the presence, often implicitly, of a significant collective element.

By employing these concepts, it is possible to identify for every transaction – which, as observed before, are classified into bargaining, managerial and rationing – the set of rights, duties, liberties and exposures which are exercised through a combination of performance, forbearance and avoidance behaviour. In particular, the relations between:

- 'market and hierarchy', which refers to the distinction between bargaining and managerial transactions;
- 'market and political economy', which alludes to the distinction between bargaining and rationing transactions;
- 'hierarchy and political economy', which can be traced back to the distinction between managerial and rationing transactions;
- as a way of synthesis, between 'market, hierarchy and political economy'.

With regard to the analysis of market-based transactions, in Commons's theory the concept of market acquires an interesting 'double' meaning, which includes not only the sphere of exchange but also that of production. In his words:

> With Ricardo, as afterwards with Marx, a market was a part of the whole process of production, and not a process of bargaining . . . This technological process of a marketing mechanism, considered as a part of the process of producing use-values, we distinguish as the technology of marketing. The other meaning is the institution of bargaining. These meanings are the difference between managerial transactions and bargaining transactions . . . This double meaning of marketing and exchanging was the root of difference between Malthus and Ricardo. It persists, with practical consequences, in modern economics. One is the technology of markets, the other is the pricing and valuing upon the markets.
>
> (Commons, 1990: 364, 365; original edition 1934)

Commons outlines a historical reconstruction along these lines of the emergence of the market, in which he underlines the importance of public intervention in its creation. The origin of the market is located in the role of the justice courts in deciding disputes and so establishing the reasonable value prevailing at the time:

> A market usually originated with a special monopolistic franchise, named a 'liberty', and granted to a powerful individual or ecclesiastical magnate, authorizing him to hold concourse of buyers and sellers, with the privilege of taking tolls in consideration of the protection afforded. These markets, thus established, were governed, eventually, by rules laid down by the common-law courts in the decisions of disputes, but originally by rules of their own making. The courts, in their decisions, developed the principle of the 'market overt', or the public, free and equal market . . . These principles were not something innate and natural but were actually constructed out of the good and bad practices of the times. The early physiocrat and classical economists thought of them as handed down by divine Providence or the natural order.
>
> (Ibid.: 775)

As we have seen, Commons's analysis of transactions embodies, in their mutual interaction, all kinds of social and economic relations – from the more individualistic to the more collective ones. In this respect, a crucial element concerns the role played by all these transactions in making up policy action. These aspects, in turn, relate to the importance of the process of social value in the dynamics of collective action. As noted before, Commons elaborated the concept of reasonable value in order to draw attention to the conflicting and evolutionary nature of the process of social valuing.

9.3 The market as a manifold entity

Now, we try to employ these concepts for the analysis of some controversial aspects of the market. In this regard, it can be useful to look more closely into its definition. The market, in its simplest and broadest meaning, can be defined as the possibility for persons to exchange their goods and services, either directly or through the medium of any socially accepted definition of 'money'.

As can be seen, this definition embodies an endless variety of economic situations: for instance, isolated, barter-based, exchanges in primitive economies, or more articulated exchanges in well-developed markets – which can be more or less capitalistic or socialistic. In the related debate, and also in psychological perception, the market appears as a manifold entity, which includes various and often contradictory features. In this sense, the market can appear, on the positive side, as:

1　An instrument for attaining more liberty and better economic co-ordination, in that it allows the unfolding of personal initiative and creativity through a system of decentralized actions.
2　A means for comparing and revealing information about the characteristics of goods and services.

On the negative side, the market can appear as:

3　A device, under the guise of equal opportunities in the labour market, for the exploitation of workers.
4　A way for devising, within the reality of pronounced market imperfections, unfair deals in the marketplace, through reduction in the quality of products and shrewd manipulation of information realized also by means of well-organized advertisement strategies.
5　As a consequence of these negative characteristics, the market is likely to constitute an ineffective system for resource allocation. Hence, the market tends to engender alienation, frustration and distorted social value process for all the participants, also through its effects on the increase of the economic inequalities, the uncertainty and disorder of the economic system, and the environmental decay.

What is the relevance of all these aspects? In our view, they can be all relevant for social life and interact among one another in a dialectic and conflicting way. The prevalence of one or the other depends on the social, economic and psychological relations underlying market structures and the related typologies of transactions occurring therein. If these relations give rise to an increasingly unequal distribution of power and income – in short, if they rest on a kind of more or less sublimated 'predatory attitude' rooted in the structure of the social, cultural and institutional framework – then it follows that the market can reinforce the negative effects outlined before. But supposing that the predatory aspects are not so predominant, the positive effects of market can, to varying degrees, outweigh the negative effects.

In our view, the real problems do not lie in the market – i.e., in the exchange activity *per se* – but in the complexity and often conflicting character of our motivations which are reflected in, and at the same time blurred by, the complexity and ambiguity of the market in any given context. For instance, a professional can sell his or her services in the market chiefly out of creative and altruistic motivations but also out of predatory and aggressive propensities aimed at increasing without limits the quest for money and power. And, in turn, market structure impinges more or less heavily on the shaping of these propensities and the related 'freedom' of individual action within the market.

Thus, different orientations, both among different individuals and within the orientations and motivations of each individual, are likely to be always present in the market and therefore constitute one of the most intricate aspects of socio-economic dynamics.

By adopting this approach, the market cannot realistically be considered as an abstract mechanism leading automatically (provided that it is perfect enough) to the maximization of individual and social utility. In fact, the market constitutes an institution which has been created and maintained by public policies and therefore is heavily embedded in the economic, social and cultural domain. This happens not only when market transactions clearly take the colour of a social and cultural phenomenon, but also, as seen in cases widely investigated in social sciences, when economic relations framed within a well-established family and social network of customs, trust, kinship, friendship and citizenship.

As a matter of fact, even the (seemingly) most atomistic and impersonal transaction occurring between individuals unknown to each other has its seat within a dense framework of collective action, with all its rights, duties, values and cultural orientations. In this sense, the 'market' involves, on the part of the actors within it, a process of social valuing which, however, can be seriously impaired in situations where the negative aspects of the market prevail. Furthermore, it is important to remember that market relations certainly constitute one important way of expressing predatory (and neurotic) attitudes but by no means the only one. In this sense, such behaviour can also be present in non-market relations and, in this regard, human history is full of these instances. Thus, the fundamental problem becomes that of understanding the psychological reasons and problems underlying predatory relations in their connections with the economic, social and cultural structure.

Likewise, the market does not constitute the sole instance for expressing personal initiative. In fact, on the one side, the market can comport with a socialist society; and, on the other side, personal initiative can unfold very well in public administration providing that the related organization is flexible enough to allow a real involvement of the workers in its activities. As emerges from Commons's analysis and, within a different context, from the literature on quasi-markets, forms of transactions and competition can exist in any kind of public or 'mixed' institution.

In that connection, it is worth noting that the more harmful effects of market relations tend to be more severe in the international domain. As investigated in particular by the literature on economic development and on 'unequal exchange', it is through the internationalization of production involving the developing and emerging countries that the worst forms of exploitation are likely to take place. There are several reasons for this. Firstly, as highlighted in particular by Veblenian contributions, the formation of modern nation-states finds its economic and cultural ancestors in ceremonial institutions chiefly rooted in emulative and predatory habits of thought and life.

In this respect, the capitalistic institutions of today, including the juridical form of nation-state, continue to express, along with other more positive orientations, these predatory attitudes. But, this being the case, then it follows that competition associated with market process comes about not only between individuals and firms but also, and perhaps even more so, between nations and larger supranational agglomerations. As a matter of fact, in the latter cases economic competition is likely to be more intense. Not only because a cultural and political rivalry is most often injected in such competition, but also for the reason that such competition – unlike national situations where in most cases economic competition is regulated and 'concerted' in many respects through legislative and contractual provisions – tends to be almost completely untrammelled in the 'globalized' world.

True, there are important initiatives for steering fair trade but they have not yet taken a strong foothold in developing and emerging economies.

9.4 The multiple meanings of 'market rigidities'

An instance of the usefulness for the structural issues of considering the microeconomic – e.g., the institution-based – foundations of macroeconomic dynamics can be found in the analysis of so-called market 'rigidities'. These rigidities, highly present in many markets, have been thoroughly investigated, particularly within institutional and regulatory economics and in the Keynesian developments of macroeconomics.

These rigidities are often depicted only as a negative factor as they are supposed to impair, by deviating the economic system away from the 'first best' world of perfect flexibility, the growth potential of the economy. Hence, in the discussion of the economic aspects of a market, synthesized in the general equation:

$$D(p) = S(p) \tag{9.1}$$

where **D** is the effective demand, **S** the effective supply and **p** the price, we can observe that the analysis[4] of all the possible rigidities is much more complex than it appears at first sight.

In fact, these 'rigidities', as relating to complex institutional relations and expectations, should not be considered only negatively as 'market imperfections', since they also perform the fundamental function of stabilizing all the 'market' and 'non-market' institution-based frameworks upon which the economic, social and cultural fabric rests.

In this sense, one of the fundamental roles of these rigidities is to reduce transaction costs which, in this light, should not be interpreted simply as a 'market imperfection' but as a highly institutionally rooted phenomenon. For instance, in examining, for a given market, the slow reaction of demand and supply behaviour to changes in 'the other side' of the market (supply and demand, respectively), institutional and Keynesian oriented theories would point out the importance, for the demand side, of the role of imperfect and asymmetric information; and, for the supply side – in particular in the theory of 'small menu costs'[5] – of the role of transaction costs and the related difficulty of promptly modifying the medium- and long-term strategy of a firm.

The difficulty or unwillingness of a firm to promptly adjust its prices whenever it would seem profit-maximizing takes, in a sense, an objective character – as when it is expensive to continually update information and/or there are administrative costs in managing too frequent changes in prices. At the same time, however, one important source of such difficulty lies in the circumstance that all the transactions wherein a firm is engaged also carry with them significant social, cultural and psychological aspects. Therefore, changing a price also implies modifying these social relations and, for this reason, too frequent changes may, at a real or symbolic level, jeopardize the stability and reliability of such relations. The same reasoning can be applied to the demand side, and to all 'managerial and rationing transactions' identified by Commons, in particular labour relations and the process of policy formulation.

In all these instances, the search for more stable and 'institutionalized' patterns of action can also express the profound need, stressed in particular by psychoanalysis, of establishing sound interpersonal relations. In that connection, the failures of the market in 'signalling' the negative effects of economic action on environmental and social objectives do not simply reflect some 'negative externalities' and 'imperfections' of an otherwise 'perfect mechanism'. Rather, according to our definition of the market, these failures witness and convey a more profound difficulty for the economy, society, institutions and policies in really embracing these objectives within their action.

In this respect, collaboration between these theories and psychoanalysis can help to locate more precisely the multifarious and conflicting ways of expressing these instances and, on that basis, to formulate policies more focused on the profound needs and orientations of society.

9.5 Implications for sustainable policies

As we have tried to outline, markets can be appraised as institutions, created and maintained by public policies, which are deeply 'embedded' in the economic, social and cultural domain. In this light, an abstract dualism between the 'State' and the 'Market', or between 'Economic Planning' and 'Capitalism', tends to miss the key feature of the economic organization: the fact that the market is not an exogenous 'mechanism' but an economic and social institution framed within, in Commons's terminology, an evolving set of 'rights', 'duties', 'liberties' and 'exposures'. And to this the multifarious realms of individuals, groups, institutions and policies corresponds, which, through the various kinds of transactions reviewed before, air their different objectives, needs and values.

These aspects were also investigated with great insight in the historical reconstruction by Karl Polanyi (in particular, 1944), where he pointed out the role of public intervention in the emergence of the market economy associated with the rise of capitalism. In his analysis, Polanyi also highlights that the rationale for increasing public intervention resides in the attempt to avert the destructive effects of an unregulated market-based economy on social structure. In this regard, Dewey (in particular, 1939) also underlines the fact that economic and social phenomena should be studied not only in their materialistic aspects but also in their psychological and cultural significance.

In the analysis of such issues, institutionalism and other heterodox theories can contribute to achieving a better insight into the features of any given market context, through the study of the following interrelated aspects:

- The structure of collective action, in particular the relations of conflict, dependence and order, and the corresponding systems of rights, duties, liberties and exposures among individuals, groups and social classes, and their means of expression in institutional, social and cultural forms.
- The analysis of public goods which, as is known, constitutes one of the most relevant instances of market failure. Particularly important, in this regard, is the preservation over time of the environment and, in that connection, the working out of adequate policies for sustainable development.
- The nature of other market failures and imperfections – in particular, as arising from the widely analysed phenomena of externalities, informational asymmetries, monopoly power, path-dependency and lock-in – in their relations with the growing complexity of economic systems.
- The role of social valuing processes associated with these developments from a historical, social, economic and psychological perspective; how explicit these assessments are; and how they can be better formulated and compared.

This approach can cast a better light on the set of policies needed for attaining environmental and social objectives.

In fact, as we have seen, the environmental crisis – which is heavily related to the structural unsustainability of our paradigm of production and consumption – constitutes one central aspect of the systemic character of the crisis discussed before.

But attaining a really sustainable economy is anything but an easy task, as we need to foster far-reaching changes[6] in production and consumption aimed at realizing a really sustainable economy and society. But, as production and consumption mostly unfold in the market system, the enquiry into how policy action impinges on its structure and evolution becomes paramount.

These issues relate to the problem of co-ordination between the various policies in an international context marked by a growing 'globalization' which, as is known, chiefly develops through a widespread system of market oriented relations. As noted before, these processes tend to be based on cut-throat economic competition, often associated with various types of cultural conflicts between nations and economic areas. In this perspective, a closer collaboration between Green Economics and other pluralistic oriented strands of social sciences can contribute to formulate policy strategies more able to pursue in an integrated way the aims of environmental and social justice.

As can readily be noted, this view embodies and encourages a thorough process of social valuing which constitutes, as we have seen, a leading concept also of heterodox economics. However, social value constitutes an evolutionary and imperfect entity, heavily rooted in consolidated habits of thought and life, which often acquires an implicit and conflicting character. For this reason, one significant explanation of financial crisis and other drawbacks pervading economic systems can be traced back to the shortcomings of the social value process – namely, of policies, institutions and, more generally, of the dynamics of collective action – in responding to the profound needs of society.

For these reasons, an improved process of social valuing involving all kinds of relevant transactions can, by casting a better light on the motivations and conflicts underlying these activities, help reach a more effective policy co-ordination. This process can be particularly appropriate in institutional settings, either private, public or 'mixed', where the multiplicity of objective is likely to engender the drawbacks typical of the 'common agency': namely, a situation in which the 'mission' of institution is only vaguely defined and the persons engaged therein follow unclear and often contradictory objectives.

In Chapter 11 we will address some of these problems in relation to the problem of policy co-ordination.

Notes

1 Refer, for instance, to Ollman (1998). For a comprehensive treatment of the issues related to the theories of communism, socialism and social justice see the encyclopedic works of Cole (2003) and Salsano (1982).
2 As already noted, for the purpose of our work we employ the term liberalism in order to denote the so-called neo-liberalism typical of the most extreme forms of neoclassical economics.

3 We are well aware that this kind of analysis is open to the following objections: (i) what do we mean when we speak of mainstream economics or liberalism? Whatever the answer, our interlocutor would promptly say that our definition is not precise because it does not consider this and that element, and so on and so forth; (ii) in considering a given set of mainstream oriented policy measures, the interlocutor would be ready to say that these measures cannot be considered 'pure mainstream' as they also contain elements of other theories, and so on and so forth. In this regard, we believe that both these objections are true but impinge little on our line of reasoning: as to the former, it suffices us to define mainstream economics as broadly corresponding to neoclassical economics which, as is known, is based on the following principles: independent economic agents tending to maximize their production or utility functions in the marketplace, which ensures – in a self-sustaining way and hence with no (or, at least, very minimal) intervention on the part of public institutions – the co-ordination of their otherwise independent actions. As to the latter, the objection is even truer but further reinforces our argument: in fact, it is easy to observe that many 'mainstream policies' contain in a disguised way, for instance, many Keynesian elements. But this happens not because policy-makers are unwilling to pursue mainstream policies but because, as we are trying to show, the contradictions of the system require the adoption of different policies. However, as there is a (supposed) lack of available alternatives, the adoption in practice of different policies cannot be easily admitted by policy-makers.

4 For this reason, the neoclassical notion of maximizing equilibrium is too narrow to take account of the complexity of these phenomena. True, if we observe a set of prices in some markets which are stable for the time being, this can be considered a kind of equilibrium. However, there is no warrant that such equilibrium is 'maximizing' some abstract utility parameter. In fact, as we are trying to show, the assessment of the 'optimality' of any situation requires a detailed analysis of the economic, social, cultural and psychological factors which combine to shape any market structure. This aspect constitutes a key contribution of institutional economics (cf., among others, Commons 1990/1934, Douglas, 1924, Hobson, 1923, Taussig, 1915). It is also pertinent to note that this kind of enquiry would not assume a 'deterministic solution' related to identification of the unquestionable 'best alternative' but would acquire a distinct pluralistic orientation aimed at an open process of social valuing of the various alternatives.

5 The theory of small menu costs was first proposed by G. Mankiw (1985) in order to highlight that firms, even in the presence of small costs of adjustment – as in the case of a restaurant's menu – often do not quickly modify their prices in response to a change in demand. The same phenomenon has been discovered in labour markets, where both firms and workers prefer to negotiate long-term contracts. This theory belongs to the strand of the 'new Keynesian economics', which tends to be considered mid-way between mainstream and heterodox economics. In fact, it also adopts, along with some Keynesian hypotheses related in particular to the rigidity of prices and nominal wages, a number of mainstream hypotheses related to the optimizing behaviour of agents in a framework of perfect competition. It can also be interesting to note that many of these issues have already been investigated by Commons in his enquiry into the emergence of unions and labour contracts in the USA (in particular in the essays contained in *Labor and Administration*, 1913), where he stresses the importance of ensuring reliable contractual relations in order to reduce the uncertainty and the transaction costs associated with it. In this sense, all the issues related to market imperfections can receive new insights by considering the concepts of institutional economics.

6 As we will also see in Part V, one key element of this transformation is constituted by
   a society in which 'the economic motive' will progressively be replaced by social and
   cultural activities.

References

Cole, G.D.H. (ed.) (2003) *A History of Socialist Thought* (7 volumes). London: Palgrave
   Macmillan.
Commons, J.R. (1964) *Labor and Administration*. New York: Kelley. First edition 1913.
Commons, J.R. (1990) *Institutional Economics: Its Place in Political Economy*. New
   Brunswick, NJ: Transaction Publishers. Originally published by Macmillan in 1934.
Dewey, J. (1989) *Freedom and Culture*. New York: Prometheus Books. First edition 1939.
Douglas, P.H. (1924) 'The Reality of Non-Commercial Incentives in Economic Life', in
   Tugwell, R.G. (ed.) *The Trend of Economics*. New York: Knopf.
Hobson, J.A. (1923) *Incentives in the New Industrial Order*. New York: Seltze.
Mankiw, G. (1985) Small Menu Costs and Large Business Cycles: A Macroeconomic
   Model of Monopoly. *The Quarterly Journal of Economics*, 100(2): 529–538.
Ollman, B. (ed.) (1998) *Market Socialism*. Abingdon and New York: Routledge.
Polanyi, K. (1944) *The Great Transformation*. New York: Rinehart.
Salsano, A. (ed.) (1982) *Antologia del Pensiero Socialista* (5 volumes). Bari, Italy: Laterza.
Taussig, F.W. (1915) *Inventors and Moneymakers*. London: Macmillan.

10 The role of 'materialistic' and psychological factors in social evolution

In this chapter we try to outline, also by building on the insights of the previous chapter, a number of relevant aspects related to the driving forces of societal evolution. We start by illustrating the main versions of historical materialism, then we consider the role of cultural and psychological factors and, finally we analyse the importance of an interdisciplinary approach for grasping the complex interlink between 'material' and the 'spiritual' aspects of social evolution.

We consider this analysis useful for our theme because, by attaining a better understanding of the complexity of factors and problems underlying economic evolution, can help devise more effective policies for addressing the problems posed by economic crisis.

10.1 Marx's historical materialism in its 'deterministic' version

As is known, Marx's theory of historical materialism can be considered a substantial breakthrough in social sciences. However, as it tends (at least in part) to acquire a monistic and absolutistic form, it can hardly be employed in this way – let alone the abstract revolutionary aspirations – for the solution of actual economic problems.

On that account, we think that it is this aspect of absolutism that has led to the failure of real communist experiences and the later and rather uncritical adoption in these countries of a neo-liberalist stance. Another, and related, problem is that Marx's theory is mostly based on the notions of perfect market and perfect competition, which are typical of the classical theory in economics.

But, we can ask, what are the aspects of absolutism we attribute to Marx's theory of historical[1] materialism? Such theory constitutes the cornerstone of the Marxist analysis and posits, in its more 'deterministic' form, that: (i) the historical epochs can be identified according to their mode of production; (ii) these modes of production tend to follow a kind of linear, 'necessary' and evolutionary sequence – from the simpler to the more sophisticated technologies; (iii) in that connection, these modes of production can be identified mainly through their modality of extracting the surplus value; (iv) the 'habits of thought and life' of persons are largely, if not totally, influenced by the role they occupy in the process of production and extraction of surplus value; (v) this implies that in each epoch the dominant ideology is that of the ruling class at the economic (and hence social, political, juridical) level.

The gist of this theory is that the evolutionary pattern outlined is considered 'necessary', in the sense that each stage, together with its evolution into the next one, is something that scarcely depends on the wills of the participants but on an array of forces external to them and over which they can exert scant control.

These situations entail social injustice and alienation, but the solution of these problems does not admit any kind of gradual action or reform. On that account, any action of this kind is sharply criticized by Marx as a useless expression of a 'bourgeois mentality'. Hence, only a proletarian revolution able to wholly dismantle the 'material mode of production' of the old system can really work. This is because, in Marx's view, a revolution in the material mode of production would 'naturally' trigger, in a kind of cathartic process, a parallel revolution in the mentality of the new society.

In this way, a truly communist society would usher in a system[2] where the division of labour is abolished and hence people will no more out-compete, exploit and dominate their fellows.

In such a classless society, people will regain their control over the mode of production, and, on this basis, products will be distributed in a fair way according to the capacity and needs of every person. Furthermore, the revolution, in order to be successful, should be realized at the world level.

In accordance with his materialistic theory, Marx specifies that this process can be accomplished only after the preceding modes of production have gone through all their potential. On that account, every form of socialization and common ownership which took place in the past was downplayed by Marx as primitive or local communism.

There are no more details in Marx's account as to when and how this new society can be realized. In particular, it is utterly unclear whether such an ideal society would assert itself spontaneously after the revolution or if it would imply, through the concept of proletarian dictatorship, an authoritarian regime. In this sense, it remains an open question whether, and to what degree, Marx would have endorsed the largely authoritarian systems that emerged in Russia after the October Revolution. There can be no precise answer, of course, but we believe that Marx's instinctive sympathy for the workers would have led him anyway to propose for them a better participation in economic, social and political life.

In this regard, even if it might seem that, from his account, all historical evolution seems to stop at the gates of the ideal communist society – a kind of Eden where everybody and every thing is perfect, there are no conflicts and every person can only be busy enjoying life – Marx was aware (often implicitly) that achieving such an ideal stage will require a long evolution.

10.2 The growing complexity of the system and the role of cultural and psychological factors

As we have just noted, the theory of historical materialism finds its inspiration in Hegelian dialectic and underscores the necessity of going beyond pure idealism by bringing to the fore the 'material and real' aspects of existence. In this respect, historical materialism has provided a decisive advance in the comprehension of the inner nature of economic and social phenomena.

However, in the extreme form of this theory, the role of economic factors in shaping human history has been appraised as a parallel unimportance of the 'non-economic factors' – in particular, the whole set of culture, values, propensities and conflicts of people in their individual and collective expression.

In this way, an abstract idealism has been replaced by a similarly abstract materialism. Abstract because, in overlooking the role of non-economic factors, it reduces economic evolution to a deterministic and rationalistic process. On that account, the dogmatic and deterministic character of this interpretation – one that was reinforced by the rather intolerant attitude of Marx towards any socialist theories different from his 'scientific communism', which were all liquidated as a disguised expression of the 'bourgeois mentality' – has impaired a full understanding of the growing multifariousness of economic and social evolution.

Furthermore, as Marx's theory rests heavily on the simplistic vision of market and competition taken from classical economics, it partly carries with it a kind of conservative flavour[3] since it seems to imply that, short of triggering a revolutionary process worldwide, any attempt to improve the conditions of the disadvantaged classes of society is largely doomed to be useless. As a matter of fact, in a classical economics-based vision such as this, the 'inexorable laws' of economics imply that capitalism can work only if wages[4] will not permanently exceed 'their value, which is equal to their subsistence level.'[5] Hence, any difficulty in suddenly realizing this magnificent and perfect revolution can easily lead to an attitude of pessimism and defeatism.

However, for good or bad, reality is much more articulated than this too simple account, since historical evolution has shown the growing importance of the mixed forms[6] of economic activities which reflect their growing complexity. This aspect contributes to explaining that a revolutionary process, at least in the way foreshadowed by Marx, becomes more and more difficult just because[7] reality is becoming more and more complex.

For instance, even supposing that a worldwide revolutionary process has just been realized under the principle 'social justice for everyone', and even supposing everybody would agree on this moral precept, there would arise in less than an hour the problems of defining, within the framework of a complex world, the meaning of social justice in relation to family, productive and social spheres.

In this sense, acknowledging the growing complexity of the system does not reduce the potential for radical change. Conversely, this process, by helping provide a more precise vision of the reality, can contribute to a more effective process of social change.

10.3 A more pluralistic orientation in Marx's and Engels's theories

In this regard, it is worth noting that Marx, while paying so much attention to the economic factors, has not completely disregarded the importance of the non-economic aspects of life.

Undoubtedly, the significance of these aspects – in having been relegated to the realm of a superstructure, which is supposed to be largely determined by the economic structure – turns out to be severely downsized in Marx's analysis. But not completely, however. In this sense, the determinism so often ascribed to Marx is more apparent than real. For instance, in theorizing the historical necessity of a transition from capitalism to socialism and communism, it is explicitly required by Marxist analysis that people – instead of letting themselves be passively outstripped by the 'deterministic stream of history' – play an active role in the very definition of these events.

This being the case, it is hardly conceivable that the culture, motivations and conflicts of the person do not enter the picture. In this light, it is no surprise that the first chapters of *Capital* are devoted to workers' struggles to obtain the ten-hour workday and that, on that account, Marx has demonstrated to be not only an acute theorist but also an effective union man.

This more comprehensive and pluralistic view was further developed by Engels,[8] who clarified that 'material' elements, although playing a prominent role in human development, interact and can be influenced by social and cultural factors. He recommended a careful study of historical situations and warned against the risk that historical materialism be (mis)used as a way for not studying real situations.

In short, what emerges from the 'milder versions' of historical materialism and from other heterodox theories of socialism, institutions and social justice is that capitalism and socialism are not only economic systems but also constitute systems of cultures and values through which the motivations and conflicts of people find expression.

In this perspective, it should be noted that while a marked differentiation between economic and social/cultural aspects of human activity has occurred over time, it is also true that the links between the two spheres have become increasingly significant. If, on the one hand, economic aspects (e.g., the evaluation of the costs and monetary benefits of the various alternatives) permeate the rest of social relations, on the other hand the opposite also holds true, in the sense that social and cultural aspects condition and find their expression in the economic realm. For instance, it is certainly true that, as effectively expounded by Karl Polanyi (1944), the establishment of capitalism has absorbed under its alienating framework the previous social relations, but the opposite is no less true, in the sense that the previous social relations, with all their aspects of despotism and prevarication, may have found an 'amplified' expression within capitalistic institutions.

10.4 The manifold patterns of economic and social evolution

The foregoing discussion suggests that any process of social change requires a thorough process of social valuing in order to foreground the profound needs, orientations and conflicts of the people and classes involved. In that connection, historical analysis shows that feudalism and capitalism, for instance, have acquired different forms in the various countries and that, in the evolutionary shaping of these forms, a crucial role was played by political and social action, with all their sets of distinctive psychological and cultural features.

For instance, it is far too obvious that different religions, with all their sets of psychological and cultural orientations, have promoted, in a more or less direct way, different economic systems. Of course, it is also very true that, in turn, the resulting modes of production have contributed to shape the prevailing 'habits of thought and life' of the time, but these elements should be studied in their complex interchange[9] in order to grasp all the specific aspects of every reality considered.

But the consideration of the psychological and cultural factors brings to light an even more fundamental limitation of this extreme version of historical materialism, which pertains to the supposed 'necessity' of the modes of production and their evolution. For instance, the system of slavery in ancient times, and even the modern one in the USA up until the nineteenth century, was considered by Marx 'necessary and inevitable' in order to realize the so-called primitive accumulation of capital. This applies also to the family sphere, where the father is held to be, at least in the past, the 'owner' of the wife and children.

In this vision, the attitude of a person who enslaves (or exploits and oppresses) another is devoid of any psychological explanation and made to derive mechanistically from an immanent and inexorable external and 'necessary' pressure of the prevailing mode of production. However, this account completely disregards the conflicts of the human mind in its economic and social unfolding. On that account, psychological and psychoanalytic studies pinpoint that the need to enslave, exploit and oppress people (and animals) is related to profound psychological conflicts which have their roots in the infantile life of the person. True, these neurotic needs can be reinforced by economic reasons, but the latter do not constitute the sole motive for slavery.

Hence, it follows that psychological factors too have played a paramount role in economic and social evolution. As indirect evidence of this circumstance, we can note that often oppression and slavery have little to do with economic reasons, as is the case in many instances of racial, ethnic and religious persecutions.

This being the case, a fundamental conclusion ensues: the modes of production of the past – with all their burdens of oppression, exploitation and slavery – were not necessary in any immanent meaning of the term. They asserted themselves also on account of neurotic conflicts, and, had these conflicts been less severe, different and more rewarding modes of production could have emerged.

But, someone may say, the past has gone and so it is useless to cry over spilt milk. However, we can learn from the past in order to avoid in the future the same errors: namely, overlooking the role of psychological and cultural factors in economic and social evolution.

10.5 The links with the debate between holism and methodological individualism

It can also be interesting to note that the issues so far discussed present significant parallels with the debate between holism and methodological individualism. More generally, this debate traverses all social sciences[10] and there arises most often a conflict between the theories centred on 'the person and individual action' and those focused on 'institutions and structures'.

Interestingly enough for our theme, the seat of this latent tension between individual and structure lies not only in the whole social structure but also in its various sub-fields. For instance, in relation to our previous discussion of the economic, cultural and psychological factors, it is easy to note that each of them can be interpreted in a more 'holistic' or 'individual' way.

For instance, one can think that: (i) it is the mode of production that actually 'determines' individual economic action or, conversely, the latter is the real driving force of economic evolution; (ii) it is the cultural structure that really shapes the values and beliefs of the person, or, instead, the person enjoys a high degree of freedom in creating the most suitable cultural patterns; (iii) it is collective psychology, with its set of beliefs and orientations, which is preponderant on individual psychology, or, conversely, what really matters is the individual will.

Furthermore, there are different opinions as to the relative importance of the economic, cultural and psychological spheres in shaping the overall evolution of the system. A visual representation of these relations is presented in the following figure:

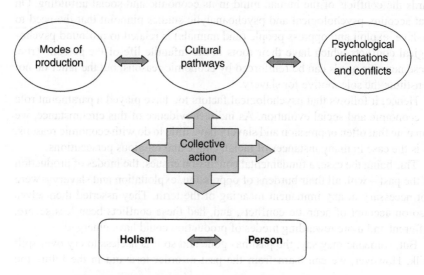

Figure 10.1 The interdisciplinary dimension of collective action

It highlights the manifold bonds between economic, cultural and psychological factors and the circumstance that both the whole structure and its-sub-fields can be interpreted in a more or less 'holistic' or 'individualistic' way.

It is also worth noting that 'holism' and 'individualism' should not be considered as separate entities but as two different but very interrelated aspects of the dynamics of collective action.

As already noted, one of the most important intuitions of John Rogers Commons (1924 and 1934) is that individual action tends increasingly to take place within institutions and organizations. For this reason, as shown in Figure 10.1, collective action embodies both the individual and collective aspects of the 'human wills in action', which unfold in the multifarious web of transactions and institutions.

The importance of a more integrated approach

In the analysis of these issues, we believe that no discipline (or field or school within a discipline) is self-sufficient and perfect. The insulation process typical of many scientific approaches can really impair a far-reaching understanding of the economic and social phenomena. In this light, a closer collaboration of Marx's theory with institutional and Keynesian economics, and with other social and psychological sciences, can help to bring out their great potential for the interpretation of socio-economic evolution.

But, at this stage, a sceptic interlocutor can ask: 'Well, an interdisciplinary approach seems very promising, but how can it be upheld in practice without ending up in a general melting pot, a situation in which everybody airs their own language and goes their own way without any fruitful interaction?' This danger is very real, and should always be kept in mind by social reformers. How can it be reduced? Of course, there is not, in the nature of the case, a straightforward answer to these questions. We think that the only way to promote scientific dialogue and to uplift our societies is to improve the process of social valuing, in particular by making more explicit the set of beliefs and values underlying any 'scientific' vision.

Another important and related issue concerns the possibility that interdisciplinarity would involve a blurring of the distinctive features of the separate disciplines. In this regard, we do not think that such approach should work in this way. As observed by the famous sociologist Karl Mannheim,[11] a landscape can be seen only from a determined perspective and without perspective there is no landscape. In this sense, observing a landscape (or phenomenon) from different angles (or disciplines) can help the observer to acquire a much clearer insight into the features of the various perspectives.

Therefore, an interdisciplinary perspective does not imply that each discipline would lose its distinctive features. Quite the contrary, a more comprehensive approach of this nature, by broadening the horizon of the observer, can contribute to a better appraisal also of the specific characteristics of his/her main areas of specialization.

With regard to social implications, a growing process of participation at the economic, social and political level appears paramount. In fact, it also acquires relevance for policy action because policy action is not limited to the governmental sphere but reaches across all the institutions and individuals concerned in one way or another with policy measures. For this reason, the problem of policy co-ordination goes to the heart of the problem of realizing an adequate social value process: namely, an adequate 'institutional' or collective co-ordination between different and often conflicting values, interests and orientations.

10.6 Historical materialism and psychoanalysis

In this perspective, capitalistic society cannot be considered as a completely 'exogenous factor' for social alienation. In fact, as society has not grown apart from the intended action of the actors involved, there arises the issue of understanding the cultural and psychological foundations of capitalistic society in their relations with its material basis.

As we have seen, psychoanalysis has provided relevant contributions which are still today largely overlooked. In this sense, psychoanalytic studies underscore that in many cases social relations are based, at various levels, on a fight for power having its focus in – at the real and/or symbolic level – 'possessing institutions'. But, since an institution constitutes an organized whole of collective action controlling, liberating, and expanding individual action, this suggests that 'possessing' an institution relates to an unconscious fantasy of omnipotent control over all the relations occurring therein. This means that, for instance, the notion of ownership in its predatory and acquisitive meaning embodies – as shown in particular by Marx and Veblen – not a person-to-goods but a person-to-person relation. According to this interpretation, the reason why, owing to these predatory and neurotic habits institutions are considered like things (or persons) to be owned does not rest in the circumstance that institutions are appraised as things in any meaning of the word, but in the fact that 'the owner' of the institutions, in trying 'to control and dominate' the social relations taking place therein, disregards all the needs and opportunities that may potentially arise from the people involved in these (frustrating and neurotic) social relations.

As we have seen previously, Freud stresses the necessity of considering not only the influence of the economic organization of society on individual psychology, but also the role of psychological factors in shaping the 'materialistic aspects' of society. In this perspective, he clearly points to a closer collaboration between Marxism and psychoanalysis:

> The strength of Marxism clearly lies, not in its view of history or the prophecies of the future that are based on it, but in its sagacious indication of the decisive influence which the economic circumstances of men have upon their intellectual, ethical and artistic attitudes. A number of connections and implications were thus uncovered, which had previously been almost totally overlooked. But it cannot be assumed that economic motives are the only ones that determine the behaviour of human beings in society. The undoubted

fact that different individuals, races and nations behave differently under the same economic conditions is alone enough to show that economic motives are not the sole dominating factor. It is altogether incomprehensible how psychological factors can be overlooked where what is in question are the reactions of living human beings; for not only were these reactions concerned in establishing the economic conditions, but even under the domination of those conditions men can only bring their original impulses into play – their self-preservative instinct, their aggressiveness, their need to be loved, their drive towards obtaining pleasure and avoiding unpleasure. In an earlier enquiry I also pointed out the important claims made by the super-ego, which represents tradition and the ideals of the past and will for a time resist the incentives of a new economic situation.

(Freud, 1990: 220–221, original edition 1933)

These remarks highlight the role of groups[12] and institutions in expressing the needs and conflicts of the person. For instance, for the person, the group may represent an idealized *ego*; and, in this connection, its 'morals' and 'code of conduct' symbolize parental figures that, through a process of 'internalization', play the role of *superego*. These processes – which operate partly at an unconscious level and may be partly driven by neurotic conflicts – can help understand the scission that often occurs[13] between 'the good and right', lying inside the group, and 'the bad and mistaken', lying outside. Hence, these psychological processes can help explain – and history is full of such instances – the neurotic roots of racism, xenophobia and other phenomena of exclusion and marginalization. As we have seen, these phenomena tend to be reinforced by economic and social crises.

An approach of this kind can cast fresh light on a number of issues underscored by Marxism and other theories of socialism. For instance, what are the psychological relations between social classes and how they interact with economic conditions? How does a social class or group interpret its social position and its links with other classes and groups?

What are the proposals for overcoming or reducing the conflicting elements between classes and groups?

This kind of analysis would also benefit from collaboration with other psychological theories, for instance: (i) the analysis of relations between the 'spiritual' dimension of personality and the process of individuation underscored by C.G. Jung (1968); (ii) the consideration of the concepts of 'social sentiment' and finalism pointed out by A. Adler (1925); (iii) the framework set forth by the 'sociology of emotions' (Turner and Stets, 2005); and (iv) the philosophy and psychology of pragmatism.

All these theories can complement in important ways the analysis of the dynamics between the individual and structural aspects of economic and social life. But someone can say that considering too many theories at the same time can lead to uncertainty and confusion. As noted before, this can certainly be true, but the solution does not lie in trying 'to eliminate' them, rather in being aware of such complexity which mirrors the complexity of the real world.

Hence, even if for every person a preference between various theories is inevitable – which also means that some of them will receive a more detailed treatment – what seems important is to be aware of the existence of different explanations of social phenomena.

Notes

1   The most clear account of this theory is contained in *The German Ideology*, which was written with Friedrich Engels in 1846 and remained unpublished until 1932. In our exposition, we refer to this theory as overwhelmingly developed by Marx, because it lays the basic principles of Marx's subsequent work. In fact, although Engels contributed to the shaping of the most extreme form of this theory as set forth in *The German Ideology*, he elaborated later on a more comprehensive and pluralistic version of this theory – a kind of 'mild or pluralistic version' of the historical materialism (cf. also later).

2   For more details on Marx's and s theory refer to *The Marx-Engels Reader* (edited by R.C. Tucker). For a more comprehensive analysis of the issues related to communism, socialism and social justice see the encyclopaedic work of Cole (2003) and Salsano (1982).

3   As also underscored by psychoanalytic contributions, in scientific investigation every theory is likely to reflect the complexity of the orientations and conflicts of their proponents. It is beyond the scope of this work to undertake a socially grounded psychoanalysis of Marx's orientations. What we can note here is that Marx had tried on many occasions to mitigate the one-sidedness of his 'materialism' (cf. also the next note and the next section) by underscoring the importance of individual action for promoting social change. In this regard, it is worth noting that, as also emerges from private letters, Marx and Engels had a wide range of cultural interests also in 'not very materialistic fields' like art and literature. In these domains, Marx and Engels developed interesting insights on the complex relations between artistic forms and the economic modes of production. On that account, Engels can chiefly be remembered for his work as a literate critic and Marx mostly for his romantic poems.

4   This does not imply, however, that in Marx's view workers should give up fighting to improve their conditions. For instance, in *Wage, Price and Profit* he clearly states that workers have the moral duty to fight to improve their conditions, even if the likely outcome in the long run would be to keep wages at their 'values' – that is, at their subsistence level (which, as is known, can acquire different meanings in different contexts). However, as just noted, in Marx's view these attempts are considered useful only insofar as they are preliminaries to the total revolution. Hence, 'in the meanwhile' there is little room in his theory for any permanent improvement of workers' conditions. However, as we do not live in the simple world of classical economics but in a complex 'mixed capitalism', it follows that workers can actually improve their conditions *here and now* and that any uplift in this way is also a progress in the building of 'the total revolution'.

5   This level, both in classical economics and in Marx's theory, depends not only on the natural needs of the workers but also on a number of 'conventional' elements.

6   In this light, it can be interesting to note that Marx's adoption of classical hypotheses has in some way limited the interpretative potential of his theory of economic crisis, and also made more difficult a useful collaboration between Marxist theories and other

important strands of heterodox economics – such as, for instance, institutional and Keynesian economics, and other theories of socialism, social justice and sustainable development.

7 Needless to say, acknowledging this complexity does not imply any kind of 'revisionistic' attempt to overlook the role of class conflicts in the development of capitalistic institutions. In this regard, these conflicts remain central in our mixed forms of capitalism too, but they assume more complex and varied expressions. For instance, in our times economic exploitation à la Marx has by no means lost its importance. But this is not the sole problem for many workers who, in the public and private domains, are overwhelmed by the problems of bureaucratic and hierarchical power, and by lack of motivation and participation. As we are trying to show, these problems can find a better understanding and solution by considering the manifold ties between economic, social and psychological factors in their historical evolution.

8 Cf., for instance, his letter to Conrad Schmidt of 27 October 1890, contained in K. Marx-F. Engels *Ausgewählte Briefe*, pp. 509–510, link https://www.marxists.org/archive/marx/works/1890/letters/90_10_27.htm

9 For instance, by referring to a famous issue, it can be true that 'the protestant ethic' may have facilitated the development of capitalism, but the reverse is no less true: namely, that the diffusion of the protestant religion has been favoured by a change in the mode of production towards a capitalistic system. Needless to say, many other factors should be taken into account in order to attain a far-reaching explanation of the characteristics that these developments have assumed in different countries.

10 There is a huge literature on that subject. See, among many others, Agassi (1960), Hodgson, Samuels and Tool (1994), Levine, Sober and Wright (1987), and the many internet resources, for instance, http://philpapers.org/browse/holism-and-individualism-in-social-science

11 For a more detailed account see Mannheim and Wolff (1993).

12 As noted by Freud (in particular, 1921) and by subsequent psychoanalysts (cf. above), group cohesion tends to be based on the following processes: (i) emotional links among the members of the group; (ii) projection of individual aggressiveness into people and/ or institutions lying outside the group; (iii) identification with the group leader – who symbolizes the parental instance (typically, the father) – in order to repress the conflicts related to the *Oedipus* complex.

13 As noted before, quite often the severity of *superego* leads – through the so-called paranoid and narcissistic transformation of personality, extensively studied in psychoanalysis – single individuals, groups or societies to carry out nasty and persecutory actions towards other individuals, groups or societies into which their aggressiveness has been projected, and so to sabotage, in the meaning reviewed before, the possibility of establishing sound interpersonal relations.

References

Adler, A. (2011) *The Practice and Theory of Individual Psychology*. Eastford, CT: Martino Fine Books. First edition 1925.

Agassi, J. (1960) Methodological Individualism. *The British Journal of Sociology*, 11(3): 244–270.

Cole, G.D.H. (ed.) (2003) *A History of Socialist Thought* (7 volumes). London: Palgrave Macmillan.

Freud, S. (1921) *Massenpsychologie und Ich-Analyse*. Leipzig, Vienna and Zurich: Internationaler Psychoanalytischer Verlag. English version, *Group Psychology and the Analysis of the Ego*. Standard Edition. New York: Norton, 1959.

Freud, S. (1933) *Neue Folge der Vorlesungen zur Einführung in die Psychoanalyse*. Leipzig, Vienna and Zurich, Internationaler Psychoanalytischer Verlag. English version, *New Introductory Lectures on Psycho-Analysis*. Standard Edition. New York: Norton, 1990.

Hodgson, G.M., Samuels, W.J. and Tool, M. (eds.) (1994) *The Elgar Companion to Institutional and Evolutionary Economics*. Aldershot: Edward Elgar.

Jung, C.G. (1968) *Man and His Symbols*. New York: Dell Publishing. Originally published by Aldus books in 1964.

Levine, A., Sober, E. and Wright, E.O. (March–April 1987) Marxism and Methodological Individualism. *New Left Review*, 1(162): 67–84.

Mannheim, K. and Wolff, K.H. (1993) *From Karl Mannheim: Second Expanded Edition*. New Brunswick, NJ: Transaction Publishers.

Marx, K. (1855–1898) (edited by Eleanor Marx), *Wage, Price and Profit*. First English edition by Charles H. Kerr and Company, 1910.

Marx, K. and Engels, F. (1978) (edited by R.C. Tucker) *The Marx-Engels Reader*. Second edition. New York: Norton.

Marx, K. and Engels, F. (1987) (edited by C.J. Arthur) *The German Ideology: Introduction to a Critique of Political Economy*. London, Lawrence & Wishart. Written by Marx and Engels in 1846 and remained unpublished until 1932.

Polanyi, K. (1944) *The Great Transformation*. New York: Rinehart.

Salsano, A. (ed.) (1982) *Antologia del Pensiero Socialista*. (5 volumes). Bari, Italy: Laterza.

Turner, G.H. and Stets, J.E. (2005) *The Sociology of Emotions*. Cambridge: Cambridge University Press.

Part IV

The economic and psychological aspects of the crisis of today

In this part we address various aspects of the economic crisis. In the following chapter we draw attention, through the employment of a simple scheme, to the paramount role played by policy co-ordination in attaining a balanced development of the economic system. In Chapters 12 and 13 we investigate the role of public spending and credit creation in sustaining aggregate demand, with particular attention to the economic and psychological implications.

11 The role of policy co-ordination in structural problems

Introduction

The idea of carrying out this exercise stems from the consideration that policy action is a complex activity, as it involves the numerous policies which are likely to impinge on the issues addressed and, consequently, on the interest groups affected in one way or another by these changes. Since different policies are likely to be designed and implemented, at least in part, by different institutions, the issue of policy co-ordination brings into the picture the issue of the institutional (and hence, social and cultural) framework.

In order to address a number of aspects related to these issues, we have constructed the 'public policies–interest groups matrix' (Table 11.1). That tool was initially conceived (Hermann, 2003) for the analysis of public utility regulation but with the aim of employing it as a general and flexible framework for the analysis of a host of economic aspects. In a sense, therefore, the application of the matrix to public utility regulation constitutes only a particular case of its more general applicability.

The aim of the matrix is to analyse the relations, as assessed by different parties, intervening between the policies affecting public utilities or other issues, with regard to their effects on interest groups. The main conclusions of the work are:

1   The problem of policy co-ordination renders more complex the issues addressed by the 'new regulatory economics', such as asymmetric information, principal–agent relations, distribution of incentives, rent-seeking behaviour and transaction costs. These issues can receive new insights by utilizing the theoretical framework of the 'old institutional economics', and, in particular, the concepts of ceremonial/instrumental behaviour dichotomy, culture, evolution, habits, learning, path-dependency, social valuing and tacit knowledge.

2   In light of the complexity and interrelatedness of these issues, the 'public policies–interest groups matrix', being conceived as a tool that can help interest groups, policy-makers and individuals to better exchange their opinions about the effects of policies in any given case, can contribute to realizing a more explicit and effective social valuing process which, in turn, can further a better co-ordination between all the policies and institutions involved.

Likewise, the matrix can be useful for bringing into focus the complex role played by the related institutional, social and cultural framework in the definition of such policies.

3   In this sense, the problems that the matrix can address are not limited to public utilities but can also involve other policy issues. In this regard, the matrix can be utilized to deal with other important socio-economic problems – for instance, economic development, competitiveness, unemployment, environmental protection, also considered in their supranational dimension.

11.1 Some insights from institutional and regulatory economics

In recent years, important contributions[1] have been provided to the analysis of regulatory problems by the so-called 'new regulatory economics'. By utilizing the incentive and contract theory, with the related concepts of asymmetric information, common agency, distribution of incentives, rent-seeking behaviour and transaction costs, these studies have addressed numerous issues concerning the role of different institutional frameworks on the effectiveness of policy action. These contributions consider the structure of institutional design as a chain of principal–agent relations which could be expressed in the following general form:

CITIZENS-USERS → GOVERNMENT → REGULATORS → PUBLIC UTILITIES

These categories are conceived in a broad sense. So, 'Government' may denote not only the ordinary governmental activity but also customs and constitutional principles. These authors conceive of institutions as an ongoing attempt to implement an incomplete Constitution or set of rules laid down by the 'Founding Fathers'. Such incompleteness stems from the circumstance that the 'Founding Fathers' – since they act under a 'veil of ignorance' about future contingencies – can lay out only a set of general principles which, for their subsequent interpretation and application, need the continual working of many other actors and institutions. In these analyses there is no specific hypothesis as to the degree of 'benevolence' of all these actors.[2] Hence, institutional actors may be either benevolent or non-benevolent and these models tend to take up both hypotheses.

In order to devise an adequate institutional design, these authors analyse the structure of incentives and of informational asymmetries of regulatory institutions in their mutual interaction. Many intertwined factors combine to define the efficiency of the institutional design: (a) the objectives and the organization of the Government; (b) the relations between the Government and regulatory agencies, and, in particular, 'how do politicians decide which agencies to create?' and 'how does regulation or deregulation come about?' (Laffont and Tirole, 1993: 503); (c) the characteristics and activities of interest groups.

In this regard, we would like to stress that many concepts utilized by these studies, and, more in general, by the 'new regulatory economics' can receive a deeper insight by applying, in an interdisciplinary spirit, the theories related to the fields of the 'old institutional economics', and also of psychology, psychoanalysis and dynamic capabilities. In particular, concepts like, among others, ceremonial/ instrumental behaviour dichotomy, culture, evolution, habits, learning, path-dependency, power, social valuing and tacit knowledge can shed new light on the complex links intervening in any given situation between the objectives of interest groups and of regulatory institutions.

The previous remarks imply that regulatory institutions such as agencies, ministries and every other body involved in regulatory activity may have, in different contexts, very different functions and structures. Another aspect which tends to complicate the picture is that regulation of public utilities is an activity involving many policies and, also for this reason, is likely to involve different institutions and impinge on several interest groups. Considering this complex situation, it is very unlikely that a first best outcome (even leaving aside the intrinsic difficulty of defining such a concept) can be achieved, and, thus, regulatory policies tend to reach only a compromise between different needs and interests.

11.2 The public policies–interest groups matrix

The remarks summarized above can be further developed by considering the problems of co-ordination between the policies influencing public utilities or other structural problems. In order to address a number of problems related to this issue, we have outlined a simple matrix showing the relations that may intervene between the policies affecting these issues considered with regard to their effects on interest groups, which are meant, in a broad sense, as any group concerned in one way or another with public utilities regulation.

The aim of the matrix (Table 11.1) is to provide a tool for facilitating the analysis of the effects of policies – as assessed by different interest groups, policy-makers and people – on public utility regulation and other structural problems.

Interest groups are indicated as follows: Stakeholders: 1j; Users, in the case of public utility regulation, or Citizens for other issues: 2j; Environmentalists: 3j, making up a 3 X 7 matrix (indicated in the matrix as Users, Citizens, Stakehol, Environ).

The matrix allows us to see the effects of each policy on each interest group. In this way it is possible to calculate the payoffs for interest groups (payoffs per line) and for policies (payoffs per column), and the overall payoff. For the sake of simplicity, we do not consider time-patterns, which, of course, would be necessary to include in a more complete analysis. The interpretation of this matrix is described below.

1   We hypothesize that there are many and complex interrelations between public policies which can hardly be identified univocally. Each policy measure can exert two types of effects on public utilities (or on other structural problems). The first one is a direct impact on the public utility (or the other issue) considered at the time, while the second one is an indirect effect on the other policies which, in turn, influence these issues. Consequently, the total effect of each policy measure on interest groups is made up of the sum of two

Table 11.1 The public policies–interest groups matrix for a public utility or other economic issues over a given period*

POLICIES / INTEREST GROUPS	REG	COMP	INDUS	R&D	ENVIR	MACR	SOC	PAYOFFS PER LINE
STAKEHOL	$\sum_j x_{1j}$	$\sum_j x_{1j}$	$\sum_j x_{1j}$	$\sum_j x_{1j}$	$\sum_j x_{1j}$	$\sum_j x_{1j}$	$\sum_j x_{1j}$	$\sum_i \sum_j x_{1j}$
USERS or CITIZENS	$\sum_j x_{2j}$	$\sum_j x_{2j}$	$\sum_j x_{2j}$	$\sum_j x_{2j}$	$\sum_j x_{2j}$	$\sum_j x_{2j}$	$\sum_j x_{2j}$	$\sum_i \sum_j x_{2j}$
ENVIRON	$\sum_j x_{3j}$	$\sum_j x_{3j}$	$\sum_j x_{3j}$	$\sum_j x_{3j}$	$\sum_j x_{3j}$	$\sum_j x_{3j}$	$\sum_j x_{3j}$	$\sum_i \sum_j x_{3j}$
								TOTAL PAYOFF
PAYOFFS PER COLUMN	$\sum_i \sum_j x_{ij}$	$\sum_i \sum_j x_{ij}$	$\sum_i \sum_j x_{ij}$	$\sum_i \sum_j x_{ij}$	$\sum_i \sum_j x_{ij}$	$\sum_i \sum_j x_{ij}$	$\sum_i \sum_j x_{ij}$	$\overline{\sum_i \sum_j} x_{ij}$

* The matrix can be denoted as P = [p_{ij}], where i = 1 . . . , k represent the interest groups and j = 1 . . . , n the policies. In the example, we utilize the following symbols: Regul: Regulatory; Compet: Competition; Indust: Industrial; R&D: Research and Development; Envir: Environmental; Macr: Macroeconomic; Soc: Social. For exposition purposes, these symbols can be further abbreviated as follows: Regulatory = i1; Competition = i2; Industrial = i3; R&D = i4; Environmental = i5; Macroeconomic = i6; Social = i7.

components: the first one is the direct effect of that policy measure, while the second one is constituted by the effects of that policy measure on the other policies which can have an impact on the issue considered. For instance, an industrial measure is likely to have effects that also influence other policies; relatedly, the overall effects of the industrial policy depend also on the effects that other policies may have on the industrial policy domain.

2   We consider such policies only with regard to their effects on the issue considered, although they usually have effects that go far beyond this scope. For instance, macroeconomic policy impinges, through its effects on interest and inflation rates, not only on each public utility but also on the whole economic system. Similarly, regulatory policy has a bearing, also through its indirect impact on macroeconomic and other policies, on the entire socio-economic system.

3   In Table 11.1, the identification of policies and interest groups has been made at an aggregate level, but, of course, each category can be subdivided into many sub-groups, and new categories can be added. Indeed, each policy is likely to comprise – especially in the complex societies of today – many measures most often applied by different institutions. In this regard, every classification of policies – and also, within this ambit, the identification of the measures considered more relevant for the analysis – assumes a conventional character, in the sense that it is made according to a definite set of criteria and objectives. This complexity of political economy was underlined in particular by Commons (1924 and 1934), where he shows that policy action consists not only of the activity of government and legislative institutions but also, in a continual interplay, of the activity of courts, and of multifarious expressions of collective action – for instance labour, environment and consumers' associations.

4   We regard the effects of policies only as evaluated by different interest groups, policy-makers and individuals. As a consequence, the assessments of each group may assume different structures and values. In this respect, identifying among all these policy assessments which could be 'the best' is a very difficult task as the policy outcome tends to be appraised on the basis of different criteria, objectives and 'visions of the world'. And, furthermore, crucially it depends on the characteristics of the 'institutional game' – based on a complex set of expectations – taking place between all the concerned actors. We are aware that this aspect can perplex the seekers of absolute certainties, but we would also note that it is in this procedure that lies the essence of democracy and pluralism.

5   Since the interaction between different policies unfolds itself in a continuous way, the matrix should ideally be able to account for all these interactions but, obviously, this is impossible. However, we should be aware that, as the initial situation from which the analysis starts also represents the outcome of previous policy action, this process presents a co-evolutionary character involving in a very complex way the relations between utilities, policies and institutions.

6   We do not consider the attempts of interest groups to obtain policy measures to their advantage even though these strategies should be carefully considered in the analysis of specific situations.

7   In these assessments every possibility is allowed: for instance, an interest group may assume that policies 'do not matter' or that there are no inter-relations between them. Such a group may care only about the effects of policies upon itself – and, in this case, the values are reported only in the corresponding line of the matrix – or else may also assess the effects upon other interest groups, and so fill all the elements of the matrix. The same holds true for the assessments of policy-makers and other observers, even though it is more likely that policy-makers have better information for elaborating a more comprehensive assessment. Furthermore, all these assessments can consist of either scant remarks or well-grounded studies of the situation. The same openness of the matrix applies to the criteria utilized to appraise the effects of policies: they could be whatever the actors deem adequate for the situation, and may be valued according to different objectives, theories and methodologies.

8   The verb 'calculate' employed before requires an explanation: although it is possible to make tentative quantitative assessments for some relevant parameters of the issue under investigation, careful qualitative assessments should always accompany and qualify such assessments (cf. also Chapter 8). For instance, considering the issue of firms' competitiveness, the available data can give a reasonable precise outline of the short-term figures but are useless at showing the effects of policies on the structural tendencies of the firm (for instance, its ability to innovate at productive and organizational levels) which, in the long run, are likely to make a substantial impact on the firm's ability to reduce its costs. The importance of such thorough policy assessments springs also from the circumstance that policy action tends in one way or another to bear on the institutional context. These effects are particularly far-reaching in the case of structural policies involving relevant changes to the institutional structure but are likely to have a considerable impact even within seemingly minor or 'routinely' policy action.

11.3 A pair of examples

In order to illustrate how the matrix could be employed in real situations, we can start by illustrating the simplest example, related to the assessment of a single policy – for instance, an industrial policy measure – by an interest group, a policy-maker or an individual (Table 11.2).

In the following table, we complicate the picture somewhat by considering two policies, an industrial measure combined with a macroeconomic measure (Table 11.3).

The example shows that the assessment of Table 11.3 obtains a better total payoff than does Table 11.2 but does not eliminate possible conflicts of interest between interest groups[3] because, for them, there are different payoffs. As can be seen, by making more explicit the points of conflict, it would become less difficult to confront different opinions and try to understand the reasons for divergences.

Table 11.2 The public policies–interest groups matrix: the hypothetical effects of an industrial policy measure on interest groups

POLICIES / INTEREST GROUPS	REG	COMPET	INDUST	R&D	ENVIR	MACR	SOC	PAYOFFS PER ROW
STAKEHOL	-1_{13}	1_{13}	2_{13}	1_{13}	0_{13}	0_{13}	0_{13}	3
USERS or CITIZENS	1_{23}	-1_{23}	1_{23}	-1_{23}	0_{23}	0_{23}	1_{23}	1
ENVIRON	-1_{33}	0_{33}	-1_{33}	1_{33}	-1_{33}	0_{33}	1_{33}	-1
								TOTAL PAYOFF
PAYOFFS PER COLUMN	-1	0	2	1	-1	0	2	3

Table 11.3 The public policies–interest groups matrix: the hypothetical effects of an industrial measure and of a macroeconomic measure on interest groups

POLICIES / INTEREST GROUPS	REGUL	COMPET	INDUST	R&D	ENVIR	MACR	SOC	PAYOFFS PER ROW
STAKEHOL	$(-1_{13}) + (1_{16})$	$(-2_{13}) + (1_{16})$	$(1_{13}) + (2_{16})$	$(-2_{13}) + (1_{16})$	$(-1_{13}) + (1_{16})$	$(-1_{13}) + (1_{16})$	$(1_{13}) + (1_{16})$	+3
USERS or CITIZENS	$(1_{23}) + (1_{26})$	$(2_{23}) + (-1_{26})$	$(-6_{23}) + (1_{26})$	$(0_{23}) + (1_{26})$	$(2_{23}) + (-1_{26})$	$(-2_{23}) + (1_{26})$	$(3_{23}) + (-1_{26})$	+1
ENVIRON	$(3_{33}) + (-1_{36})$	$(1_{33}) + (0_{36})$	$(1_{33}) + (-1_{36})$	$(2_{33}) + (-1_{36})$	$(3_{33}) + (-2_{36})$	$(-1_{33}) + (0_{36})$	$(1_{33}) + (-1_{36})$	4
								TOTAL PAYOFF
PAYOFFS PER COLUMN	4	1	-2	1	2	-2	4	8

It is also important to stress that in the tables we have provided numerical examples, where the numbers can be related to the various parameters as utilized and assessed by each interest group, but, as observed before, the matrix may also contain qualitative or non-measurable assessments. As already noted, the assessments of each interest group reflect only this group's opinion as to what it holds to be the effects of a given set of policies. Needless to say, the real effects of such policies may turn out to be quite different from these assessments, also for the intrinsic difficulty of policy analysis.

Conclusion

In this regard, the public policies–interest groups matrix – since it is conceived as a tool that can aid the interested individuals, groups and institutions to better exchange their opinions and information about the effects of policies affecting public utilities or other problems – can contribute to realizing a more explicit and effective social valuing[4] process which, in turn, can further a better co-ordination between all the policies and institutions which are likely to have a bearing on public utilities.

As already noted, the issues which can be addressed by the matrix are not limited to public utilities regulation but, as a consequence of the interrelatedness existing between policies, reach out to other policy domains. Hence, the matrix could also be utilized for dealing with other important economic issues and, with regard to our theme, it seems particularly appropriate for addressing in a comprehensive way the manifold aspects of economic crisis. As we have seen, the crisis involves several dimensions – economic, social, cultural, psychological, extending virtually across every nation and region of the world – that acquire both a short-term and a more structural dimension. For these reasons, as many policies, institutions and interest groups (in the broad meaning of the term) have been affected by the economic crisis and, at the same time, can play a role in its overcoming, the problem of policy co-ordination in devising an effective policy strategy can hardly be exaggerated.

The process of policy co-ordination calls for an adequate involvement of individuals and groups affected in one way or another by economic crisis. Such participation could be beneficial to policy action for the following reasons:

1   It can be a useful source for the exchange and diffusion of knowledge and experience regarding all the aspects of the issue under examination. In particular, these groups can play a central role in the definition and application of numerous aspects of these provisions.
2   Relatedly, this participation, by performing a monitoring function on policy action in its institutional articulation, can contribute to reducing the problems of asymmetric information and multi-principal structure outlined above.

By furthering the process of social valuing in this way, it would become possible to gain more knowledge on the complex interplay between institutional frameworks, interest groups and policies, and thus to provide with a more precise content the notion of public purpose and of the related process of social valuing.[5] In this way, it would become easier to reduce the typical problems of policy action, which refer to the following interrelated factors:

- complexity, uncertainty, incomplete and asymmetric information of policy action, also due to the interrelations between policies, institutions and interest groups;
- different opinions and objectives of the actors involved in policy-making, who are often concerned, as noted before, only with one or a few aspects of policies;
- efficiency and efficacy of public administration;
- difficulty – also due to path-dependency and lock-in phenomena – of prompting the economic and institutional changes which may be necessary for the effectiveness of policies.

In the presence of these problems, the criteria according to which collective decisions are made are likely to be correspondingly 'shadowy', because in these situations the clarity and the explicitness of social valuing process tend to be impaired. As a consequence, policy action – by tending to become overwhelmingly biased in favour of the stronger groups and/or less able to have an actual 'grip' on the situation – may fail, to a greater or lesser extent, to respond to the profound needs of society.

As acutely observed by Dewey (1939), a situation of this kind, in which policies are unable to cope effectively with the economic and social problems, could raise a call, in absence of a clear recognition of the real causes of the problems, for an authoritarian 'solution' which, however, for the reasons we have tried to set forth, would end up worsening the capacity of the system to understand and solve the real problems of society.[6]

As can be easily noted, these problems tend to become more critical in situations – occurring with great frequency in less developed countries and backward areas – of structural problems that render the trade-offs and conflicts between policies more acute. Indeed, in these circumstances, an adequate process of policy formulation would be all the more important, but the capacity of policies to master these problems is likely to be dramatically insufficient. This may happen because the 'quality' of policies is not independent of the other characteristics of the social and economic context but, rather, is partly determined by them. In this sense, the 'quality' of policies should not be regarded as a totally exogenous variable but as a collective (institutional) and evolutionary pattern of action which is, at least in part, endogenously determined by the conflicts, values and motivations of all persons and institutions involved.

Notes

1 For an analysis of these issues see, among others, Dixit, Grossman and Helpman (1997), Laffont (2000), Laffont and Martimort (1998), Laffont and Tirole (1993), Martimort and Moreira (2010).

2 An additional problem is that, as shown in particular by the theory of social value addressed before, defining 'benevolence' constitutes a very difficult task, especially in the presence of numerous individuals and groups – characterized by different values, theories and objectives – acting within a context of relevant informational asymmetries. As we shall see presently, this situation very often leads to a multi-principal institutional structure of 'common agency'.

3 According to our perspective, we do not make any simplistic hypothesis with regard to the 'egoism' or 'altruism' of the interest groups and their ways of achieving their goals (meant in the broad sense, and which can also include their social awareness). Only a careful study of the context can give more precise clues on these issues.

4 The theory of social value has a long tradition in the history of economic theory, and, in its simplest form, stresses that the system of social and individual values plays, more or less explicitly, a crucial role in policy action. The following passage expresses effectively this concept: 'To conceive of a problem requires the perception of a difference between "what is going on" and "what ought to go on". Social value theory is logically and inescapably required to distinguish what ought to be from what is; indeed, it is implicit in modern methodology' in Hodgson, Samuels and Tool (1994, vol. I, p. 406). The evolutionary, conflicting and relative character of social value is underlined by Commons through his concept of reasonable value (cf. above). Regarded in this light, a full understanding of the concept of reasonable value would require a far-reaching analysis of the historical, economic, legal, ethical and psychological aspects which, in their complex interplay, concur to shape the characteristics of collective action – and the corresponding nature of the whole set of public policies involved – in any considered situation.

5 In relation to these problems, it is interesting to note that the theory of social value might seem to run into the typical problem of 'cultural relativism': in fact, it could seem that, if what matters is the adequate expression of social value, then any kind of value (and of corresponding policies and public purpose) – for instance, even social values based on predatory and acquisitive attitudes – so expressed should receive, on the grounds of ensuring equal respect to each context considered, equal legitimacy no matter how ethical we deem it to be. In this respect, the central question becomes how to identify the ethical foundations of social value and policy action. On this matter, as also shown in the Part I, the ethical foundations of social values and policies can be found not so much in some kind of abstract universal principles (or moral duties) of kindness and solidarity but, rather, in rooting these principles in the actual needs of the person. In this sense, psychological sciences, in a mutual collaboration with institutional economics, can play a paramount role in identifying these needs and the policies most adequate for their attainment. For instance, if we assume, following the insights of Veblen and of many psychological studies (see before), that the propensities of workmanship and parental bent – or, in the terminology of contemporary psychology and psychoanalysis, the need to establish sound interpersonal relations – lie at the heart of the true expression of the needs of the person, the ethical principles of solidarity, democracy and participation can be endowed with a more precise content as they would be based on a continual scientifically based observation of the characteristics of human needs.

6 In this light, the issue of participation can be considered equivalent to the problem of creating an institutional system ensuring the growth of more and more effective democratic structures in the political, economic and social spheres. In this regard, we can observe that an insufficient process of participation – by bringing about an inadequate expression of the structure of 'reasonable value', that is, of the conflicts and motivations underlying

social life – can constitute an important explanation of the failure of policies to respond to the profound needs of society and of the corresponding phenomena of 'anomie', alienation and insufficient socio-economic development.

References

Commons, J.R. (1995) *Legal Foundations of Capitalism*. New Brunswick, NJ: Transaction Publishers. Originally published by Macmillan in 1924.

Commons, J.R. (1990) *Institutional Economics: Its Place in Political Economy*. New Brunswick, NJ: Transaction Publishers. Originally published by Macmillan in 1934.

Dewey, J. (1989) *Freedom and Culture*. New York: Prometheus Books. First edition 1939.

Dixit, A., Grossman, G.M. and Helpman, E. (1997) Common Agency and Coordination: General Theory and Application to Government Policy Making. *Journal of Political Economy*, 105(4): 752–769.

Hermann, A. (2003) Il ruolo del coordinamento delle politiche nella regolamentazione delle *public utilities*. *Studi Economici e Sociali*, 38(3): 45–60.

Hodgson, G.M., Samuels, W.J. and Tool, M. (eds.) (1994) *The Elgar Companion to Institutional and Evolutionary Economics*, Aldershot: Edward Elgar.

Laffont, J.J. (2000) *Incentives and Political Economy*. Oxford: Oxford University Press.

Laffont, J.J. and Tirole, J. (1993) *A Theory of Incentives in Procurement and Regulation*. Cambridge, MA: MIT Press.

Laffont, J.J. and Martimort, D. (1998) Transaction Costs, Institutional Design and the Separation of Powers. *European Economic Review*, 42: 673–684.

Martimort, D. and Moreira, H. (2010) Common Agency and Public Good Provision under Asymmetric Information. *Theoretical Economics*, 5: 159–213.

12 Public spending and credit creation as the drivers of aggregate demand

12.1 Some structural reasons for the economic crisis

The aim of this chapter is to identify a number of structural elements in the emergence of the recent economic crisis. As is known, such crisis had built up silently and exploded in 2008 with the failure of the banks involved on ill-advised speculative ventures. Since then, several authors, who had in most cases already pointed out the unsoundness of the speculative fever, have stressed the inadequacy of neoclassical theories in addressing these phenomena. The main aspect of these theories has been (and still is) to place an unconditioned emphasis on the rationality of economic man and on the maximizing virtues of free markets. The chief drawback of this account lies in its excessive simplification of economic phenomena which prevented these economists from detecting the complexity and imperfections of the markets and of human behaviour.

Reality, in fact, has proved to be very different from these simplified pictures. It became apparent that, in particular but not only, in the financial sector, economic behaviour was often driven by irrational or non-rational elements and that, relatedly, markets not only did not adequately signal the risk of certain ventures but in some cases provided perverse incentives to go on with these initiatives.

For this reason, many authors[1] have pointed to a number of factors in the explanation of the economic crisis. Foremost among them is the marked redistribution of income in favour of the wealthier classes that has occurred in the last decade. This phenomenon has had an adverse effect on aggregate demand because, as is known, the marginal propensity to consume tends to be higher with lower incomes. Furthermore, as this redistribution has been accompanied by a growing economic precariousness and insecurity, the overall effects of this trend have been much worse, as it has affected the (relative) stability of the economic and social fabric.

But, owing to the unconditional faith in the market virtues, little importance had been given to these imbalances, which tended to be considered a sort of 'necessary evil' of economic development. Likewise, and by the same token, little importance was paid to the massive speculative operations taking place in the financial sector. In this situation, no wonder that an economic crisis was bound to emerge. Starting from these insights, we will address in the next paragraphs and in Part V a number of contradictions that have contributed to determining the systemic character of the crisis.

As also noted before, economic institutions – in particular, markets, firms, and also public administration – are becoming increasingly complex and for this reason are moving away from any simplistic conception of 'public' and 'private' economy.

There are many reasons for this phenomenon, an important group of them referring to the need of the public sector to grow and diversify its functions in order to try to manage the complexity and contradictions of the 'mixed economies' of our days. Among its many functions, the public sector plays a relevant role – directly through public spending and more indirectly through credit creation – in the formation of aggregate demand.

Now we focus attention on this aspect, by analysing a number of macroeconomic features of public intervention.

12.2 The chronic insufficiency of effective demand and the impressive increase of the ratio of public spending on GDP

One leading aspect of the growing role of public intervention is the increase in public spending (PS), not only in absolute but also in relative terms, as shown by the ratio of public spending to GDP. The available data clearly make evident this trend. The average value of the ratio has shifted, for the OECD Countries, from 20–30 per cent in the 1970s to 40–50 per cent in recent years. Some of these data are reported in Table 12.1.

As for credit creation, the available data show (Tables 12.2 and 12.3) for the OECD countries high values of the ratio of public and private debt to GDP. Moreover, these figures have considerably increased[2] in the last decade, from, in average, approximately 50–100 per cent for public debt and from approximately 20–50 per cent for private debt.

What are the structural reasons for such an impressive increase in public spending and credit creation? As regards public spending, this phenomenon was first highlighted by Adolph Wagner, who observed that economic and social development carries with it an enlargement and diversification of the functions of the public sector. With regard to credit creation, its role in creating effective demand[3] was spelled out by J.M. Keynes and many authors in the Keynesian tradition. These authors also made clear the role of the public sector (meant in a broad sense, and then also including Central Banks) in guaranteeing the value of money and in orienting the banks in their policies of credit creation. The reason why we accept banknotes of intrinsic minimal value is that we are fairly confident that their real purchasing power is monitored and guaranteed (up to a certain degree, of course) by public action. In this sense, as underscored by many authors, money is a highly institutional phenomenon.

Hence, the public sector performs an irreplaceable role in providing public goods, including the legal and institutional framework; in managing and/or regulating important economic sectors; in redistributing resources; and in promoting research and innovation.

These insights have evolved into three lines of research, which often tend to be blurred: (i) public choice, chiefly belonging to the mainstream domain, which investigates the role of interest groups in lobbying the political system in order to

Table 12.1 Total public spending as a percentage of GDP

Nations	Year 2009
Australia	37.19
Austria	52.97
Belgium	54.11
Canada	44.37
Chile	24.62
Czech Republic	45.95
Denmark	58.42
Estonia	45.17
Finland	55.86
France	56.74
Germany	47.50
Greece	52.85
Hungary	50.54
Iceland	51.05
Ireland	48.17
Israel	44.27
Italy	51.83
Japan	42.03
Korea	33.08
Luxembourg	42.19
Mexico	23.51
Netherlands	51.35
New Zealand	42.33
Norway	47.31
Poland	44.51
Portugal	49.85
Slovak Republic	41.54
Slovenia	49.16
Spain	45.80
Sweden	55.15
Switzerland	34.15
Turkey	39.44
United Kingdom	51.45
United States	42.18

Source: Based on data from OECD (2011), 'General government expenditures', *in Government at a Glance 2011*, OECD Publishing. http://dx.doi.org/10.1787/gov_glance-2011-10-en

obtain more public resources in their favour. The limitations of these studies lie in the circumstance that they tend to consider public spending only as a negative phenomenon – a kind of unwelcome departure from the perfect world of mainstream hypotheses; (ii) a number of theories belonging to the fields of institutional and evolutionary economics, which point out the potential of the institutional framework for the unfolding of the national system of science and innovation, and of the related framework of human and social capital; (iii) Keynesian

Table 12.2 Debt of general government as a percentage of GDP

Nations	Year 2012
Australia	56.3
Austria	85.2
Belgium	106.4
Canada	109.7
Chile	18.7
Czech Republic	55.7
Denmark	59.3
Estonia	13.2
Finland	64.5
France	109.3
Germany	88.5
Greece	164.2
Hungary	89.6
Iceland	Na
Ireland	125.7
Israel	80.0
Italy	141.7
Japan	235.8
Korea	37.5
Luxembourg	30.1
Mexico	Na
Netherlands	82.7
Norway	34.7
Poland	62.3
Portugal	127.8
Slovak Republic	56.8
Slovenia	61.4
Spain	92.8
Sweden	48.8
Switzerland	46.1 (2011)
Turkey	46.3
United Kingdom	101.5
United States	123.0

Source: Based on data from 'Financial Indicators – Stocks' http://stats.oecd.org/Index.aspx? DataSetCode=FIN_IND_FBS in OECD.StatExtracts http://stats.oecd.org/

oriented theories, which investigate the role of public spending and credit creation in ensuring macroeconomic stability and the full employment of the labour force. Especially in the last three decades, strands (i) and (ii) have received surely more attention than point (iii). In particular, both critics and advocates of public spending implicitly agree that today's level of public spending is 'too high' and should be abated in one way or another. And this opinion has gained some ground even among Keynesian macroeconomists, chiefly as a result of the supposed 'failure' of the 'Keynesian' oriented policies of the post Second World War period.

Table 12.3 Private sector debt as a percentage of GDP

Nations	Year 2011
Australia	184.4
Austria	179.5
Belgium	251.8
Canada	233.7
Chile	166.4
Czech Republic	147.0
Denmark	261.1
Estonia	166.6
Finland	207.4
France	221.9
Germany	159.5
Greece	142.7
Hungary	219.5
Iceland	Na
Ireland	411.6
Israel	132.0
Italy	188.5
Japan	243.0
Korea	251.3
Luxembourg	451.5
Mexico	Na
Netherlands	252.2
Norway	254.8
Poland	119.6
Portugal	331.0
Slovak Republic	113.9
Slovenia	176.4
Spain	279.8
Sweden	295.2
Switzerland	221.4
Turkey	Na
United Kingdom	204.2
United States	198.7

Source: Based on data from 'Financial Indicators – Stocks' http://stats.oecd.org/Index.aspx?
DataSetCode=FIN_IND_FBS in OECD.StatExtracts http://stats.oecd.org/

However, since the data indicate that such massive increase of PS/GDP ratio has been fully compatible with the development of capitalistic system (in reality, 'mixed economies'), a macroeconomic explanation along Keynes's insights is highly needed to cast more light on the profound reasons for such increase.

In this respect, it should also be stressed that Keynes has never been a blind advocate of public spending as such. He investigated the importance of public spending as a component of the aggregate demand and, on that account, was well aware of the contradictions of the system. In his view, as set forth in particular in

Essays in Persuasion and in *The General Theory*, any increase in public spending should minimize its impact on (a) the real interest rate and (b) the level of taxation on productive activities. The first goal can be attained by gradually increasing the supply of money, the second by shifting taxation from productive activities to rent-based sources of income and wealth.

Public spending is important for the private sector not only as a component of the aggregate demand but also because such component is paramount (along with credit creation) in forming the profit of firms. Since this aspect, however central in Keynes's theory, remains partly implicit in his analysis, in the next paragraph we try to 'disentangle' the macroeconomic components of aggregate profit.

12.3 A Keynesian oriented interpretative framework

Let us consider some macroeconomic effects of public spending and credit creation. As can be inferred in particular from Keynesian theories, these elements become vital for generating the aggregate demand, and hence the profit for private firms. On that account, it is interesting to note that, in the absence of such policies, no significant aggregate profit[4] would be possible for firms.

As a matter of fact, labour cost constitutes an aggregate cost for the system of firms. This cost can be brought to zero if employees spend all their earnings but can never become a source of profit. But, very interestingly, not even the entrepreneurs' investment expenses can create an aggregate profit for the firms as a whole. In such a case, in fact, the profit of an entrepreneur must correspond to the expense of another, so that the net result for the firms would be zero.

As a consequence, aggregate profit[5] must derive from sources 'external' to the system of firms: these sources – not considering, for the sake of simplicity, international trade whose balance[6] is zero at world-level – take two interrelated forms: public spending and credit creation. We can express these relations in the following way:

$$P + L \equiv Y = C + I + G \equiv amG + bmCD + (1 - a)mG + (1 - b)mCD + C_p + I_p \tag{1}$$

where P denotes the aggregate profit for the system of private[7] firms, L the sum of 'labour' incomes, including the 'executive salaries', G public spending and CD the amount of aggregate demand generated by credit creation, m the value of multiplier, a and b, and $(1 - a)$ and $(1 - b)$ the ratios of the effective demand generated by public spending and credit creation accruing to private profits and to labour incomes, $C_p + I_p$ the sum of consumption and investment originated[8] in the private sector. CD indicates that, in a monetary economy, credit (both short- and long-term based) is created through the provision of new purchasing power (e.g., of money creation) made available to borrowers. In this context, P constitutes a fraction of the aggregate income and is equal to:

$$P \equiv amG + bmCD \tag{2}$$

Now, considering a 'pure system' of private agents, we obtain that:

$$P + L \equiv C_p + I_p \equiv C + I \tag{3}$$

such identity implies that in a private system, without public spending and credit creation, the sum of consumption and investment tends to be equal to wages and salaries and, therefore, there is little room for aggregate profit, in the meaning described above.

12.4 Can a cut in public spending improve the public budget?

Let us now analyse with simple examples the possible effects of a reduction in public spending on the public sector's budget. We wish in this way to assess if, apart from other social considerations, these measures can be effective in improving public sector accounts.

For instance, by reducing the salaries of civil servants by an amount, say, equal to 100, this entails a saving of 100 in the public sector. But, on the other side, the cut in salaries will induce a parallel reduction of effective demand. By hypothesizing a marginal propensity to consume equal to 0.8 and an average income tax equal to 0.3, we obtain, by applying the income multiplier:

$$\frac{1}{1-c(1-t)} = \left(\frac{100}{1-0,8+0,24}\right) = -\left(\frac{100}{0,44}\right) \approx -227 \tag{4}$$

If, then, we assume, as a reasonable hypothesis, that the total taxation (direct + indirect) is approximately equal to 50 per cent, the reduction of public spending will cause a reduction of fiscal revenue equal to $-227*0,5 = 113,5$. The net balance of this operation for public finance is then $-113,5 + 100 = -13,5$ and is only the role of the 'social absorbers' that can mitigate this effect.

Needless to say, in real situations we need to specify much better, among others, the following aspects: (i) the characteristics of the 'consumption functions' for the various groups and classes, in order to consider the social, cultural and psychological elements which combine to shape a given consumption pattern; (ii) the characteristics of the 'social absorbers', and their links with other policy objectives which, as shown in the previous chapter, need to be studied in their manifold interrelations. Being aware of all these aspects, we believe that this example can depict an important aspect of macroeconomics.

The reduction of income tax

Let us consider the instance of an income tax reduction, say, from 30 to 20 per cent. The new income, by assuming an hypothetical starting value of 100, will be equal to:

$$\frac{100}{1-0,8+0,16} = \frac{100}{0,36} \approx 278 \tag{5}$$

The difference between the new income (278) and the old income, indicated by:

$$\frac{100}{1-0,8+0,24} = \frac{100}{0,44} \approx 227 \tag{6}$$

is equal to 51. The level of fiscal revenue remains almost unchanged: in fact, supposing as before a total amount of direct and indirect taxation equal to 0,5 we get in the first case $227*0,5 \approx 113$ and in the second $278*0,4 \approx 111$. But, to what extent is this hypothesis realistic? As can be easily noted, it is realistic to assume a GDP increase of approximately 22 per cent (51/227).

If, as it seems much more plausible, for a number of reasons the aggregate supply curve is likely to be steeper for a sudden and large increase in the effective demand, the increase in GDP will be much lower than 22 per cent and the result will be a worsening of public accounts. As in the previous case, this example is only indicative of a much more complex reality.

To what extent can private investment replace public spending?

This analysis is linked to the following central question, namely, whether in the familiar identity

$$Y \equiv C + I + G \tag{7}$$

the terms I and G are mutually replaceable. As a matter of fact, it is on this (more or less explicit) assumption that the neoclassical economists base their reasoning – namely, that the economic space now 'ineffectively occupied' by the public sector can easily be replaced by private investment. But to what degree is this alternative feasible (and advisable)? For instance, let us suppose that we have, at the time zero:

$$Y_0 \equiv 800 + 50 + 150 \equiv 1000 \tag{8}$$

In this case, neoclassical oriented theories tend to posit that a diminution, say, by 100 in public spending would entail a parallel increase in I. In the opinion of many, if 1000 is an equilibrium of underemployment, the reduction in public spending would generate an increase in I even higher than the correspondent reduction in public spending. In this way, the new level of Y_1 would be higher than Y_0. By assuming, for the same marginal propensity to consume 0.8, that the decrease in public spending by 100 is accompanied by an increase of I equal to 150, we obtain:

$$Y_1 \equiv 1000 + 200 + 50 \equiv 1250 \tag{9}$$

However, this idyllic result for mainstream economics is hard to be attained as the hypothesis of perfect substitutability between I and G is very far from reality. In fact, as we have seen, public spending and credit creation are the main drivers of aggregate profit. Furthermore, a perfect substitutability[9] between I and G finds a limit in the circumstance that the amount of investment goods needs to be geared to the amount of consumption goods that firms plan to produce which, in turn, depends on the available income of the labour force. We can represent this situation with the general equation:

$$C = f(I) \tag{10}$$

We define this equation general to imply that, in order to produce a given amount of consumption goods, many methods of production are possible. However, the possibility of choosing different productive techniques does not imply the perfect flexibility of productive factors postulated by neoclassical economics.

Quite the contrary, this formulation takes into account that any kind of productive process – with their present and prospective techniques – is highly evolutionary and path-dependent as it is fully ingrained in the complexity of the social and cultural context. In any event, and for whatever productive technique employed at the time, a fundamental implication of the Keynesian theory of aggregate demand is that investment expenses are made with a view to producing a programmed amount of consumption goods. Hence, the trend of the demand for consumption goods will affect, positively or negatively, the demand for investment goods.

12.5 The unrealistic hypothesis of a 'pure private economy'

A general implication of this analysis is that a 'perfect' private economy is unlikely to be attained in the modern world. Such an economy, in allowing little growth, little innovation and little change, can have as its correlate only very simple economic systems, based on vicinity and direct personal relations. But, as soon as these systems start growing, the role of the public sector becomes paramount. Both public spending and credit creation originate from public intervention. This is evident for public spending, but for credit creation too the role of the public sector is no less important. In fact, as just noted, the public sector (meant in a broad sense and then including also the Central Bank) plays an exceedingly pivotal role in creating and guaranteeing the value of money.

Public spending and credit creation can accrue to aggregate demand in numerous ways: as for public spending, in particular, (i) classic multiplier effects related to public consumption, public investment and civil servants' incomes; (ii) subsidies and incentives to firms, which can accrue both to firms' consumption and to investment expenses. And, (iii) as for credit creation, the various types of consumer credit and investment credit, which also combine to shape the level and forms of public spending.

For these reasons, it appears clearly that the neoclassical idea of a *crowding-out* effect of public spending on the private sector can display, if anything, only a limited effect in our economies. As we have tried to show, in a 'pure private economy' aggregate profit is unlikely to be very high. Public spending and credit creation play the fundamental role of pushing the growth of the system, also because they contribute to creating an important part of the aggregate demand, which accrues to the private sector.

It can also be interesting to note that these conclusions hold true whatever be the elasticity[10] to prices of the aggregate supply function. As a general remark, we believe that the aggregate supply function is in most cases elastic enough in the short run, and even more in the medium and long run, due to the effects of technological progress.

Notes

1 Cf., among others, for an account of a heterodox perspective on these phenomena, Harcourt and Kriesler (2013), Keen (2011), Minsky (2008), Stiglitz (2009).
2 For more information refer to the following link: http://stats.oecd.org/Index.aspx?DataSetCode=FIN_IND_FBS
3 Refer in particular to Keynes (1930, 1931 and 1936) and the authors mentioned in the previous note.
4 By the expression aggregate profit we mean an amount of profit which exceeds the 'normal' incomes of all the workers engaged in the private sector, including the so-called executive salaries. Needless to say, a kind of aggregate profit can be present also in a hypothetical pure private economy, but in this case it is difficult for it to acquire the nature of the extra-profits typical of expansionary period driven by public spending and credit creation. As a matter of fact, in a 'pure private economy', the income differences between people and classes find a limit in the principle of effective demand. For instance, if entrepreneurs want to increase their profits by reducing real wages, they must also make up for the reduction in the effective demand caused by wage reduction. In a private economy, as investment goods are intrinsically related to consumption goods, the only available way for increasing the effective demand is to attain a higher level of the entrepreneurs' consumption. However, this process finds many limitations, especially in the presence of scale-economies associated with mass consumption (the entrepreneur can buy himself a yacht, but for the class of entrepreneur buying, say, one thousand iPads each in order to sustain effective demand is likely to be a bit less practical). This aspect can help explain why the marginal propensity to consume tends to be lower for the richest sections of populations. For these reasons, we consider the consumption of entrepreneurs in the formation of aggregate profit as a relatively unimportant phenomenon. It is important to underscore that all these economic relations embody, at the same time, also a social, cultural and psychological aspect, the study of which becomes paramount for a full understanding of the real features and problems of the contexts examined.
5 Another condition for the existence of profits as defined above is the presence of some kind of market power on the part of entrepreneurs. This can arise in the labour process, where normally entrepreneurs have strong contractual powers over the workers, and in the market for goods, when firms hold various forms of monopoly power.

6 Needless to say, this is a gross simplification. In fact, as well underscored by the theories of unequal exchange, the total effects of international trade tend to adversely affect the weaker countries.

7 Also in this case, the multifarious aspects of the growing complexity of the system comport with a parallel articulation of the structure of ownership of the firms, with the presence of many 'mixed' forms. It is interesting to note that this analysis will apply also to the case of state-owned enterprises, provided that they are organized as administratively independent bodies.

8 We are aware of the difficulty of 'disentangling' the various components of aggregate demand in real economies. Besides, in our complex credit-based economies, it seems really arduous to find significant instances of a pure private economy: namely, an economy in which credit creation and public spending play a minor role in creating aggregate demand. Such realities can perhaps be found in simple economic arrangements, like local markets based on craftsmanship and typical products.

9 As noted in Part III, the notions of public and private action, markets, competition and efficiency are determined by the complex and evolutionary systems of norms, institutions and policies in their relation with the cultural and psychological orientations at the individual and collective level. In this respect, one noteworthy phenomenon is the growing importance of the 'mixed forms' of economic activities. They are characterized by an articulated presence of 'stakeholders' which carry different objectives and systems of value. Also for this reason an adequate level of coordination between institutions and policies becomes more and more necessary in order to take into due account the multifariousness of these issues.

10 It can be worth noting that the classic hypothesis of the vertical aggregate supply curve, corresponding to full employment, in which there is perfect flexibility of prices and wages, is quite unrealistic for a host of reasons: (i) Full employment is hard to achieve not because of too high wages but owing to an insufficient level of effective demand; (ii) Technological progress can contribute, in a complex way, both to the rise of the unemployment and to the shifting of the 'supply functions' at firm at industry level (cf. also Part V); (iii) The role of expectations, which makes the distinction between short run and long run more blurred; (iv) The phenomenon of sticky prices, which do not depend only on 'market imperfections' but are often needed in order to provide the system with a minimum of stability and reliability: if everything were wildly flexible, no stable economic and social life would be possible (see also the previous chapter); (v) Also for this reason, the decision to change prices necessitates some planning activities in order to foreshadow the possible consequences. As this activity should be made in advance, it constitutes a good explanation, set forth in particular by the theory of 'small menu costs', of the reason why firms do not quickly adjust their prices even when it would seem more profitable to do so; (vi) The same phenomenon has been observed in labour markets, where both firms and workers prefer to negotiate long-term contracts. As can easily be seen, all these relations do not take place in a *vacuum* but are heavily interlinked in the social and cultural domain. For all these reasons, an interdisciplinary approach can help to look more deeply into the microeconomic foundations of the macroeconomic aggregates.

References

Harcourt, G. and Kriesler, P. (eds.) (2013) *The Oxford Handbook of Post Keynesian Economics*. Oxford: Oxford University Press.

Keen, S. (2011) *Debunking Economics – Revised and Expanded Edition: The Naked Emperor Dethroned?* London: Zed Books.

Keynes, J.M. (1930) *A Treatise on Money*. London: Macmillan.

Keynes, J.M. (1936) *The General Theory of Employment, Interest and Money*. London: Macmillan.

Keynes, J.M. (1963) *Essays in Persuasion*. New York: Norton. Originally published in 1931 by Macmillan.

Minsky, H. (2008) *Stabilizing an Unstable Economy*. New York: McGraw Hill.

Stiglitz, J.E. (2009) The Current Economic Crisis and Lessons for Economic Theory. *Eastern Economic Journal*, 35: 281–296.

13 Economic and psychological implications

13.1 The growing contradictions of the system

The pivotal role of public spending and credit creation in ensuring an adequate level of aggregate profit engenders many contradictions, which tend to become more and more unmanageable.

As we have seen, there has been, since the inception of the industrial revolution, a rather stable increase of public spending, both in absolute and relative terms, also on account of the role of public spending in increasing the aggregate demand, and, hence, the profit of firms. In this regard, the present economic crises do not depend on the Keynesian policies of the past and/or on an alleged inefficient and lobbyist nature of public intervention – even if, of course, it is true that public spending is not always effective and/or can be driven, to a greater or lesser extent, by the dynamics of various interest groups: rather, they depend on the need to manage the growing contradictions of the system. In this regard, we can mention two major, and interrelated, contradictions:

(I) As just noted, public spending and credit creation play a paramount in the formation of effective demand and aggregate profit of the economic systems, and this aspect constitutes a key explanation of their impressive growth over time. The relevance of these aspects is, however, only imperfectly acknowledged in our societies. Both for this reason and because of the influence of neo-liberalist attitudes, public spending is in general appraised (cf. also Chapter 15) in a negative way, as a kind of obstacle which crowds out resources from the private sector. This has been accompanied by an even more negative attitude towards taxation. Every candidate, of whatever political orientation, knows that in order to win elections he/she must promise a tax reduction and that the worst and most fatal accusation that can be levelled at a government is that it has increased taxation. Consequently, as the increase in taxation has fallen systematically behind the level of the increase in public spending, public budget deficits in OECD Countries have reached considerable values (Table 13.1).

In order to finance these deficits, a huge accumulation of public debt followed. The increase of public debt is particularly detrimental for economic development owing to a different type of crowding-out effect. As a matter of fact, the payment of interest on public debt diverts to rent-based incomes a good deal of public

Table 13.1 Government deficit/surplus as a percentage of GDP

Nations	Year 2014
Australia	−2.5
Austria	−2.8
Belgium	−2.1
Canada	−2.1
Czech Republic	−2.1
Denmark	−1.5
Estonia	−0.2
Finland	−2.2
France	−3.8
Germany	−0.2
Greece	−2.5
Hungary	−2.9
Iceland	−2.0
Ireland	−4.7
Israel	−3.9
Italy	−2.7
Japan	−8.4
Korea	+0.1
Luxembourg	+0.3
Netherlands	−2.7
New Zealand	+0.1
Norway	+10.7
Poland	+5.6
Portugal	−4.0
Slovak Republic	−2.7
Slovenia	−4.1
Spain	−5.5
Sweden	−1.5
Switzerland	+0.1
United Kingdom	−5.3
United States	−5.8

Source: Based on data from OECD (2014), 'Government deficit/surplus as a percentage of GDP',
Economics: Key Tables from OECD, No. 20, http://dx.doi.org/10.1787/gov-dfct-table-2014-1-en

resources which could have been devoted to objectives of public utility. This constitutes, in our view, the crux of the supposed inadequacy of public spending to pursue economic and social objectives. The gross inadequacy of this situation both for stimulating the economy and for addressing economic and social imbalances is self-evident.

In this sense, we believe that the issue related to the difficulty of payment of public debt is largely exaggerated. Conversely, what seems urgently needed in order to solve the public debt problem is: (a) to restore a climate of trust, so that people would reinvest in bonds once their assets come due. (b) To reduce the public sector deficit by rationalizing public spending and/or by realizing a more progressive taxation, especially for rent-based incomes and wealth. In this regard, it is important to recall from 'Haavelmo's theorem' (1945) that public spending is likely to positively influence aggregate demand even with a corresponding level of taxation, since the marginal propensity of consumption of the public sector is likely to equal unity, whereas that of the private sector is likely to be less. (c) To lessen as much as possible the real interest rate, in order to reduce the burden for the public sector and promote investments. (d) Of course, more radical solutions can also be envisaged, such as a partial or total debt cancellation. In our view, these measures are interesting but, taken in the absence of a far-reaching perspective of economic and social change, run the risk of acting only as a temporary relief. What seems really necessary is a structural transformation of the system in which the need for public debt will be gradually eliminated. In this regard, the attainment of the previous points, together with other measures oriented to ensure an equitable and sustainable growth, seem particularly important.

(II) Another macroscopic and disruptive contradiction – which has paved the way for the eruption of the present-day economic and financial crisis – can be found in the relation between (a) most credit policies, which aim to uplift, also through well-organized advertisement strategies, people's spending capacity well beyond their real earnings; and (b) business strategies which, in order to gain 'competitiveness', tend to reduce employees' incomes and work conditions to a minimum. Under these growing burdens, personal bankruptcy is likely to arise, with the spreading of all its negative consequences on the whole system.

It can be interesting to note that these contradictions can find a relevant explanation in the relations of accumulation in a monetary economy, which are indicated by the expression $\mathbf{M} \rightarrow \mathbf{C} \rightarrow \mathbf{M'}$, where $\mathbf{M}$ indicates money and $\mathbf{C}$ the commodities. As is known, this formulation was proposed by Marx and was then taken up and elaborated by Veblen, Keynes and many other scholars. In this sense, it represents one of the cornerstones of economic theory. It means that, in a capitalistic economy, all economic transactions are, at the same time, monetary transactions, and hence, for a growing economy this means, for the same level of prices, a continual accrual of their monetary value.

In order to carry out a more precise theoretical and empirical analysis on these issues, a careful study of the following factors is needed: the labour and goods markets and the institutionally based 'mechanisms' of prices and salaries formation; the organization of firms, industrial structure, and any other relevant aspect of the social, legal, policy and institutional framework.[1]

Bringing together macroeconomic objectives and sustainable development

In the analysis of these problems, and also on account of the interrelations between policies discussed in Chapter 11, it seems pertinent for our issue to look into the interrelations between macroeconomic policies (typically, more short-term targeted) and structural policies (typically, more long-term oriented). As a matter of fact, on the one hand, macroeconomic policies, as is widely recognized and analysed, impinge on structural policies – for instance, environmental, industrial, competition, innovation and regulatory. But, on the other hand, structural policies also bear on macroeconomic policies. Indeed, structural policies also influence, in a complex interlink, (i) the effects of macroeconomic policies on the short-term targets of employment, inflation and interest rates and (ii) the economic and social framework in which the macroeconomic policies are interlaced. As underscored in particular by institutional and evolutionary economics, political economy is profoundly bound up with the social and cultural domains. For this reason, a comprehensive approach also embracing other important fields of social sciences – in particular, sociology, psychology and anthropology – would be of particular value for enquiring into the intrinsic multifariousness of policy action.

In this regard, one aspect that emerges from our institutionally rooted analysis is that policy co-operation does not acquire only a 'technical character' but involves a profound 'cultural revolution' of the historical, political, institutional, social, economic and psychological dimensions of any given context.

13.2 The difficulty of devising alternative paradigms: a psychoanalytic interpretation

This interdisciplinary and encompassing character of policy action, while prospecting new avenues of progress, can help explain, at the same time, the difficulty of its accomplishment. In fact, owing to this complexity, policy measures taken in an uncoordinated and piecemeal way are unlikely to be successful. As a result, a feeling of frustration and pessimism can ensue. For this reason, it can be pertinent to get a closer look at how psychological and social phenomena are interlaced.

As regards the recent economic crises, an interesting strand of research, often labelled 'socioanalysis', has pointed out the role of unconscious fantasies and group behaviour in the analysis of the phenomena of money, finance and capital, with particular reference to speculative behaviour on the part of financial institutions and citizens. These studies (cf. in particular, Compton and Ozler, 2011; Long and Sievers, 2012; Tuckett, 2011) underline that financial investments are unlikely to be 'rational' owing to the strong emotional involvement and the role of psychological conflicts in this respect. A marked ambivalence characterizes these mental states, in which aggressive behaviour plays a relevant role. Typically, the first stage is one of greedy euphoria, which often spreads out on account of some optimistic stories relating to the quotations of the financial assets. In this honeymoon stage there tends to be a total identification with the 'good object', and any warning on the risk of the investment is strongly denied. Then, when the quotations start to go down, a depressive and pessimistic phase follows in which the 'good object' has now transformed itself into a 'bad object' and nothing, it is supposed, can be done to help the situation.

In this sense, a psychoanalytic perspective can also be employed for the study of other economic and social issues. On that account, it can be very interesting to analyse how people perceive and interpret their economic and social realities and the reasons that can hinder the attainment of a more equitable and sustainable society. We can see these aspects by investigating how people tend to perceive and interpret the increase in public spending of the past decades.

In this situation, a vicious circle tends to arise: as a result of the structural tendency towards an increase in public spending, the opinion has gained ground, even across various sectors of the progressive domain, that the only remedy to the present crisis consists in a progressive reduction of public spending and public deficit. Needless to say, these targets[2] are quite different, but in the conventional wisdom, and also in the unconscious perception, they tend to be equated. The basic and widespread perception is that public spending is 'too high' anyway and so must be abated at any cost.

In these situations, in which the only faith in economic progress rests on a kind of wild and unregulated competition, the market tends to be psychologically perceived as an inflexible and punitive *superego*. In that vision, the only possible thing we should do is to comply with the 'needs of the market', without any further enquiry as to the adequacy of the system to respond to the profound needs of the economy and society.

In order to better appraise these complex phenomena, an enquiry into how people tend to perceive market phenomena becomes paramount. For instance, if, as just noted, the market is perceived as an inflexible and punitive *superego* this implies that persons try to repress their neurotic aggressiveness, which, however, can find many expressions in the marketplace in a more or less disguised way. A typical instance is the behaviour towards financial assets reviewed before.

A psychoanalytical interpretation can make light of the unconscious reasons lying behind the need to reduce public spending.[3] Such a need may refer to the child's desire to possess its mother's affection and nourishment and to the feeling of guilt[4] that often arises in relation to such a desire. As well expounded by the contributions of Sigmund Freud, Melanie Klein and many others, the child, in its early relation with the mother, is likely to experience complex feelings[5] – which can include anger, ambivalence and frustration – related to its utter desire to be nourished and protected.

For these reasons, the attempts to reduce public spending are unlikely to really improve the situation. Our impression, instead, is that these measures are likely to worsen a vicious circle of economic and social crises, most often accompanied by an increase – as we have seen before, mostly neurotic-driven – of xenophobia, intolerance, prejudice, localism and disruptive rivalry[6] in international relations.

13.3 A (supposed) lack of alternative theories

This leads us to the following fundamental questions: is the level of social participation in collective issues satisfactory? If not, for what reasons? And what can we do to improve the situation? Let us consider, for instance, financial speculation. It is well known that the sources of this speculation originate from the large capacity for credit creation by big banks and other financial institutions. They often act through a concerted action which, if carried out on an extensive scale, can spell uncertainty and turbulence for the social and economic fabric. Also, many of these speculative attacks are backed by the opinions of rating agencies and supranational institutions, which are not precisely heterodox oriented.

However, critical analysis of these facts is largely absent from public debate and even in street protests. For instance, when a government, also as a result of a speculative attack, applies a drastic cut to public expenditure in order to keep the public sector's budget 'in order', all the protests tend to be directed only towards the direct effects of these measures. True, many protesters would criticise the action of the 'big powers' and would uphold very different systems, such as socialism or communism.

The problem, however, is that, when confronted with the policy measures that need to be taken here and now in order to handle comprehensively the problems at stake, there is a lack – short of triggering an unlikely revolutionary process – of viable alternative proposals to mainstream oriented policies. Even when there are alternative proposals on specific aspects, it is in general difficult to go beyond the ingrained habits of thought and life prevailing at the time. In this sense, the arguments of the protesters and of progressive public opinion do not always square with the heart of the questions: what are the profound reasons for the steady increase in public spending? If (for the reasons illustrated above) it is virtually impossible to diminish public spending without lessening effective demand and profit, is it really so frightening to slightly increase taxation in order to allow effective and transparent public spending? And why is progressive taxation still considered an 'intolerable sign of socialism'? Why should we allow disruptive financial speculation? Should we consider such speculation as 'a free play of market forces' or as an unscrupulous activity made possible within a definite set of institutional and legal frameworks? And, as a way of synthesis, how can we build a viable alternative economic and social system, really based on democracy and participation in economic, social and political spheres?

These issues converge towards the basic fundamental theme: why has a steady deterioration of relevant aspects of the quality of life occurred over time – for instance, difficulty in finding and retaining a motivating job, environmental decay, lack of participation and highly uneven distribution of incomes and power?

In the analysis of these problems, even within the progressive domain, few alternatives are left open: in fact, as the policy of 'public spending' is associated with the theory of John Maynard Keynes and, since this theory is often considered to have been a failure, the theories that have survived are mainstream economics and Marxism. Of course, we cannot agree with any of these points.

First, as we have tried to show, public spending is a key driver of capitalistic growth and Keynes was the first scholar to spell out this aspect. But Keynes was not a superficial advocate of public spending as he was well aware of the many contradictions of the capitalistic system and the corresponding need for long-term solutions to these imbalances (cf. also the next chapter).

And second, there are important theories, which are most often overshadowed in public debate, which highlight the role of norms and institutions in the provisioning process of society. As we are trying to show, institutional and Keynesian theories can usefully interact for a better understanding of the structural tendencies of our economic systems.

Notes

1 The importance of these aspects was highlighted in particular within the field of institutional economics, see Commons (1913, 1924 and 1934); Hodgson, Samuels and Tool (1994), Veblen (1899, 1914 and 1919).

2 As a matter of fact, public budget deficit can be reduced not only by cutting expenses but also by increasing taxation.

3 In this regard, the attitude towards public spending tends often to assume the typical trait of a neurotic disturbance, namely, a compromise between the 'desire' and the 'defence'. For instance, some persons can express their greediness and related aggressiveness by showing an exploitative attitude towards public spending. Others persons, instead, can air their greediness and aggressiveness by denying their need of the mother and identifying themselves with omnipotent and aggressive parental figures. Needless to say, the latter category of persons is also often ready to take advantage of public spending, if the occasion presents itself, but they try to strongly deny it. Both patterns of behaviour tend to be profoundly destructive: in the first case, people display indirectly their aggressiveness by being 'lazy' and trying to live on public spending. The inner sense of guilt expresses itself by keeping them in a passive and dependent condition, which of course hinders the true expressions of their personalities. In the second case, people tend to be overactive, but often in destructive ways: for instance, by making career and money in an unscrupulous way and letting little room in their life for affective and social relations. In this case, the feeling of guilt creeps up on people by leaving them always discontent, no matter what they have achieved, and preventing them from having a rewarding social and affective life.

4 Of course, such feeling can also be related to the characteristics of our 'affluent societies' – which induce people to consume more and more in order to keep the productive process going – when compared with the realities of the poorest countries. In this instance, however, it is quite appropriate to enquire as to the adequacy of our provisioning process in ensuring a real possibility of development for everyone. What we are referring to here is the neurotic feeling of guilt (cf. also the previous note). As we will also see in the next part, J.K. Galbraith and other heterodox economists have pointed out that, owing to the massive increase in labour productivity, the real problem in our societies relates not to real scarcity but to artificial scarcity (cf. Chapter 7), the latter being created by the legal and institutional frameworks of our economies – and also, we can add, by their intertwining with psychological conflicts and orientations. Of course, one significant element of reality in the discourse on scarcity refers to the wild exploitation of natural resources. However, as just noted, in the typical negative attitude towards public spending the elements of real 'scarcity' are only imperfectly appraised: what is 'scarce', in conventional wisdom, are not natural resources and the associated patterns of conspicuous consumption, but the supposed 'easy and lazy life' made possible by public spending.

5 In this regard, it can be interesting to note (see also the previous notes) that the aggressive attitude towards public spending as a symbol for a maternal figure can help explain why we tend all too often to think of the problem of scarcity as if it involved a real lack of goods. This feeling is conveyed through the following expressions, 'by now, there is no money left', 'we cannot afford these expenses', 'we need to tighten our belt', and so on. As well expounded by Melanie Klein, the child, as a result of an early feeling of abandonment, can react very angrily and so develop a neurotic and aggressive reaction consisting of excessive greediness – and a corresponding feeling of guilt – which can

express itself by the fantasy of destroying or exhausting the mother's breasts. It can easily be noted how such early experiences can impinge on adult life, for instance, on their ambivalent attitude towards public spending.

6 It can be interesting to note that these aspects have been spelled out by Veblen also (in particular 1899, 1915, 1917, 1919, 1921, 1934) in his historical reconstruction of the emergence of modern nation-states. In this sense, there is a promising area of convergence between institutional theories, psychology and psychoanalysis.

References

Commons, J.R. (1964) *Labor and Administration*. New York: Kelley. First edition 1913.

Commons, J.R. (1995) *Legal Foundations of Capitalism*. New Brunswick, NJ: Transaction Publishers. Originally published by Macmillan in 1924.

Commons, J.R. (1990) *Institutional Economics: Its Place in Political Economy*. New Brunswick, NJ: Transaction Publishers. Originally published by Macmillan in 1934.

Compton, A. and Ozler, S. (2011) A Psychoanalytic Approach to Explanation of the Housing Bubble: from Individual to Group. University of California, mimeo.

Haavelmo, T. (1945) Multiplier Effects of a Balanced Budget. *Econometrica*, 13(4): 311–318.

Hodgson, G.M., Samuels, W.J. and Tool, M. (eds.) (1994) *The Elgar Companion to Institutional and Evolutionary Economics*. Aldershot: Edward Elgar.

Long, S. and Sievers, B. (eds.) (2012) *Towards a Socioanalysis of Money, Finance and Capitalism*. Abingdon and New York: Routledge.

Tuckett, D. (2011) *Minding the Markets: An Emotional Finance View of Financial Instability*. New York: Palgrave Macmillan.

Veblen, T. (1899) *The Theory of Leisure Class*. New York: Penguin.

Veblen, T. (1915) *The Imperial Germany and the Industrial Revolution*. New York: Macmillan.

Veblen, T. (1917) *An Inquiry into the Nature of Peace*. New York: Macmillan.

Veblen, T. (1919) *The Place of Science in Modern Civilization*. New York: Viking Press.

Veblen, T. (1921) *The Engineers and the Price System*. New York: Huebsch.

Veblen, T. (ed. by Leon Ardzrooni) (1934) *Essays In Our Changing Order*. New York: Viking Press.

Part V

The structural transformation of economic systems and the social and psychological implications

In this part we investigate a number of structural transformations of economic and social systems and their effects on economic and social life. In the next chapter we focus on the reasons underlying the growing difficulty of aggregate demand to reach the level of full employment (however defined). In this light we consider the opportunity for the economic system to move towards a society in which the exclusive search for monetary gain will gradually lose relevance and be replaced by a system of activities which better express the needs and inclinations of people.

Then, in the next chapter we continue this line of enquiry by analysing the main aspects of John Kenneth Galbraith's *The Affluent Society*.

14 The structural tendency of aggregate demand to lag behind the aggregate supply of full employment

Introduction

As we have seen, a central trait of capitalistic institutions lies in the chronic tendency of aggr.emand to lag behind the aggregate supply of full employment (however defined). There are a number of reasons for this tendency: in particular, both the growing productivity of labour and the satiation for certain categories of goods combine to render the objective of full employment more difficult to achieve.

In the former case, this happens because the increase in productivity signifies that, for a given level of production, fewer jobs are required; and that, in order to keep up with the same level of employment, more products should be produced and sold in the market. In the latter case, it happens because, since the needs of consumers are becoming increasingly tied to the immaterial and intellectual side[1] of consumption, their fulfilment tend to depend less and less on the 'material and quantitative' aspects of consumption. In fact, we do not buy books by kilos and cultural activities by mere numbers. Also, if we buy a high-tech product, we are likely to be more interested in learning well how to use it, than to change it with every new model.

These aspects constitute a significant explanation of the tendency of the socio-economic system (see also later) to move from work activities resting on 'the economic motive' to activities – social, cultural, scientific, artistic – based on the true expression of people's real needs and inclinations. In this regard, what are the effects of technological progress on job creation? Considering the complexity of the issue, what we hope to do is not to provide precise answers but – on the basis of the most important theories – to stimulate a debate on the most relevant tendencies.

As just noted, the increase in productivity requires a growing amount of goods to guarantee the same level of employment. Of course, firms can introduce new products to the market, but this would not solve that structural issue. In fact, even if new jobs are created in these fields, in the medium and long run the increase in productivity also extends, and perhaps even more so, to the new products. This could help to explain why every innovative wave tends to create fewer and fewer jobs. For instance, it is easily observable that, whereas the durable goods typical of the 1960s and 1970s involved hundreds of thousands of workers, the innovative cycle of today's high-tech products would employ no more than several thousand workers.

All this suggests that a kind of 'forced' over-consumption is the only and very imperfect way, in our present economies, for attaining some kind of full employment level. How many high-tech items, cars, clothes, etc. should we buy to sustain the aggregate demand? For a host of economic, social and environmental reasons, this system is untenable in the long run. In this respect, the problem becomes to identify the set of institutional and policy arrangements for moving along a new avenue of economic and social progress.

14.1 The nature of the problem in a nutshell

We can delineate some aspects of these problems by developing a very simple scheme which, of course, needs to become far more complex in the analysis of specific issues. Let us denote with N the number of workers – who are supposed to work approximately for the same time and with same productivity – π the average labour productivity and Y the aggregate product. Supposing that, for the sake of simplicity, the product is homogeneous, consists of additive units and is sold at the unit price, we obtain:

$$N\pi = Y \tag{1}$$

For instance, supposing $N = 1000$ to be the level of full employment (however defined), and $\pi = 5$, the corresponding value of Y for a given time span will be equal to:

$$1000*5 = 5000 \tag{2}$$

Now, if, for instance, the productivity increases by 20 per cent the potential product will be equal to:

$$1000*6 = 6000 \tag{3}$$

As can be easily seen, in order to maintain the same level of employment, it is necessary that the new product of 6000 will be produced and sold in the market. Conversely, if, with the new level of productivity, the product sold would remain at 5000, the productive capacity could not run at full blast. As a result, the new level of occupation will be:

$$N = \frac{Y}{\pi} = \frac{5000}{6} = 833,3 \tag{4}$$

with a corresponding drop of occupation of 166,6; which is equal to the previous level of occupation minus the new one (1000 – 833,3).

In this way, 166–167 labour units will be made redundant. Thus, in order to secure full employment, it is necessary to sell on the market 6000 units. How can this be accomplished? There are two main ways, with all the degrees of intermediate cases: (a) a corresponding reduction of prices, in which case the benefit of the productivity increase will be transferred on to consumers; (b) the invariance of prices, which implies that the benefit of the productivity increase will be retained by firms.

As for case (a), which more closely corresponds to neoclassical economics, the required flexibility of the factors of production rarely occurs in practice. For a number of reasons, some of them illustrated in Chapter 9, prices, wages and mark-ups tend to be rather sticky, also because these 'prices' tend to reflect the social and institutional arrangements upon which economic activity is framed. But also supposing a sudden realization of that condition, the problems of satiation pointed out before would still remain and even get worse over time. As a matter of fact, the increased vent of product would compel us to buy a growing quantity of goods in order to afford full employment. As for case (b), its realization demands nothing less than a parallel increase in the demand, in the form of disposable income of the consumers. As we have seen, the main channels for attaining such increase are a continual expansion of the share of public spending and credit creation on GDP.

14.2 Can prices and wages flexibility solve economic problems?

From the previous account it appears that the prevailing productive paradigm, based on ever-growing consumption and on an unlimited supply of natural resources, is becoming more and more unfit for ensuring a sustainable and equitable development of economic systems. For this reason, measures aimed only at increasing aggregate demand are important but not sufficient to address these problems thoroughly.

As for the neoclassically oriented policies of cutting spending and tax reduction, we have seen in the previous chapters that – although it can be possible and advisable to realize a better rationalization and accountability of the public sector – it is utterly unrealistic to believe that public spending can be easily and massively substituted by private spending. For these reasons, policies based on these premises are unlikely to be effective in sustaining aggregate demand.

At this stage, it can be interesting to wonder if the other central prescription of neoclassical economics can work in our economies. As we know, such prescription relates to the importance of realizing an adequate flexibility[2] of productive factors, and in particular of prices and wages.

For instance – and even setting aside the circumstance outlined in Chapter 9 that sticky prices also reflect the complexity of socio-economic relations embedded therein and hence cannot be properly explained through the lens of a simple maximization hypothesis – in the presence of a rate of unemployment (however defined) of 20 per cent, can a corresponding reduction of labour cost restore full employment?

Our impression is that it is possible for this measure to have some positive effect on employment in the short run. Such effect, however, tends to vanish over a longer period. Why? First, even in the short run, there is no guarantee that a reduction of wages of, say, 20 per cent would entail a corresponding increase in employment. In fact, if the entrepreneurs perceive that this reduction is due to the weakening of workers' contractual power, they would be induced to increase the intensity and duration of the workday. This measure can be accompanied by the attempt of further reducing the wages, which can be made more effective by prospecting a delocalization of production in lower labour cost countries.

But even supposing that such a reduction can work in the short period, in the long run the effects are likely to disappear because the factors just depicted – in conjunction also with the growing difficulty for aggregate demand to reach the full employment level discussed before – tend to become stronger over time. In fact, as observed in the previous chapters, in the capitalistic, or 'mixed', systems of today, the 'natural' tendency of entrepreneurs is to reduce as much as possible labour costs in order to try to be competitive and enable profits to accrue.

In this regard, we can also note that, as underscored by many studies on technological accumulation, a policy action based only on the reduction of labour cost will – by disregarding the need for the proper development of human and social capital[3] in order to upgrade the capacity of a country to compete in the higher levels of the value chain – contribute to marginalizing and impoverishing that country.

14.3 Towards an alternative paradigm

For these reasons, we believe that much more than a simple *laissez-faire* option is needed to realize full employment and economic development. What is fundamentally required for effective policy action is an adequate process of co-ordination of the related policies. For instance, let us suppose that the main goal of policy action is to promote a better efficiency of productive system. In this framework, the objective of labour cost reduction can also be contemplated in order to gain competitiveness in the marketplace. But that reduction can work, if deemed necessary, only in conjunction with other policies involving aspects of utmost relevance for the development of the system.

We can mention, among others: (i) policies for promoting human capital in the workplace, in particular through an ongoing upgrade of the workers' competencies coupled with the improvement in their motivation and participation; (ii) policies aimed at fostering scientific, cultural and technological development in public and private institutions and in the society at large; (iii) macroeconomic and structural policies directed at aiding the building of a more and more equitable and sustainable society.

As noted before, a central aspect of a novel economic system relates to building a society that is based less on the 'economic motive' and more on the unfolding of the true inclinations and potentialities of persons. This means that this system will be fully compatible with limited growth, steady state, or de-growth. As also remarked in the conclusions, the objective of our work is not that of indicating what option is preferable but how to facilitate the move towards this path of progress.

It can be interesting to note that this more 'qualitative' tendency was noted by important economists, and now we mention two significant examples. The first one can be found in the most 'heterodox' classical economist, John Stuart Mill. In his appraisal of the long-term economic evolution, he remarks that the structural tendency towards the stationary state not only does not imply a static way of living but, on the contrary, constitutes the necessary condition for the full expression of the more advanced aspects of personality. The central element for attaining such a state is the control of population. In his words:

> There is room in the world, no doubt, and even in old countries, for a great increase of population, supposing the arts of life to go on improving, and capital to increase. But even if innocuous, I confess I see very little reason for desiring it . . . .I sincerely hope, for the sake of posterity, that they [the future generations] will be content to be stationary, long before necessity compels them to it.
> It is scarcely necessary to remark that a stationary condition of capital and population implies no stationary state of human improvement. There would be as much scope as ever for all kinds of mental culture, and moral and social progress; as much room for improving the Art of Living and much more likelihood of its being improved, when minds ceased to be engrossed by the art of getting on. Even the industrial arts might be as earnestly and as successfully cultivated, with this sole difference, that instead of serving no purpose but the increase of wealth, industrial improvements would produce their legitimate effect, that of abridging labour. Hitherto it is questionable if all the mechanical inventions yet made have lightened the day's toil of any human being . . . .Only when, in addition to just institutions, the increase of mankind shall be under the deliberate guidance of judicious foresight, can the conquests made from the powers of nature by the intellect and energy of scientific discoverers, become the common property of the species, and the means of improving and elevating the universal lot.
> (Mill, 1994 (1871): 128, 129–130)

Another relevant contribution[4] to these issues has been provided by J.M. Keynes, in particular in the final part of the *Essays in Persuasion*. This can appear a bit surprising because, owing to his proposals for recovering from economic depression, Keynes is often depicted as the theorist of the short period. This opinion tends to be reinforced by his famous expression 'in the long run we will all be dead'. However, from the reading of the *Essays* we discover that the long-term perspectives of economy and society play a central role in his analysis.

For Keynes, focusing the analysis on short-term problems constitutes only a part of a more profound awareness of the structural transformations of society. The pith of these changes will be a substantial shortening of the working time, made possible by the increase of productivity. The main obstacle to the attainment of this potential rests not in technical but in psychological difficulty. He notes, with great psychological intuition, that the latter obstacle relates to the difficulty for people to employ leisure time for a better realization of their personalities. In his words:

We are being afflicted with a new disease of which some readers may not yet have heard the name, but of which they will hear a great deal in the years to come – namely, *technological unemployment*. This means unemployment due to our discovery of means of economising the use of labour outrunning the pace at which we can find new uses for labour.

But this is only a temporary stage of maladjustment. All this means in the long run *that mankind is solving its economic problem* . . . [but, despite this opportunity] . . . Yet there is no country and no people, I think, who can look forward to the age of leisure and of abundance without a dread. For we have been trained too long to strive and not to enjoy . . . [hence, in this perspective, economics] . . . should be a matter for specialists – like dentistry. If economists could manage to get themselves thought of as humble, competent people, on a level with dentists, that would be splendid!

(Ibid.: 364, 368, 373)

In the next chapter we shall see how J.K. Galbraith's *The Affluent Society* complements in interesting ways this analysis.

Notes

1 See, for instance, Skidelsky and Skidelsky (2012) and the next chapter on J.K. Galbraith's *The Affluent Society*.
2 In this discussion, of course, we do not refer to the opportunity that 'productive factors' should possess a degree of flexibility but to the idea that their unlimited flexibility, coupled with a *laissez-faire* attitude, would be able to realize an economic growth with full employment.
3 For more detail on these issues see the references indicated in Note 7 of the concluding chapter and in particular Dosi, Nelson and Winter (2000); Dunning and Lundan (2008); Nelson (1993); Woolcock (1998).
4 For more detail refer also to Hermann (2014).

References

Dosi, G., Nelson, R.R. and Winter, S.G. (eds.) (2000) *The Nature and Dynamics of Organizational Capabilities*. Oxford: Oxford University Press.
Dunning, J.H. and Lundan, S.M. (2008) *Multinational Enterprises and the Global Economy*. Cheltenham: Edward Elgar.
Hermann, A. (2014) 'The Essays in Persuasion of John Maynard Keynes and Their Relevance for the Economic Problems of Today'. In J. Hölscher and Klaes, M. (eds.) *Keynes's Economic Consequences of the Peace: A Reappraisal*. London: Pickering and Chatto.
Keynes, J.M. (1963) *Essays in Persuasion*. New York: Norton. Originally published in 1931 by Macmillan.
Mill, John Stuart (1994) *Principles of Political Economy*. New York: Oxford University Press. Originally published by Longmans in 1871.
Nelson, R. (ed.) (1993) *National Innovation Systems*. Oxford: Oxford University Press.
Skidelsky, R. and Skidelsky, E. (2012) *How Much Is Enough?: Money and the Good Life*. New York: Other Press.
Woolcock, M. (1998) Social Capital and Economic Development: Toward a Theoretical Synthesis and Policy Framework. *Theory and Society*, 27(2): 151–208.

15 The 'affluent society' of John Kenneth Galbraith and its relevance for the problems of today

Introduction

The Affluent Society, published for the first time in 1958 and then in 1998 with an author's update, addresses a number of issues central to the development of the 'societies of abundance' of the post Second World War period. It proposed an innovative interpretation of the main aspects and contradictions that have characterized this development: in particular, (i) the imperative of production and consumption, with the excessive use of credit and pervasive advertising; (ii) the presence of a powerful technostructure; (iii) the systematic downplaying of public expenditure and of public goods; (iv) the growing economic and social insecurity; (v) the environmental decay; (vi) the limited ability of 'conventional policies' to influence these phenomena. As can be observed, these aspects are also extremely relevant for our theme, since they can explain the profound reasons for the current economic and social crisis.

In the analysis of the main aspects and problems of the developed economies, Galbraith addresses the following questions: how is the affluent society perceived by current opinion, and how is it interpreted in economic theory?

A first notable element is that the growth of productive capacity that has made possible mass consumption has not been accompanied by a parallel development of the theories needed to interpret these phenomena. Such theories, in fact, have remained largely anchored to an earlier time of 'scarcity' and low productivity, where poverty, deprivation and uncertainty were the rule for the majority of the population. Although considerable 'material' progress has been made, the legacy of social and cultural periods of scarcity still prevails. He highlights some common traits of what he names the 'central tradition in economics' and that includes the Classical, Marxist, Neoclassical and Keynesian Schools. This definition – with which of course one need not agree – includes not only the classical tradition of mainstream but also important sectors of heterodox economics.

Let us now look[1] in more detail at what are the main aspects of the 'conventional wisdom' characterising the 'affluent society'.

15.1 The main characteristics of the 'affluent society'

The imperative of production

One aspect that unites, in academic debate and in common perception, the economic systems that emerged from the industrial revolution, from the oldest to the most modern, is the 'imperative of production'. In his words:

> On the importance of production as a test of performance, there is no difference between Republicans and Democrats, right and left, white and minimally prosperous blacks. It is common ground for the Chairman of Americans for Democratic Action, the President of the United States Chamber of Commerce and the President of the National Association of Manufacturers.
>
> (Galbraith, 1958: 99–100)

Of course, conventional wisdom often also calls attention to the qualitative aspects of life, but these aspects tend, in general, to take on a residual and separated character from production. The profound thought that tends to pervade our society is 'First come the needs of production, then the rest.'

The primacy given to production does not imply, however, that attention is actually paid to the policies to uplift it. In fact, it is assumed that 'the market mechanism' will ensure the increase of production, no matter how 'perfect' markets are in real situations.

Another typical feature of the conventional wisdom is that 'real production' is identified almost exclusively with the private sector. The action of the public sector is considered, at best, a necessary evil, and, at worst, a cost and an obstacle to the 'free operation of market forces'.

In this appraisal, 'public services rarely lose their connotation of burden. Although they may be defended, their volume is almost certainly never a source of pride' (ibid.: 110). This view leads to a chronic shortage of a number of public goods that would be needed for a balanced development of economic activities.

The apparent autonomy of consumer preferences

While, as we have just seen, in the 'affluent society' great importance is attributed to production, little attention is paid to what is produced: whether the product is more or less educative, more or less harmful to the environment, is considered something that comes 'after'. What matters, 'in the meantime', is only to produce, because, in the general appraisal, the income of citizens should depend only on production.

As regards consumption, the 'conventional wisdom' assumes the hypothesis of 'consumer sovereignty': the goods produced and sold in the market would mirror the preferences of consumers, and therefore any intervention in that sphere is considered more harmful than beneficial.

In this perspective, it is held that, with the increase of real income, the 'utility' of the goods does not decrease. While in fact, for a basket of goods and income at a given time, it is assumed that the marginal utility diminishes along the same indifference curve, this does not happen with different baskets of goods, higher incomes and different times. In this appraisal:

> The concept of satiation has very little standing in economics. It is held to be neither scientific nor useful to speculate on the comparative cravings of the stomach and the mind . . . that, as of a given time, an individual will derive lesser satisfaction from the marginal increments to a given stock of goods, and accordingly cannot be induced to pay as much for them, is conceded. But this tells us nothing of the satisfactions from such additional goods, and more particularly from different goods, when they are acquired at a later time.
>
> (Ibid.: 117, 121)

In fact, the basic idea of this theory is that the needs of the consumer originate autonomously in the person. It assumes a world of completely independent and rational individuals who maximize their utility functions.

The dependence effect and the role of technostructure

This description of the consumer in terms of a subject completely free from external influences is, however, very far from the mode of operation of our societies based on 'consumption at all costs'.

In the affluent society, notes Galbraith, the needs of consumers for the products are largely created by big business, through massive advertising campaigns. The complex of large enterprises, which Galbraith names the 'technostructure', thus acquires a leading role in the creation and satisfaction of consumer needs.

One of the indicators of this phenomenon consists in the costs of promoting the product, which often tend to be equal or superior to the costs of production. In this sense, 'as society becomes increasingly affluent, wants are increasingly created by the process in which they are satisfied' (ibid.: 129).

The creation of ever new consumer needs, by stimulating the feelings of emulation associated with new products, takes on a largely symbolic role. We often buy a new product not so much for its technical and functional characteristics, but for the 'social message' associated with it.

Hence, the main characteristics of the affluent society can be summarized as follows: (i) the centrality of production as an indicator of economic and social progress, accompanied by lack of attention to what is produced and to the social and environmental effects; (ii) the predominant role of producers and of 'technostructure' in the continual creation of new needs; (iii) the role of production in ensuring a satisfactory, or at least acceptable, level of employment.

The third factor, of course, constitutes a relevant aspect of the centrality attributed to production, which, in the current economic systems, becomes almost the only way to secure an income for citizens.

As can be observed, the affluent society has, along with some positive aspects, a number of problematic elements that raise serious doubts about its sustainability in the medium and long term.

The growing indebtedness of consumers

The aim of producers to promote their products is limited by the spending capacity of consumers. This happens especially in the case of durable goods, where it is not always easy to have cash in relevant amounts. In the production chain, consumer credit plays a central role and has become an integral part of business strategies. In a passage of great interest, he notes:

> It would be surprising indeed if a society that is prepared to spend thousands of millions to persuade people of their wants were to fail to take the further step of financing these wants, and were it not then to go on to persuade people of the ease and desirability of incurring debt to make these wants effective. This has happened. The process of persuading people to incur debt, and the arrangements for them to do so, are as much a part of modern production as the making of goods and the nurturing of the wants.
>
> (Ibid.: 145–146)

In this context, consumer credit has grown exponentially in the post Second World War period and can be an important explanation of the economic crisis of today. But after the benefits of consumption (assuming they are relevant) come the pains of payments, especially for lower income families. In this regard:

> One wonders, inevitably, about the tensions associated with debt creation on such a massive scale. The legacy of wants, which are themselves inspired, are the bills which descend like the winter snow on those who are buying on the installment plan. By millions of hearths throughout the land, it is known that when these harbingers arrive, the repossession man cannot be far behind. Can the bill collector or the bankruptcy lawyer be the central figure in the good society?
>
> (Ibid.: 146–147)

The remarkable aspect of this process is its steady increase over the last decades. Evidently, credit creation is so necessary for the development of the system that nothing seems to lessen its role, even during periods of tight credit policies. But how is it possible to induce consumers to borrow even when real interest rates are high? In the first place, the payment periods may be prolonged. Moreover, an increase in the real interest rate, even remarkable, is perceived by the consumer with greater difficulty, because the total amount to pay increases, in percentage terms, to a lesser extent than the increase in the interest rate. We can see this phenomenon with an example: for a price of an item purchased on a loan, say, of €1,200 with an interest rate of 6 per cent on an annual basis, the annual amount charged will be equal to €1272, with monthly payments of €106. If the interest rate doubles to 12 per cent, the total amount to be paid will be €1,344 with monthly payments of €112.

The percentage increase of this amount (€1344) to the previous one of (€1272) is 'only' 5.6 per cent, compared with an increase of the interest rate of 100 per cent. These phenomena can help explain the difficulty of reducing the excess of credit creation.

The imbalance between public and private goods

The aspects considered above – the focus on the quantitative aspects of production and the growing indebtedness of households – are accompanied by a parallel lack of attention to (and of adequate resources for) the provision of essential public goods. This situation is aggravated by the fact that a substantial proportion of public resources is destined for military spending.

The result is the lack of an adequate 'social balance' between public and private goods. As we have seen, in the 'conventional wisdom' production takes place mainly in the private sector. In this view, the public sector tends to be relegated to the background and regarded as a place of inefficiencies and privileges. If public services are efficient, this is considered as 'something due' and therefore will not win the admiration that accompanies, for example, the launch of a new product.

This imbalance causes a situation of social and environmental degradation, and exacerbates the tensions of the 'affluent society'. In a famous passage, Galbraith notes:

> The schools are old and overcrowded. The police force is inadequate. The parks and playgrounds are insufficient . . . The family which takes its mauve and cerise, air-conditioned car, power steered and power braked automobile out for a tour passes through cities that are badly paved, made hideous by litter, blighted buildings, billboards and posts for wires that should long since have been put underground. They pass on into a countryside that has been rendered largely invisible by commercial art. They picnic on exquisitely packaged food from a portable icebox by a polluted stream and go on to spend the night at a park which is a menace to public health and morals. Just before dozing off on an air mattress, beneath a nylon tent, amid the stench of decaying refuse, they may reflect vaguely on the curious unevenness of their blessings. Is this, indeed, the American genius?
>
> (Ibid.: 187–188)

In this sense, the insufficiency of important public goods goes in tandem with a parallel reduction of the potential benefits of private property.

Considering, for example, the sector of private housing, it is more than obvious that it can grow in a balanced way only in the presence of adequate public services. The negative effects of the lack of public goods are evident not only in the 'material' aspects of the lack of infrastructure, but also, and perhaps even more so, in the lack of public investment in the fields of education, science and culture.

These effects are particularly negative for the young, who are increasingly exposed to cultural models of little educational value. Thus:

> Schools do not compete with television and the movies. The dubious heroes of the latter, not Ms. Jones, become the idols of the young . . . Comic books, alcohol, narcotics and switchblade knives are, as noted, part of the increased flow of goods . . . An austere community is free from temptation. It can be austere in its public services. Not so a rich one.
>
> (Ibid.: 191)

The limited role of monetary and fiscal policies

In this situation, Galbraith underscores the limited role of monetary and fiscal policies in abating macroeconomic imbalances, in particular, inflation and unemployment. For instance, in a situation of rising inflation, monetary policy of the classic type would prescribe credit restrictions, to be implemented mainly through an increase of the real interest rate. A policy of this kind would generate a considerable drop in the effective demand, which could start a depressive phase of the economy. Another major limitation of these policies is that they act in an unequal way on the various sectors of the economy.

In fact, an increase in the real interest rate affects primarily small firms, by making their activities more onerous owing to the phenomenon of 'credit rationing'. Conversely, large companies can withstand much better an increase in the real interest rate. First, it is likely that they have a much greater bargaining power with the banks. Furthermore, they can also issue bonds to finance their activities and thereby avoid the phenomenon of credit rationing. And, last but not least, they can more easily transfer price increases to consumers.

For all these reasons, it is unlikely that a 'normal' restrictive monetary policy is able to significantly reduce large firms' investment decisions. The likely result of these policies will be, as witnessed by the events of the last decades, the concentration of the economic and financial power of large groups, accompanied by an increasing downsizing of the weaker productive sectors. Restrictive monetary policies are also disadvantageous for the provision of public goods, because these policies are likely to increase the debt burden for public institutions.

As for expansionary monetary policies, there is little to be added to the conclusions already reached by Keynes: a decrease in the real interest rate, although necessary and advisable, is not a sufficient factor to stimulate investment.

Similar reasoning can be carried out in part for fiscal policies. These measures, unlike monetary policies, impinge more directly on the components of aggregate demand and are therefore more easily scrutinized in their immediate effects. The reasoning clearly becomes more complicated if we consider the overall effects on the system. For example, reducing taxes often leads to a reduction of resources for essential public services. The reduction of these costs does not, however, represent a guarantee of a parallel reduction of the possible inefficiencies in public spending.

In this regard, Galbraith acutely notes that:

> It is far easier to cut the function than the waste, and this is what occurs . . . [and moreover] . . . in time of inflation the situation of the public services is certain to be even more tenuous because of the inevitable tendency for public budgets to lag behind the general increase in prices.
>
> (Ibid.: 178–179)

Also to be considered is the fact that any change in the tax regime unfolds, in a much more direct and visible way than for monetary policies, a redistributive effect. This condition implies that – in contrast to what happens for monetary policies, whose redistributive effects tend to go largely unnoticed – any proposed change in taxation is likely to trigger an extensive debate between liberals and conservatives on the desirability of such change. As a result, fiscal policies tend to play a limited role because they will usually achieve a compromise that will not alter significantly the existing equilibrium.

Macroeconomic policies, therefore, have little opportunity to really solve the problems of the affluent society. To do this, it is necessary to enquire into the economic and social roots of these contradictions.

The increasing economic and social uncertainty

As appears from the above discussion, the perspectives of the 'affluent society' are not very positive. Such a society is based on the primacy of production and, for this reason, the employment and income of workers increasingly tend to depend on the production of goods that are often of little use, if not harmful, to physical health, mental education and the environment. The prominence of private production chimes with a structural shortage in the supply of public goods essential for economic and social life. These circumstances effect an increase in insecurity of economic and social life, which is paralleled by urban and environmental degradation.

The basic limitation of private production is that the wealth produced rests on a concept of 'scarcity' typical of previous economic systems. For this reason, focusing attention only on the production aspect as such tends to give rise to a society based less and less on the real needs of the person.

For instance, in 'conventional wisdom' voluntary unemployment is regarded as the worst of sins, like a fraud against the community. But, says Galbraith,

> if the goods have ceased to be urgent, where is the fraud? Are we desperately dependent on the diligence of the worker who applies maroon enamel to the functionless metal of a motorcar? The idle man may still be an enemy of himself. But it is hard to say that the loss of his effort is damaging to society.
>
> (Ibid.: 215)

In our affluent society, the imperative of 'efficiency' tends to prevail over emotional ties and quality of life, over the security and satisfaction of jobs, and, more generally, over the soundness of human relationships. This is expressed in the following passage:

> [In the conventional wisdom] . . . If a locality is declining . . . then one should encourage the people to leave. Mobility means efficiency. It is true that the ties of family, friends, pastor and priest, countryside and mere inertia may make this a Draconian and even cruel prescription. Until relatively recent times, a large amount of industrial and occupational disease could be justi-fied on the grounds that considerations of cost did not permit of its elimina-tion . . . [hence] . . . A good deal of practical heartlessness was what served the social good . . . no tears should be wasted on the farmers who go bank-rupt. This is the path to more efficient farm production.
>
> (Ibid.: 212, 213, 215)

The importance of loosening the dependence of income on production

In order to solve these problems, it becomes central to reduce the paramount role of production. In order to realize this objective, Galbraith observes, there is no other way than to loosen the dependence of income on production. This can be achieved, firstly, by increasing the duration and the amount of unemployment benefits and other forms of support for people who cannot profitably carry out work activities. And, secondly, by increasing public spending on essential public goods, in order to achieve a better 'social balance' between public and private property, and thus abate or eliminate the phenomena of social and environmental decay.

But how these measures can be financed? In this regard, an increase in taxation, both direct and indirect, is the only way to attain a better-balanced economic and social system. There is, however, as noted above, a general reluctance to increase tax, both in progressives' and conservatives' domains. In fact, any change in the tax regime will trigger the debate on equality, with the likely result that the recip-rocal vetoes will render it arduous to achieve significant changes.

Furthermore, the conventional wisdom is prone to cut taxation in any case, even if this involves a reduction of essential public services. Therefore, a tax cut for the poor, although it may seem more equitable, threatens to undermine the central goal of the elimination of the causes of poverty and degradation. In this sense, Galbraith complains: 'The modern liberal rallies to protect the poor from the taxes which in the next generation, as the result of a higher investment in their children, would help eliminate poverty' (ibid.: 230).

To eradicate poverty, in fact, not only is a higher income needed, but so too is a thorough understanding of the social causes that determine such a plague. These negative factors, such as, for example, insufficient resources for primary and sec-ondary education, can be eliminated mainly through higher public investment. In this sense, 'Poverty is partly self-perpetuating because the poorest communities are the poorest in the services which would eliminate it' (ibid.: 240).

Conclusion

As emerges from the above discussion, the analysis of Galbraith proposes a brand new interpretation of the affluent society that, in underscoring the negative aspects, broadly indicates the necessity for a more equitable economic system. There arise, then, the central problems of (i) specifying in more detail the main features of a better society, and (ii) identifying the most suitable policies for achieving these goals.

In this regard, the text is not intended to deal specifically with policy issues. The solutions to the problems of the affluent society, he notes, can only be based on a growing awareness of these problems, and this is the main objective of his contribution. On that account, he does not show excessive optimism on the possibility of realizing in short time this potential. In this sense, the book closes with a rather negative note:

> To furnish a barren room is one thing. To continue to crowd in furniture until the foundation buckles is quite another. To have failed to solve the problem of producing goods would have been to continue man in his oldest and most grievous misfortune. But to fail to see that we have solved it, and to fail to proceed thence to the next tasks, would be fully as tragic.
>
> (Ibid.: 260)

We can conclude this chapter by noting that the fundamental insights of Galbraith on the problems of the 'affluent society' can interact with the contributions of institutional and Keynesian economics addressed previously[2] in order to identify a more comprehensive course of policy action.

Notes

1 We have also dealt with these issues, in a partly different way, in Hermann (2012).
2 See in particular Commons (1924 and 1934), Keynes (1931 and 1936), Veblen (1899, 1914, 1919).

References

Commons, J.R. (1995) *Legal Foundations of Capitalism*. New Brunswick, NJ: Transaction Publishers. Originally published by Macmillan in 1924.

Commons, J.R. (1990) *Institutional Economics: Its Place in Political Economy*. New Brunswick, NJ: Transaction Publishers. Originally published by Macmillan in 1934.

Galbraith, J.K. (1958) *The Affluent Society*. New York: Mariner Books. Second edition 1998.

Hermann, A. (2012) La *Società opulenta* di John Kenneth Galbraith e la sua rilevanza per i problemi attuali. *Il Pensiero Economico Moderno*, 1–2: 31–55.

Keynes, J.M. (1963) *Essays in Persuasion*. New York: Norton. Originally published in 1931 by Macmillan.

Keynes, J.M. (1936) *The General Theory of Employment, Interest and Money*. London: Macmillan.

Veblen, T. (1899) *The Theory of Leisure Class*. New York: Penguin.

Veblen, T. (1990) *The Instinct of Workmanship and the State of the Industrial Arts*. New Brunswick, NJ: Transaction Publishers. Originally published by Macmillan in 1914.

Veblen, T. (1919) *The Place of Science in Modern Civilization*. New York: Viking Press.

Concluding chapter

How can heterodox economics and psychoanalysis interact to address the complexity of the economic crisis?

Where have we arrived?

As is evident from the previous discussion, we have addressed in our work a number of contributions from heterodox economics and psychoanalysis, with particular attention to their insights for understanding the systemic character of the economic crisis. In this respect, the usefulness of these contributions is twofold: (i) on the one side, a good deal of them can aid in achieving a better understanding of the 'more encompassing aspects' of the socio-economic system which are also likely to have a bearing on the dynamics of the economic crisis. And, on the other side, (ii) a good number of these contributions can help explain more specific aspects of economic systems that are still today very relevant for a better appraisal of the economic crisis.

Having this end in view, we started our interdisciplinary journey by providing an outline of the main concepts of psychoanalysis. We have tried to illustrate the richness and articulation of psychoanalytic theories, and their usefulness in the analysis of a host of economic and social phenomena.

In the second part we treated the contributions of institutional economics (in particular in its 'old' tradition) by pointing out the potential of its key concepts – habits, transactions, working rules, collective action, instincts (or propensities), evolution, culture, social value – of getting inside the 'living hearts' of institutions.

In the third part we continued our journey by elucidating the institutional nature of the market and the role of 'material' and psychological factors in social evolution.

Then, in the fourth part, we analysed the role of policy co-ordination in structural problems, and the role of public spending and credit creation in sustaining effective demand, with particular attention to the economic and psychological implications of these phenomena.

Finally, in the fifth part we considered a number of structural transformations of economic systems and their implications for the economic and social system.

One implication of our analysis is that, although short-term policies aimed at sustaining aggregate demand and employment are of utmost importance, they are not sufficient for solving the structural character of the crisis. This happens because the systemic character of the economic crisis involves a crisis of the old-fashioned production paradigm based on (i) unlimited growth; (ii) over-consumerism;

(iii) marked differences in income and opportunities accompanied by numerous instances of poverty and destitution; and (iv) uncontrolled exploitation of natural resources.

For these reasons, such paradigm becomes less and less sustainable in every considered dimension: economic, social, environmental, psychological. This means that a real solution of the crisis demands nothing less than a real integrated approach to the various dimensions of the crisis. However, these transformations are anything but easy to accomplish, because they also imply getting rid of long-standing habits of thought and life based on the existing production paradigm.

In this light, our approach is not focused on the issues related to the ideal characteristics of a new society. Whether, for instance, it should be better to build a particular kind of socialism or co-operative economy; and whether such economy should be oriented towards a de-growth, a moderate growth, or a steady state.

This is because we concentrate more on the ways to overcome the shortcomings of our economic systems and then on how to steer the construction of a really sustainable and equitable society. Such society can be compatible with various economic organizations based on co-operative and equitable relations, which are likely to vary according to the unique characteristics of any considered context.

On that account, we have tried to explore the potential of an interdisciplinary approach in understanding the problems of our economic systems and the ways for charting a new course of policy action. In this perspective we try now to outline, as a way of synthesis and conclusion, a number of relevant aspects for attaining these objectives.

The individual and collective aspect of psychological dynamics

A first observation coming to the fore is that heterodox economics has established a fairly systematic collaboration mainly with pragmatist and cognitive psychology.[1] Conversely, collaboration between institutional economics and psychoanalysis has until now assumed an unsystematic character that has been unable to provide a comprehensive treatment of many relevant issues.

The same is true, more generally, for collaboration between psychoanalysis and social sciences. This does not mean, however, that psychoanalysis has not tried to wage the collective dimension of life. As we have seen, both Freud and later psychoanalysts have stressed the importance of the collective dimension of life and they have provided significant contributions to a number of social phenomena.

In this regard, we believe that psychoanalysis is too rich and complex a discipline to be encapsulated within the boundary of a number of too narrow assumptions. Thus, psychoanalysis can contribute to a deeper understanding of the conflicting elements associated with each collective context by applying a pluralistic oriented scientific approach, which has also been developed within the institutionalist and pragmatist perspectives.

As seen early on, a number of studies have shown, from a psychoanalytical perspective, how people tend to regard institutions. In fact, institutions are important for people not only with regard to their real functions but also on account of their symbolic meanings. This suggests that, to varying degrees, people may regard institutions not in their reality but according to their own unconscious conflicts and fantasies which, in turn, are partly socially determined. Hence, the characteristics of every culture – including, of course, the characteristics of the family setting – are likely to play a pivotal role in determining the course that individual conflicts will take.

In this respect, it is interesting to observe that even psychological disturbances, since they are in part socially and culturally determined, present an evolutionary character.[2] Within this field of research, important psychological and psychoanalytic concepts[3] can help to reach a more complete understanding of the complex meanings of habits, which combine to determine their typical unconscious, evolutionary and rather 'sticky' nature. For instance, as noted earlier, the multifariousness of instincts, the role of internalization of norms and models of behaviour in child development, the role of Freud's notion of 'compulsion to repeat', the importance of symbols and fantasies in individual and collective life and the multiple and interrelated levels (in particular, individual, family-based, social and cultural) of the concept of identity.

In this respect, psychoanalysis can help throw light on the fact that habits, despite their rather sticky nature, should be regarded not merely as a means for the unconscious and passive adaptations of individuals to external pressures but, rather, as complex psychological procedures of interactions between individuals and societies. For this reason, in their mutual interaction people also play an active role in maintaining and modifying habits.

It is also worth noting that this account does not imply a negative role for institutions but, rather, takes into account their conflicting and complex functions. Within this scope, the manifold role of institutions as a necessary medium for the individual to establish object and interpersonal relations would deserve paramount attention.

In fact, institutions are in many cases a necessary means for liberating and expanding individual action. Moreover, psychological disturbances should not be regarded as something 'bad or abnormal' but as the typical expression of the structure of the human personality, with all the related problems, weaknesses, contradictions and ambivalence. As appears from this outline, some of the reasons why we believe the interaction between institutional economics and psychoanalysis to be useful is because it can shed a stronger light on the following interrelated issues:

1   The evolutionary interaction between individuals and institutions in the formation of interpersonal relations, expectations, identity and values, and the role of conflicts and aggressiveness in the dynamics of these processes;
2   The evolutionary and conflicting nature of habits, customs, routines, organizations, institutions and collective knowledge;
3   The evolutionary and conflicting nature of ethics and morality, also in their connections with social value process.
4   The possibility of economic and social reforms, and the role of policies in these projects.

This kind of analysis would help us to look more deeply into the decision-making process underlying economic action by observing that the typical provinces of this action – consumption, work, investment, saving – embody profound psychological meanings which go beyond the strict economic maximization principle. As a matter of fact, economic action constitutes an aspect of the relations that the person establishes with his or her context and, as such, is influenced by the complexity of the social, cultural, psychological and ethical aspects which, in their complex links, combine to define the context-based character of economic action.

In this perspective, it is certainly true that society heavily impinges on 'the habits of thought and life' of the person. But the reverse is no less true, in that the related ISEF should not be appraised as a totally exogenous element, completely beyond individual control, but as a complex framework of legal, institutional and social relations which are partly moulded by the values, actions, expectations and conflicts of every individual concerned. Hence, psychological motivations are likely to play an important role in both directions: (i) the 'material' and psychological influence of the ISEF on the person; and, relatedly, (ii) the influence of every person's thoughts and actions on the related ISEF.

The multifarious links between individuals, institutions and policies

In the exploration of these aspects, the central point we wish to stress is that the structure of the ISEF is intrinsically linked to policy dynamics. This implies that collaboration between institutional economics and psychoanalysis could also be utilized for the analysis of the manifold aspects of policy action, with particular attention to the problem of co-ordination between different policies.

Since, as noted before, policy action is not limited to governmental activity but involves all the institutions and individuals concerned in one way or another with policy measures, the problem of policy co-ordination goes to the heart of the problem of 'institutional' or collective co-ordination between different values, interests and orientations.

This issue raises an interesting question which, of course, is related to every policy domain: should public policies be aimed at reducing psychological disturbances and, if so, which are the most suitable actions? With regard to the first question, we think favourably of policies addressed to lessening psychological disturbances.

As we have seen, psychological disturbances, although occurring in the mind of the person, acquire an intrinsic social character, owing to the person's need (and possible difficulty) to establish affective and intellectual relations with others. Also for these reasons, psychological disturbances tend to be, to a greater or lesser extent, a widespread feature of human beings. Moreover, the most impairing forms[4] most often occur among the disadvantaged section[5] of the population.

In this sense, psychological disturbances partly embody, as outlined before, an intrinsic social and evolutionary character. This signifies that public policies can play an effective role in reducing psychological disturbances and, in virtually every industrialized country, there are examples of policies addressed to the therapy of these disturbances. Although the analysis of such policies is beyond the scope of this work, our general impression is that there is still need for substantial advancement, especially in the areas of prevention and diffusion of psychological and psychoanalytic knowledge.[6]

This process, however, should not be confined only to the 'individual dimension'. As we have tried to show, individual needs and conflicts also acquire a collective dimension through their unfolding in the institutions and organizations where personal interaction comes about. And, furthermore, this collective dimension has grown more important over time. In this respect it seems appropriate to stress that the ISEF is likely to play a far-reaching role in orienting, fostering or frustrating the various propensities, values, conflicts and needs of the person. For this reason, a thorough social value process, based on an interdisciplinary approach, of the various institutions and organizations that go to make up the social fabric would deserve particular attention.

By furthering the process of social valuing in this way, it would become possible to shed more light on the complex interplay between institutional framework, interest groups and policies, and thus to provide the notion of public purpose with a more precise content. In this way, it would become easier to reduce the typical problems of policy action, which, as also noted before, refer to the following interrelated factors:

- complexity, uncertainty, incomplete and asymmetric information of policy action, also due to the interrelations between policies, institutions and interest groups. This entails, in a vicious circle, a corresponding uncertainty about the 'mission' of every institution involved;
- different opinions and objectives of the actors involved in policy-making;
- the difficulty – also due to path-dependency and lock-in phenomena – of prompting the economic and institutional changes which may be necessary for the effectiveness of policies.

In consequence of these problems, the criteria according to which collective decisions are made are likely to be correspondingly 'shadowy', because in these situations the clarity and the explicitness of the social valuing process tend to be impaired. As a result, policy action – by tending to become overwhelmingly biased in favour of the stronger groups and/or less able to have an actual 'grip' on the situation – may fail, to a greater or lesser extent, to respond to the profound needs of society.

As acutely observed by Dewey (1939), a situation of this kind, in which policies are unable to address effectively the economic and social problems, could raise a call, in the absence of a clear recognition of the real causes of the problems, for an authoritarian 'solution' which, however, for the reasons we have tried to set forth, would end up worsening the capacity of the system to address the real problems of society.

Culture, participation and democracy

In this light, the issue of participation chimes with the problem of creating an institutional system enabling the growth of more and more effective democratic structures in the political, economic and social spheres. We can observe that an inadequate process of participation – by bringing about an inadequate expression of the structure of reasonable value, that is, of the conflicts and motivations lying at the heart of social life – may constitute an important explanation for the failure of policies to respond to the profound needs of society and for the corresponding phenomena of 'anomie', alienation and insufficient socio-economic development.

These problems tend to become more critical in situations – occurring with great frequency in less developed countries and backward areas – of structural problems that render the trade-offs and conflicts between policies more acute. Indeed, in these circumstances, an adequate process of policy formulation would be all the more important, but the capacity of policies to address these problems is likely to be dramatically insufficient. This may happen because the 'quality' of policies is not independent of the other characteristics of the social and economic context, but, rather, is partly shaped by them. For this reason, the 'quality' of policies should not be regarded as a totally exogenous variable but as a collective (institutional) and evolutionary pattern of action which is, at least in part, endogenously determined by the conflicts, values and motivations of all individuals and institutions involved.

The systemic character of the economic crisis and the need for an encompassing approach

The foregoing discussion has several implications for economic crisis. In fact, as we have seen, the economic crisis of our times presents a systemic character which reaches across many dimensions. For this reason, the objective of realizing better policy co-ordination constitutes a paramount aspect for devising an effective course of policy action.

In order to realize this objective, we think it important to realize an interdisciplinary oriented collaboration within the various theories treated before, because it can help attain a more complete understanding of the factors at play in determining the structure and evolution of social valuing.

In fact, social value structure, as being deeply rooted in the habits of thought and life typical of every society, tends to take, at individual and collective level, a (partly) unconscious, symbolic and implicit character. Consequently, the nature of the problems and conflicts associated with these evaluations may render arduous the identification of all the aspects of these problems and their possible solutions.

In this respect, this interdisciplinary approach would also lead to a deeper understanding of the multifarious aspects of concepts such as capitalism, socialism, market, democracy, participation and competition which are at the heart of policy action and which tend, by embodying different values and visions of the world most often having a strong emotional component, to constitute an important part of the individual and collective social value process.

The issues of social and psychological sciences are so complex, we do believe, that the collaboration of many disciplines is necessary for understanding economic and social phenomena. This comports with a pluralistic approach, in order to also surmount the fragmentation so often present in psychological and social sciences. Bringing together psychological and socio-economic analysis can help to throw more light both on the role played by social and economic factors in shaping the person's course of life and on the role performed by each person in influencing these factors. As noted before, such collaboration does not imply a blurring of the distinctive aspects of each discipline.

In fact, if we consider, say, the nature of economic systems we are dealing, there is no doubt, with economics, not with psychoanalysis. And when we employ psychoanalysis in order to understand our psychological life we are dealing, no doubt, with psychoanalysis, not with economics.

However, it is one thing to stress the distinctiveness of each discipline and then, in our example, to remark that economics is different from psychoanalysis. It is quite another thing to claim that each discipline does not need the aid of other disciplines for a more complete understanding of the phenomena under investigation. In this sense, collaboration between economics and psychoanalysis can prove itself useful because, as we have tried to show, economic action embodies also a psychological (and social and cultural) dimension. For this reason, such dimensions need to be appraised in their complex intertwining in order to attain a more complete account of economic life.

This suggests that, in relation to collaboration between heterodox economics and psychoanalysis, on the one side, psychological conflicts and orientations concur to shape the characteristics of the economic system. And, on the other side, the psychological conflicts and orientations of the individual do not unfold in a *vacuum* but within a well-defined economic system which, for this reason, is likely to play a central role in moulding – in its 'material', social and cultural dimension – the ways these individual aspects are expressed. The same remarks can be made with regard to collaboration within and between other related fields of economics, psychoanalysis and psychology.

Overcoming economic crisis by building a sustainable and equitable society

We can note the far-reaching scope of this interdisciplinary approach. In fact, it can be employed to address, at the local, national and supranational level, virtually every social and economic issue, even the (apparently) most 'technical' ones. Instances of these topics include the following interrelated issues: (i) industrial, research and innovation, labour and welfare policies; (ii) the various kinds of collective bargaining; (iii) regulation of the banking and financial sector;

(iv) the problems of sustainable development; (v) macroeconomic policies; (vi) other structural issues, also related to the enquiry into the complexity of factors at stake in explaining the severity of the present economic crisis.

In the same spirit, a useful synergy can also be established with, among others, the following interrelated theories:[7] (a) theories of scientific and technological innovation, with particular attention to the phenomena of path-dependency and of the cumulative character of the accumulation of knowledge; (b) theories of globalization, with particular attention to the complex role of multinational enterprises in fostering development in the emerging countries; (c) theories of human and social capital, with particular attention to their manifold expressions and their role in economic and social development; (d) the various attempts to define measures of sustainable well-being that go beyond the narrow criteria of GDP.

In concluding this work, we can remark that our approach is not in agreement with the view that little can be done to abate economic maladjustments and social injustice.

In fact, so the latter reasoning goes, human history has always been characterized – also in our days – by violence and prevarication, marked class and groups distinctions, poverty and other social problems. The reasons for this are to be found in an inherent wickedness of human nature and/or in the inescapable 'laws' of economic development.

In this regard, the theories addressed in the book portray a different reality. They highlight that human nature is neither immutable nor perfect and that it interacts in a complex way with the social setting. Hence, if we build a social setting more conducive to the true expressions of personality, a parallel improvement of the latter is likely to occur. Or, alternatively, if we are able to improve personality, a like change in social setting is likely to occur.

Needless to say, we are aware that *natura non facit saltus* and that, therefore, social change is difficult and slow. Within these limits, however, there is ample room for charting a policy action targeted at building a sustainable and equitable society. In this perspective, past events were 'necessary' only in the presence of a given balance of positive and negative aspects. If this balance had been different, a different historical course would have ensued. Hence, human development does not assume a deterministic character in which a 'Darwinian competition' is the only possible way of survival. As we have seen, in human society many choices are possible and then the problem becomes to identify the most suitable ones for economic and social progress.

We can note that aggressive behaviour aimed at harming, at physical or psychological level, one's fellows – and also animals, plants[8] and the habitat – is not only unnecessary for survival but is likely to seriously jeopardize the attainment of such objective. As we have seen, this behaviour largely finds its roots in neurotic conflicts,[9] and it is in this aspect – as witnessed by too many historical events – that lies its destabilizing and destructive significance.

The issue then becomes how to frame a society in which the negative aspects of personality will progressively fade away and the positive aspects will progressively be reinforced. In this light, the theories analysed above can be usefully employed, in particular by overcoming fragmentation and promoting their synergic interaction, in order to attain this objective.

Notes

1   The fact that institutional economics shares many elements with pragmatist and cognitive psychology constitutes an enriching factor that can contribute to a more fruitful collaboration between these theories and psychoanalysis. Furthermore, significant exchanges of ideas have already occurred among these disciplines and psychoanalysis.

2   For instance, it is well known that in the feudal economy neurosis acquired a distinctive nature, rather different from the prevailing nature of modern-day neurosis. In this regard, an interesting field of research applies psychoanalytic concepts to historical analysis. For an in-depth treatment refer, among others, to Gay (1985).

3   As also observed earlier on, it is important to note that (i) not every conflict is neurotic-driven; (ii) as observed by Freud (1937) and many others, the neurosis-free state tends to be more an ideal type than an observed reality. For this reason, personal conflicts are likely to be complex phenomena in which many intertwined factors are at play. In this regard, there has been over time a growing attention to the complexity of the objectives of psychoanalysis (see, in particular, the interesting study of Sandler and Dreher, 1996). For our purpose, we can consider psychoanalysis in its general meaning of a science aimed at reaching a better self-understanding at both individual and social level.

4   It is interesting to note that even severe psychological disturbances do not necessarily imply a corresponding difficulty for the person concerned to carry on an apparently 'normal life'. In fact, neurotic behaviour can express itself even within an 'ordinary life' if the deep-seated reasons underlying that behaviour are rooted in the neurotic conflicts of the person. As observed before, the reasons why a psychological disturbance may find expression in one form rather than another – that is, in psychoanalytic terminology, the reasons underlying 'the choice of neurosis' – are very complex as they involve the whole set of personal and social factors in their complex interaction.

5   Refer, for instance, to Desjarlais and others, 1995, and to the initiatives promoted by *The Lancet*, http://www.thelancet.com/series/global-mental-health-2011.

6   For an analysis of these issues refer to, among others, Fine (1979); Desjarlais and others (1995); Klein, Heimann and Money-Kyrle (1955). In this regard, Freud (in particular, 1926 and 1933) considers paramount the psychoanalytic treatment of children because, as we have seen, their development is likely to undergo several difficulties. This treatment has a number of differences in respect to the standard psychoanalytic treatment but, owing to the much greater flexibility of the child's mind, is also more promising. It is realized by employing the typical children's play activities for the analysis of early psychological conflicts. Pivotal contributions to child analysis were provided, among others, by Anna Freud, Melanie Klein, Margaret Mahler, Edith Jacobson and Donald Winnicott.

7   For some significant references for the points (i)–(iii) see Banfield (1958); Buckley and Casson (2009); Casson (1987, 1991); Dicken (2010); Dosi, Nelson and Winter (2000); Dunning and Lundan (2008); Dunning and Tsai-Mei (2007); Eisenhardt and Martin (2000); Hall and Rosenberg (2010); Ietto-Gillis (2012); Lall (1985); Mowery and Rosenberg (1979); Nelson (1993); Nelson and Winter (1982); Rosenberg (1976, 1982); Rugman (2012); Schmookler (1966); Woolcock (1998).

8 For point (iv) refer to the links http://www.oecd.org/site/ssfc2011/48606921.pdf http://www.wikiprogress.org/index.php/Main_Page; Stiglitz, Fitoussi and Sen (2011) and for the Italian experience, to Istat (2014).

9 Exceptions can be made for the strictly necessary quantity of animals and vegetables needed for human alimentation. We believe, however, that the consumption of animals in particular can be drastically reduced (or hopefully eliminated) and that a more humane treatment should be reserved for the animals employed to that purpose.

10 As we have seen, these conflicts can be traced back to a distorted expression of life instinct.

References

Banfield, E. (1958) *The Moral Basis of a Backward Society*. New York: Free Press.

Buckley, P.J. and Casson, M. (2009) *The Multinational Enterprise Revisited: The Essential Buckley and Casson*. London: Palgrave Macmillan.

Casson, M. (1987) *The Firm and the Market*. Oxford: Blackwell.

Casson, M. (ed.) (1991) *Global Research Strategy and International Competitiveness*. Oxford: Blackwell.

Desjarlais, R. et al. (1995) *World Mental Health. Problems and Priorities in Low-Income Countries*. Oxford and New York: Oxford University Press.

Dewey, J. (1989) *Freedom and Culture*. New York: Prometheus Books. First edition 1939.

Dicken, P. (2010) *Global Shift: Mapping the Changing Contours of the World Economy*. London: Sage Publications.

Dosi, G., Nelson, R.R. and Winter, S.G. (eds.) (2000) *The Nature and Dynamics of Organizational Capabilities*. Oxford: Oxford University Press.

Dunning, J.H. and Lundan, S.M. (2008) *Multinational Enterprises and the Global Economy*. Cheltenham: Edward Elgar.

Dunning, J.H. and Tsai-Mei, L. (ed.) (2007) *Multinational Enterprises and Emerging Challenges of the 21st Century*. London: Edward Elgar.

Eisenhardt, K. and Martin, J. (2000) Dynamic Capabilities: What Are They? *Strategic Management Journal*, 21: 1105–1121.

Fine, R. (1979) *A History of Psychoanalysis*. New York: Columbia University Press.

Freud, S. (1926) *Die Frage der Laienanalyse. Unterredungen mit einem Unparteiischen*. Leipzig, Vienna and Zurich: Internationaler Psychoanalytischer Verlag. English version, *The Question of Lay Analysis*. Standard Edition. New York: Norton, 1990.

Freud, S. (1933) *Neue Folge der Vorlesungen zur Einführung in die Psychoanalyse*. Leipzig, Vienna and Zurich: Internationaler Psychoanalytischer Verlag. English version, *New Introductory Lectures on Psycho-Analysis*. Standard Edition. New York: Norton, 1990.

Freud, S. (1937) Die endliche und die unendliche Analyse. *Internationale Zeitschrift für Psychoanalyse* vol. 23. English version, Analysis Terminable and Interminable. *International Psychoanalytical Association*. First edition 1987.

Gay, P. (1985) *Freud for Historians*. Oxford: Oxford University Press.

Hall, Bronwyn H. and Rosenberg, N. (eds.) (2010) *Handbook of the Economics of Innovation*, 2 volumes. Amsterdam: Elsevier.

Ietto-Gillies, G. (2012) *Transnational Corporations and International Production: Trends, Theories, Effects*. Cheltenham: Edward Elgar.

Istat (2014) *Il benessere equo e sostenibile in Italia*. Rome: Istat.

Klein, M., Heimann, P. and Money-Kyrle, R. (eds.) (1955) *New Directions in Psycho-Analysis*. London: Tavistock Publications.

Lall, S. (1985) *Multinationals, Technology and Exports*. London: Macmillan.

Mowery, D. and Rosenberg, N. (1979) The Influence of Market Demand upon Innovation: A Critical Review of Some Recent Empirical Studies. *Research Policy*, 8(2): 102–153; also in Rosenberg, 1982.

Nelson, R. (ed.) (1993) *National Innovation Systems*. Oxford: Oxford University Press.

Nelson, R. and Winter, S.G. (1982) *An Evolutionary Theory of Economic Change*. Cambridge, MA: Harvard University Press.

Rosenberg, N. (1976) *Perspectives on Technology*. Cambridge: Cambridge University Press.

Rosenberg, N. (1982) *Inside the Black Box: Technology and Economics*. Cambridge: Cambridge University Press.

Rugman, A. (2012) *The End of Globalization: What It Means for Business*. Amazon: Cornerstone Digital. New edition.

Sandler, J. and Dreher, A.U. (1996) *What Do Psychoanalysts Want?* Abingdon and New York: Routledge.

Schmookler, J. (1966) *Invention and Economic Growth*. Cambridge, MA: Harvard University Press.

Stiglitz, J.E., Fitoussi, J.P. and Sen, A. (2011) *MIS-Measuring Our Lives*. New Delhi: Bookwell Publishers.

Woolcock, M. (1998) Social Capital and Economic Development: Toward a Theoretical Synthesis and Policy Framework. *Theory and Society*, 27(2): 151–208.

Index

absolutism, and historical materialism 121
abstract idealism 123
abstract materialism 123
accumulation, technological 172
action, individual/collective *see* collective
   action; individual action
Adler, Alfred 3–4
advertising 177
affective relations, and human action/
   motivation 7
affluent society 164n.4, 175–83
Affluent Society, The 175
age of leisure 174
aggregate analysis 95
aggregate demand: and aggregate supply
   92; and credit creation 86, 146–55;
   and forced over-consumption 170; and
   full employment 169–74; generation
   of 151; and income redistribution
   146; Keynesian theory of 91, 154; and
   policies 180, 185; and public spending
   86, 146–55, 160; sustaining 171
aggregate profit 151, 152, 155, 158
aggregate saving, and aggregate
   investment 92
aggregate supply 92, 155, 156n.10, 169–74
aggressive behaviour 19–21, 50, 192
aggressiveness: and death instinct 50, 52n.5;
   difficulty of lessening 34; and *eros* 46;
   institutionalised 47; neurotic 20, 36, 47,
   50, 51, 192; public/private dimensions of
   19–21; and repression 48, 51
alienation 122, 128, 190
American Academy of Psychoanalysis 11
Ammon, G. 21
analysis, theoretical/empirical 93–6

animal spirits 92
anomie 145n.6, 190
Association for Heterodox Economics
   (AHE) 102
authoritarian, defined 40n.3
authoritarianism, of patriarchal family
   40n.5
authoritarian relations, unconscious need
   for 31–2
authoritarian systems 122

banking system, and credit economy 86
bankruptcy, personal 160
bargaining transactions 81, 82, 111, 112
behaviour: aggressive 19–21, 50, 192;
   analysis of 105n.10; ceremonial 61;
   complexity of factors at play 50;
   genuine and prejudices 77; improving
   personal 60; instrumental behaviour 61,
   68; and technological progress 68, 69
behaviourism 94–5, 97–8, 100
behaviouristic psychology 97
beliefs, and scientific vision 127
benevolence, social valuing process 144n.2
biological component, of psychology 84
Bion, W.R. 21
bubbles, speculative 72
budget deficits 91, 158, 159, 164n.2
business cycles, analysis of 57, 98
business enterprise 70–3

Capital 124
capital: marginal efficiency of 87;
   primitive accumulation of 125
capitalism: and alienation 128; concerted
   86, 93; development of 83; economic

For Product Safety Concerns and Information please contact our
EU representative GPSR@taylorandfrancis.com Taylor & Francis
Verlag GmbH, Kaufingerstraße 24, 80331 München, Germany